Ancient Africa — Fully Explained

Coming soon

Precolonial Africa — Fully Explained

Early Modern Africa — Fully Explained

This is the first of a series of books about African history. To get updates, and preview samples of future publications, sign up at muksawa.com/email-list.

Ancient Africa — Fully Explained

Geography, Prehistory, Early History and the Rise of Its Civilizations

Adam Muksawa

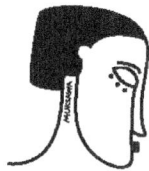

To my father (Abba), to all Africans, to all those who have documented Africa's past (in one way or another), and to all those interested in history as a whole. Here's to learning about those that came before us!

Contents

Figures

Maps

Introduction / Preface

When people read or study any subject, African history or not, they often just dip into bits and pieces without having an understanding of the bigger picture. And so, what they read they can recite, but none of it really makes sense — nothing clicks in. The truth is, to truly understand African history — you have to go back to the roots.

The roots of African history go back many years, to the beginning of man, when man could not speak or write. Thanks to science, we have some picture of what life would have been like for the earliest humans — who first populated Africa and then the world. Science also allows us to understand how the African continent was formed. The nature of this very formation, gave us the varied landscapes and climatic conditions seen throughout the continent. It is these geographic factors that man first learned to live with, and subsequently exploit in different ways. This exploitation eventually gave rise to the many languages and cultures seen throughout Africa today.

Depending on geography, some Africans went on to form urban cultures — leading to the development of some of the first civilizations in the world. This urban way of life presented a whole host of new problems — problems that needed to be dealt with. And so Africans were forced to constantly innovate — leading to rapid improvements in technology. It is this knowledge and technology that the people of today continue to build upon.

This is not a scientific or academic textbook (although in terms of the information within, it is as good as). This is a book that answers a lot of the "hows" and "whys" of Ancient African history. It does this by boiling down the science into language that can be understood, by almost anyone, while keeping the essential facts in order. In keeping in line with the books audience, the general reader, referencing is kept at a bare minimum. However, for those that want to read further, you will find a list of suggested texts at the end. Language is also kept plain and simple — where possible.

Although this book focuses on Ancient African history, once you've read it, you'll have a much clearer picture of African history in general. It is the author's belief, that there are very few books that go into Ancient African history (in much detail at all). Most books simply focus on the last 5000 years or so, going back to the building of the Pyramids of Giza. Even then, for most people, an understanding of why those pyramids came about is lacking. In the grand scheme of things, 5000 years is an insignificant amount of time, compared to the age of man or of Africa itself. Consequently, the years from the formation of the continent, up until the arrival of the Romans — is the main focus of this book.

I think I've said enough for now, hopefully, I've given you a taste of what is to come. So buckle up and enjoy the read.

Abbreviations and Dating System

e.g. – for example

fig. – figure

km – kilometer(s)

m – meter(s)

c. – circa (approximately)

Millennium / Millennia – a period of a thousand years

Century – a period of 100 years. For example 13th century means anything from 1201 to 1300

BP – years before present

mya – million years ago

kya – thousand years ago

CE – Common Era

BCE – Before the Common Era

AD – Anno Domini (Latin — year of the lord)

BC – Before Christ

The Common Era begins with year 1 in your standard (Gregorian) calendar. CE is the same as AD. BC is the same as BCE. Unspecified dates are to be taken as the Common Era (CE).

Glossary

Prehistory – refers to the period prior to written records or documentation i.e. history before c. 5000 BP.

Antiquity – the ancient past, particularly before the Middle Ages (c. 500 CE).

Ice Age – any geologic period during which thick ice sheets cover large areas of land — corresponding to significant drops in global temperatures.

Holocene – name given to the last 11,700 years of the planet's history — the time since the end of the last major glacial period (Ice Age).

African Humid Period (AHP) – spanning from the early to middle Holocene. This was a time when the Sahara Desert was much wetter. And was covered by grasses, trees and lakes (the so-called "Green Sahara").

Homo – genus (a category) that emerged as part of human evolution. Homo sapiens (humans) fall under this genus. You also have Homo habilis, Homo erectus and Homo neanderthalensis.

Lithic – relating to or consisting of stone.

Proto – the earliest form of something.

Culture – the ideas, customs, and social behavior of a particular people or society.

Subsistence – the condition of having (just) enough food (or money) to stay alive.

Domestication – process of adapting wild plants and animals for the benefit of humans.

Pastoralism – a subsistence strategy dependent on the herding of animals, particularly sheep, goats and cattle.

Stone Age – a time when stone was used to make tools. It starts around 3 mya and ends with the beginning of the Bronze Age.

Bronze Age – a period marked by the use of bronze, writing, and other early features of more urban societies. In (North) Africa c. 3400–1200 BCE.

Iron Age – follows on from the Bronze Age, starting c. 1200 BCE. Marked by the production and more extensive use of iron.

Neolithic – a period, in the stone ages, marked by a shift from mainly hunting wild animals and gathering plants, to the development of agriculture, and the manufacturing of pottery. In parts of Africa, it starts in the early Holocene.

Levant – refers to an area, in the Middle East, which includes parts of modern Lebanon, Jordan, Palestine, Israel and Syria. These countries are positioned along the Eastern Mediterranean shores.

Near East – a geographical area that includes the Levant and the rest of the Middle East.

Cataracts – the Cataracts of the Nile are a series of six whitewater rapids (water is shallow and flows fast). Small boulders and rocks also lie on the river bed. Hence these cataracts have been historically used as key checkpoints.

Map 1. Political map of Africa. Source: Wikimedia Commons/CC BY-SA 4.0 (Author: mapswire).

Map 2. African rivers and lakes. Source: "Own Work".

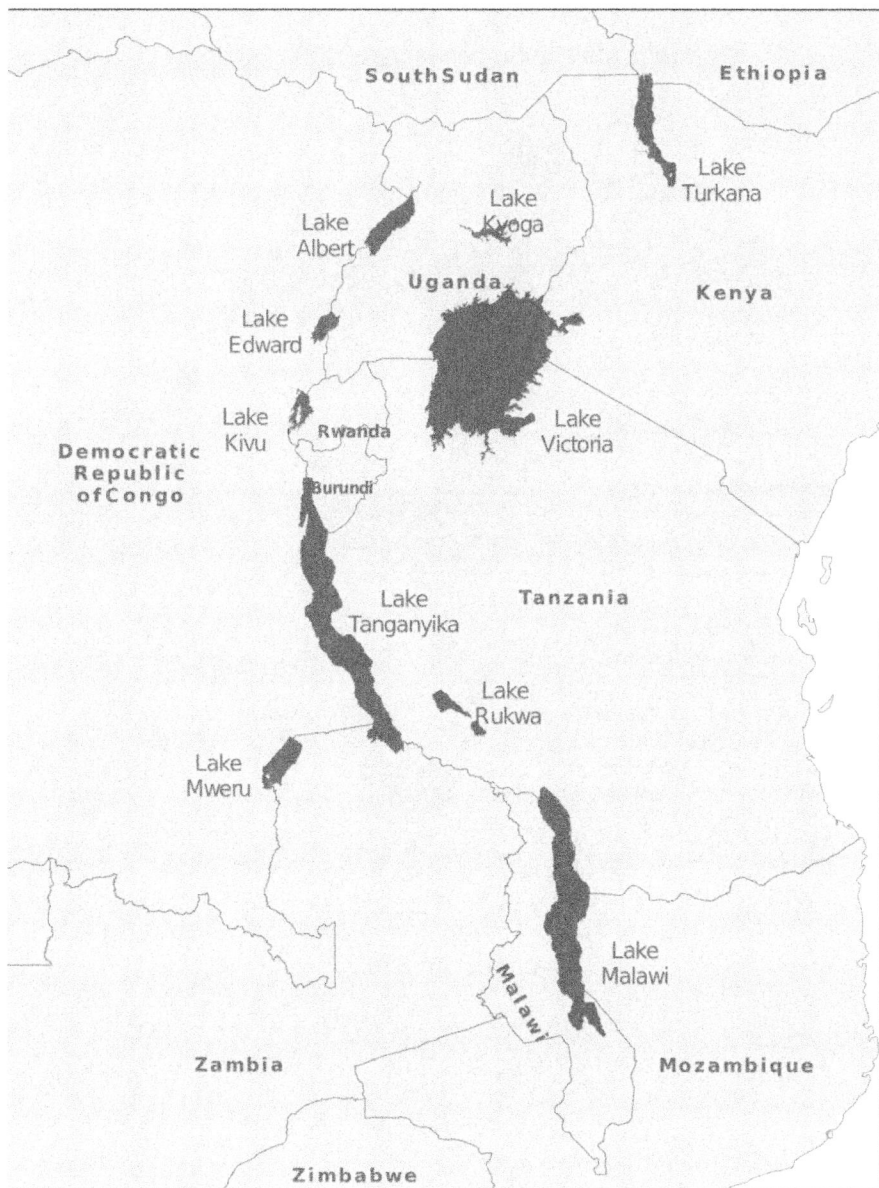

Map 3. African Great Lakes. Source: Wikimedia Commons/CC BY-SA 4.0 (Author: MellonDor).

Africa map of Köppen climate classification

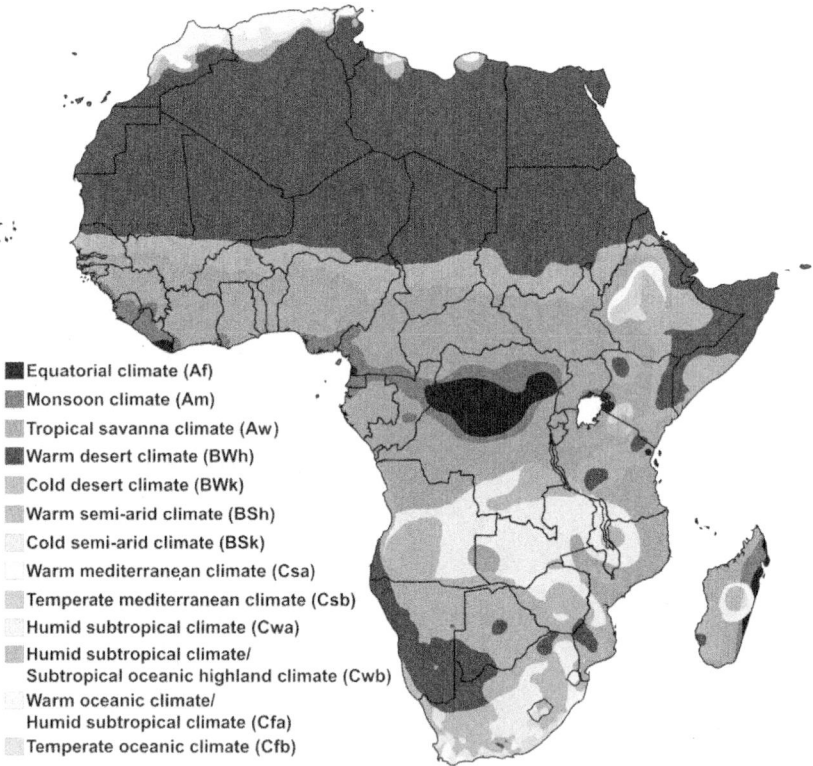

Equatorial climate (Af)
Monsoon climate (Am)
Tropical savanna climate (Aw)
Warm desert climate (BWh)
Cold desert climate (BWk)
Warm semi-arid climate (BSh)
Cold semi-arid climate (BSk)
Warm mediterranean climate (Csa)
Temperate mediterranean climate (Csb)
Humid subtropical climate (Cwa)
Humid subtropical climate/
Subtropical oceanic highland climate (Cwb)
Warm oceanic climate/
Humid subtropical climate (Cfa)
Temperate oceanic climate (Cfb)

Map 4. Climate map of Africa. Source: Wikimedia Commons/CC BY-SA 4.0 (Author: Ali Zifan).

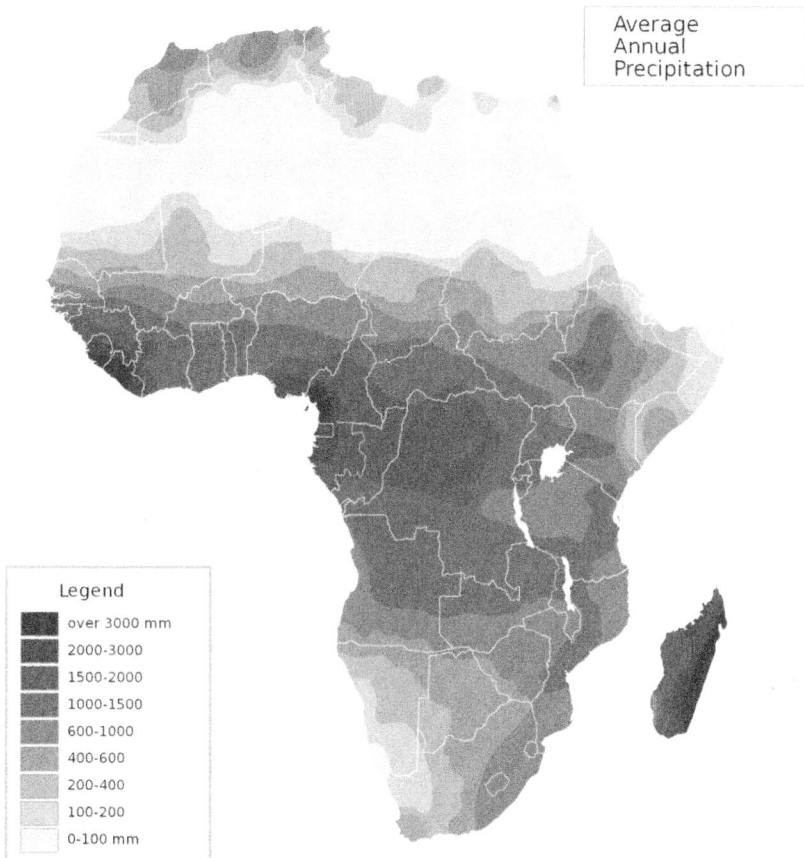

Map 5. Average precipitation (rainfall) in Africa. Source: Wikimedia Commons/CC BY-SA 4.0 (Author: Delphi234).

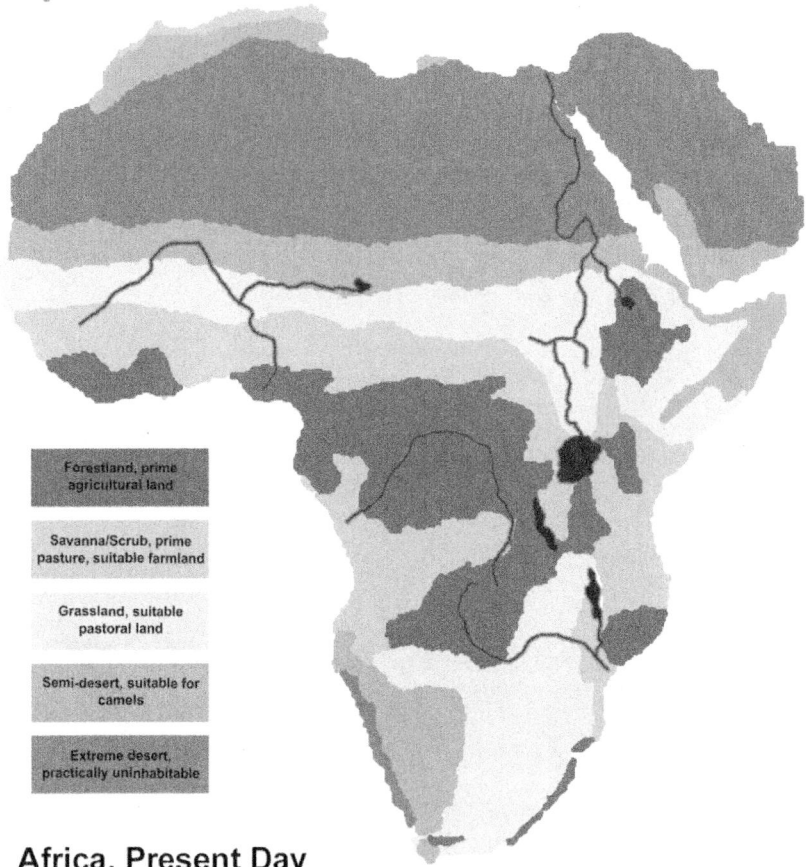

Forestland, prime agricultural land

Savanna/Scrub, prime pasture, suitable farmland

Grassland, suitable pastoral land

Semi-desert, suitable for camels

Extreme desert, practically uninhabitable

Africa, Present Day

Map 6. Vegetation map of Africa today. Source: Wikimedia Commons/Public Domain (Author: Ingoman).

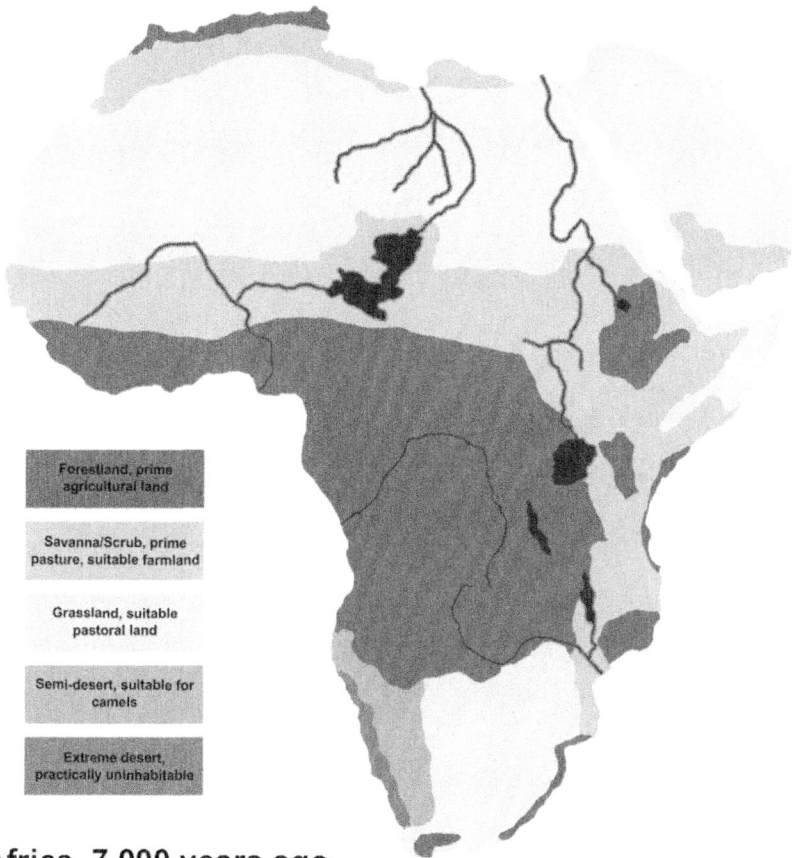

Africa, 7,000 years ago

Legend:
- Forestland, prime agricultural land
- Savanna/Scrub, prime pasture, suitable farmland
- Grassland, suitable pastoral land
- Semi-desert, suitable for camels
- Extreme desert, practically uninhabitable

Map 7. Vegetation map of Africa c. 7000 BP. Source: Wikimedia Commons/Public Domain (Author: Ingoman).

1. Setting the scene

Origins of the name "Africa" — who named the continent?

If you were to open a dictionary, to look up the definition of the word "Africa", what would you find?

Well according to the Cambridge English Dictionary, Africa is:

> the continent that is to the south of the Mediterranean Sea, to the east of the Atlantic Ocean, and to the west of the Indian Ocean.

While this is somewhat of an accurate definition, I'm sure that it is not the thought that crosses the mind of 99% of people. The fact is — Africa means different things to different people. Your thoughts will primarily be shaped by your past experiences with the continent. For some it's the lions, leopards, elephants, and buffalos — found on a safari adventure. For others it's the desert nights, the beaches or a place to do business. Or perhaps Africa is simply a powerful word — one that relates to freedom, hope, mystery and more. Arguably, and for most, Africa is simply home.

There are other facts that you may find when looking up the definition of Africa. It is the second biggest continent on earth, which is true both in terms of size and the number of people. It is home to around 16% of the world's human population, with the average age of the populace being the youngest of all the continents. If you do the math, over 1.1 billion people may call themselves African. That is including both those that actually live on the continent itself, and those in the diaspora.

Now that we have somewhat defined and described Africa — where does the name actually come from? Given the fact that millions of people identify as African, knowing where the name comes from is in order — particularly for those concerned with Africa's history.

Roman origins of the word Africa

The precise origins of the word Africa is still debated by historians. However, there is much that we do know. The majority of scholars agree that the term Africa came into Western use and by extension the English language, through the Romans.

At the time, the Romans used the term to refer to parts of Carthaginian North Africa — the Carthaginians being among Africa's greatest civilizations, with their capital "Carthage", centered on present day Tunisia. After the Romans conquered Carthage c. 146 BCE, the province of *Africa Proconsularis* was soon declared, with the province becoming one of the wealthiest in the entire Roman Empire.

The Romans are said to have got the name Africa from a Berber tribe, living just to the south of Carthage. There are a number of sources as to the name of this particular tribe, with the most common being *Aourigha* or *Afarik.* Accordingly, some claim the Romans first called this land *Afri-terra* (land of the "Afri"). Some have also made the case that the suffix "ica" (in Africa) could also refer to the same "land of the Afri". Case in point *Celtica*, named after the region of Ancient Gaul (modern day France) inhabited by the Celts.

A common myth is that Africa was named after the Roman general Publius Cornelius Scipio, also known as Scipio Africanus. However, Scipio got his honorary nickname "Africanus" after his victory over Hannibal Barca, and the Carthaginians, in the Second Punic War c. 202 BCE.

Other origins of the word Africa

Leo Africanus (not related to Scipio) was one of the most famous travellers and scholars in the 16th century. He was best known for his book *Descrittione dell'Africa* (Description of Africa), which focused on the geography of both North and West Africa. Africanus had it that the name Africa came from a town called *Afrikyah* (founded by a Yemenite chief). However, it is likely that the Arabic term for Africa, *Ifriqiya*, stems from the word "Africa" itself.

Other suggestions include that it came from the Greek word *a-phrike* (without cold), or the Latin adjective for sunny *aprica*.

So we have mentioned the Roman theory, the Africanus theory and the weather theory. There are a whole host of other theories including the Phoenician (*pharika* — land of fruit, *faraqa* — diaspora) and Sanskrit/Hindi (*apara* — geographically comes after (Asia) i.e. the western continent).

Lastly, some also argue that the word is indigenous to the continent, with the word coming into Greek/Roman use only after they came into contact with Africans. For example you have the Egyptian word *Afru-ika*, meaning birthplace or motherland.

Other names for the continent (apart from Africa)

The word Africa originally referred to only North Africa, before later expanding to cover the entire landmass south of the Mediterranean Sea. Other parts of Africa went by very different names, according to different people — both within and outside the continent. Common names used to describe different parts of Africa include *Aethiopia*, *Guiné*, *Libya* and *Sudan*. These names primarily referred to regions in the northern half of the continent, as the southern half was not as well known or explored at the time.

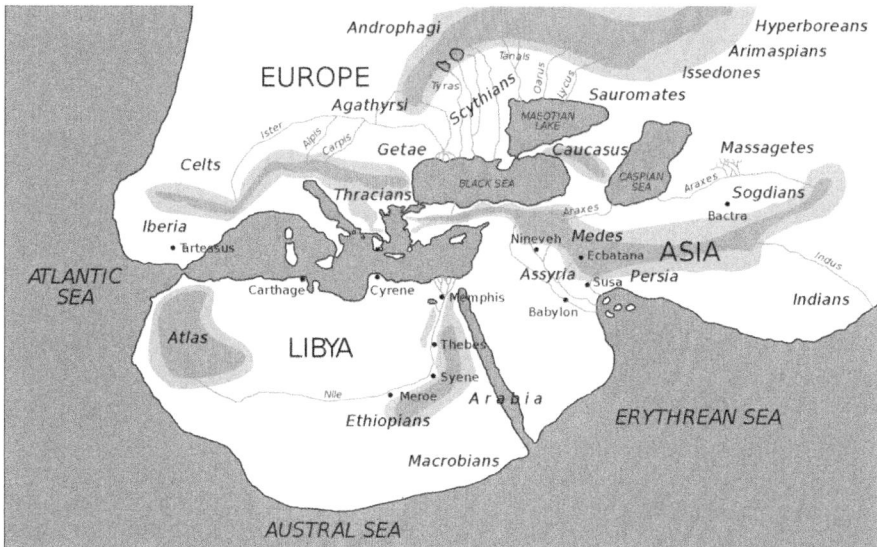

Map 8. Possibly what the world looked like, according to Herodotus in the 5th century BCE. Source: Wikimedia Commons/Public Domain (Author: User:Bibi Saint-Pol).

The Arabs called the Sahara/Sahel region *Sudan*, from the Arabic *bilād as-sūdān* (Land of the Blacks). This is where the modern nation of Sudan (and of course South Sudan) gets its name from.

The Ancient Greeks called the land stretching from the far west of Carthage, to the western borders of Ancient Egypt *Libya*. However, the Greeks did use the term Libya in a number of ways. Sometimes, Libya also referred to the entire landmass south of Greece i.e. the whole (known) African continent (apart from Egypt). The Greeks believed their world was split into three greater regions Europa (Europe), Asia and Libya (Africa) — all centered on the Aegean Sea. Early Greek maps often placed the dividing line between Libya and Asia at the Nile River. In other words, half of Egypt was placed in Africa, while the other half was placed in Asia.

To the south of Libya and Egypt was the land *Aethiopia* (Ancient Greek for "burnt-face" i.e brown/dark skinned) — home to the "Ethiopians". This term was used to refer to most of the near-tropical areas below the Sahara Desert (initially nearer the East African Coast).

In West Africa, around the 15th century, Portuguese explorers started to call lands below the Sahara as *Guiné*. This was a general term that referred to lands inhabited by the *Guineus* (black Africans south of the Senegal River). It is from the word Guiné that we get the English word "Guinea", and the subsequent nations of Guinea and Guinea-Bissau — as well as the Gulf of Guinea (and more).

Indigenous names for Africa

None of these words would have been what the ancient inhabitants of these regions, called the landmass upon which they lived. And there was likely no concept of continental geography, at the time anyway. During these early times, the whole of the African continent, as we know it today, had not been mapped. Each cultural or ethnic group, likely thought of their land as the center of the world.

This makes it impossible to identify a universal name, for what the entire continent was called, before it started to be fully mapped (by cartographers) around the 15th and 16th centuries.

The name Africa takes root

The European Age of Discovery or Age of Exploration (c. 15–17th century), brought about the notion of continents as we know it today; and so entire continents started to be given names.

Around the 18th century the name Africa, for the whole continent, had firmly taken root. As such names like Aethiopia, Guinea, Sudan and Libya lost out. Why was Africa chosen over the others? This was likely due, in part, to historians of the time having a preference for words with a Latin character.

The concept of an "African" (a person with roots from the continent) has only recently become a thing. In prehistoric, ancient and medieval times it was pretty much an unknown concept — with the world being far less globalized and connected than it is today.

Who was and is an African

Although I have touched on this briefly in the previous section, a discussion on who was and is an African — is important for anyone that truly wants to understand African history.

When one thinks about such a question, one may find the answer blatantly obvious — an African is someone that comes from Africa.

But then don't we all?

If the first humans are said to have come out of Africa, then by default that makes everyone an African. No?

Technically, yes, that is true. However, the term African is one of those English words that have been, to put it plainly, misused. This misuse of the term African makes the answer to the question, of who was and is an African, not so obvious. In other words, the answer is rather complicated. Ultimately, like the term Africa, an African means many different things, to many different people.

A brief discussion on how people's perceptions of Africa, has been shaped, is in order.

A continent that stands as one, but yet at the same time differs

Historically Africa, as a whole, is not a continent that has been isolated from the wider world, nor has it been inhabited by one group, or set of people. That is the impression one may have gotten, initially, from reading general books and newspapers, as well as watching TV. Backed up (of course) by schooling systems — that do not really explain history in a way that allows kids to connect the dots. Instead, bits and pieces are presented in a "vacuum" — seemingly unrelated to any prior or future events.

The truth is — Africa is diverse. In fact, it is the most diverse continent on the planet. The sheer number of languages in Africa proves this fact. Nowhere on earth is there such linguistic diversity as in Africa. Language, culture and ethnicity are all related concepts. Accordingly, the people of Africa cannot be one and the same.

This fact is not appreciated enough, primarily because of the lack of limelight given to Africa today — particularly with regards to its history. Instead, apart from Ancient Egypt, focus has primarily been on "Africanness" when there was no such thing as Africanness (until relatively recently).

This also links to the concept of the nation state. Most African nations are both new and artificially created. Consequently, common identities in relation to the nation (country) are weak, and what you have instead is more loyalty to ethnicity. So when you look at what it means to be a Frenchman, and compare that to what it means to be a Tanzanian — there are clear differences (with the former having much more meaning).

This lumping together of Africa as one, tends to result in individual African societies, cultures and civilizations, getting little to know recognition in the Western world. You may occasionally hear a thing or two about nation states such as Ghana or Kenya. But what percentage of Western people know that nobody speaks "Ghanaian" or "Kenyan"?

People have been moving in and out of Africa for thousands of years

If you look at a map of Africa, to the far north east, there is a small land bridge called the Sinai Peninsula. This peninsula is what has connected Africa to Asia and Europe, enabling people to move between the three continents (overland). Movement via the sea was also possible, as demonstrated by Carthaginian invasions of Spain, and the Ancient Greek colonies in (modern) Libya. Undoubtedly, along with the movement of people, historically there has always been the movement of goods and ideas. This is comparable to how people move and trade with one another today (although on a much greater scale in this day and age).

Contacts between different regions of Africa varied

East Africa, for example, had a significant trade network with Arabia and Asia — across the Indian Ocean (by the first millennium CE). This meant that East Africans influenced, and were influenced by the peoples of Asia — namely Arabs, Persians, Indians and Indonesians. This contact and influence gave birth to the Swahili city-states, and the resulting language of Swahili (an indigenous African language, with a great deal of Arabic loan words).

There was also a significant trade network across the Sahara, in West Africa. Caravans of goods would be sent up, through the desert, to ports in modern day Morocco, Algeria, Tunisia, Libya and Egypt. From these ports the goods would be transported by sea to Europe. Trade equally flowed the other way. While this trading network flourished, Europeans did not actually know the original sources of some of these exported goods, and so for example Hausa Nigerian leather was labeled

"Moroccan leather". The search for the direct sources of such goods, led to the European Age of Exploration.

Thanks to Africa's geography (as we shall see a bit later on) not all parts of the continent developed in the same way. Due to natural barriers (deserts, jungles, mountains etc.) and large distances — contact and subsequent trade between people in certain parts of Africa was difficult. For that matter, groups from parts of the continent would often have more links with external people, than with other groups within Africa itself. This was particularly true in the case of Southern Africa — a region where people migrated to much more slowly. This all played a part in the vast differences in language and culture we see today, across the continent, sometimes even in places more or less "next door" to each other.

A European example

Due to Britain's position, on the fringes of Europe, it developed much more slowly than both the mainland (of Europe) and the civilizations centered on the Mediterranean Sea. One such civilization was the Roman Empire. With Rome's conquest of Britain, the Romans brought the technology, architecture and way of life — that ultimately forms the basis of much of British society today.

Before the Romans, Brits lived a mostly tribal life in scattered villages. The Romans brought the concept of permanent settlements or towns, laying the foundation for the City of London as we know it today. The Romans themselves borrowed greatly from the Greeks — including ideas on art, literature, religion and architecture. While the Greeks in turn borrowed from the Egyptians (and many other cultures).

All this borrowing could not have taken place in a vacuum. In other words, there must have been the movement of people from place to place. Africans to Asia, Asians to Europe and Europeans to Africa, and vice versa.

The answer to — who was and is an African?

The prior discussion now sets the stage for finally answering the question of — who was and is an African? And like initially answered, an African is just someone that comes from Africa.

Africa has always been home to people of different skin colors and physical characteristics. Being African, has nothing to do with the way a person looks. As detailed above — isolation, migration, trade, conquest and more have all shaped what Africa has become today — a melting pot of different cultures, religions and languages.

Simply put — the people that identify with Africa, and call it home, are the true Africans. This has been the case in the past, is the case now, and will be the case in the future.

Africa's place in history — a continent that has always been part and parcel of the "known world"

The continent's place in (recent) world history, has been greatly influenced by Europe (as to has Europe been influenced by Africa). This influence has had a great effect on the perception of Africa as a continent, and the people living here — be it perceptions in academia, media or politics.

You may often hear the term "Sub-Saharan Africans" i.e. black Africans living south of the Sahara Desert. Taking the term at face value — who then are the Saharan Africans? What's the difference between the Saharan and the Sub-Saharan Africans (if any)? And finally who are those Africans above the Sahara?

This term Sub-Saharan implies some sort of separation, or isolation between Northern and Southern Africa. Some have even argued that it has been an attempt to shift the northern boundary of Africa, from the Mediterranean Sea, south, to the edge of the Sahara. That's not to say that there are no natural barriers in Africa — there are. And the Sahara is one of them, but there are others. One of the others is the Congo Rainforest, which as we shall see, was arguably the bigger barrier to movement in Ancient African history.

The Sahara itself has not always been a desert — archaeologists, historians, linguists and scientists have all attested to this. 11,000 years ago the Sahara was green and lush, meaning multicultural Africans used to live across its plains — trading with one another. As highlighted before, this Saharan Trading Network was in place well before the coming of the sea routes. And it is this trade that formed the backbone of several West African civilizations e.g. the Mali and Songhai Kingdoms.

People often make the mistake or assumption that how the world is today, is how it has always been (and how it will be in the future). It is all too easy to forget that the world is millions of years old, and that the average human does not live up until a 100 years of age. A 100 years ago (the 1920s) horse and carriage was still a popular means of travel. Further, we had just come to the end of World War 1, and most African and Asian countries had not even got their independence yet. Go back 500 years, and there was pretty much no European presence in what is today the United States.

Ancient Egypt's place in Africa

When one talks about African history, you cannot get away from the Ancient Egyptians. The topic of Ancient Egypt has a particular charm worldwide, especially in the West. So much so that the average American or Brit, probably knows more about Ancient Egypt, than the modern nation state of Egypt itself. Countless films, plays and stories have been told, with some of the more famous characters and figures being Tutankhamun (King Tut), Cleopatra, Ramses II, Hatshepsut and Imhotep. These famous figures go along with the mummies, the pyramids, the treasures, the hieroglyphics and more.

What is particularly fascinating is the fact that, to the Ancient Greeks and the Romans, Egypt was already an Ancient civilization. To put this in context, Ancient Egypt's beginnings can be traced back to well before the unification of the two lands i.e. Upper and Lower Egypt c. 3100 BCE. Rome itself was only founded in 753 BCE. In other words, the Ancient Egyptians had well over 2000 years on the Romans! In fact, Ancient Egypt and by extension Africa as a whole was part of the earliest cradle of civilization. This cradle is known as the "Fertile Crescent" — spanning the Nile Valley and the Near East.

Was Ancient Egypt the only great African civilization? No, it was not.

Why then is Ancient Egypt talked about so much? Well, I have already given you the answer to that above, even so let me clarify.

When you talk about the roots of Western civilization, two civilizations are almost always mentioned — Ancient Greece and Ancient Rome. Together they are often referred to as the "Greco-Roman" civilization. This period of history, between 800 BCE and 600 CE, is known as classical antiquity (or the classical era). It is a roughly 1400 year period, during which both Greek and Roman societies flourished.

The Persians (modern day Iran) were the ones to have ended almost 3000 years of native Egyptian rule, in c. 343 BCE, with their (second) invasion of Egypt and overthrow of the 30th Dynasty (headed by Pharoah Nectanebo II).

Let's do some math. 3000 years, of (almost) exclusively indigenous rule over Egypt, is more than twice as long as the entire classical era. Even if we were to extend classical antiquity to the final fall of Byzantiuym (Eastern Roman Empire) in 1453 — the Ancient Egyptian civilization still lasts longer (by a few hundred years).

This is but one of the reasons why, Ancient Egypt is (deservedly) talked about so much, no other civilization (except perhaps the

Chinese) has lasted as long. Most of the other reasons have their roots in Egyptian contributions to the world, which are arguably unrivalled to this very day.

2. The African beginnings of human life

It is widely acknowledged that life for us as humans started in Africa. However, the specifics are yet to be determined. The science of evolutionary theory is an ever changing one. New studies are always being undertaken, as are new discoveries being made, both giving rise to new theories. Sometimes these newer theories support existing ones. Other times they completely contradict what we thought we knew.

Despite this, the theory that mankind came out of Africa holds true, and has held true (for most scientists) for a few decades now. It is from Africa that humans went on to colonize the world; leading to the almost 8 billion people we have today — spread across the continents.

In evolutionary theory our ancestors are said to have been roaming the earth millions of years ago. Some say 3 mya some say 6 and others say 12. Either way, that's a long time ago. To put that into context, civilization as we know it, is only around 6000 years old. And the first industrial revolution occurred less than 300 years ago. These ancestors of ours were not the modern form of humans we know today. Instead, they were different forms of hominins (humanlike beings). As to what made these hominins special, compared to other beings, it was their ability to both walk upright (on two legs) and their larger brains.

We know that humans evolved in Africa, through scientific study of ancient bones, fossils, stone tools and related artifacts. With modern technology, scientists are also able to conduct DNA analysis to study the genetic profiles of ancient peoples, and subsequently trace their movement around, and out of the continent.

Until recently, the oldest remains or fossils of modern-humans (Homo sapiens) had been found in East Africa — dating back to c. 200,000 years. However, recent dating of a skull found in *Jebel Irhoud*, Morocco was put at c. 300,000 years old. These findings suggest that around 300 kya, early forms of Homo sapiens could be found spread across the continent. Researchers say "early" because the "brain case" (back of the head) is noticeably longer than humans of today. In those 300,000 years, leading up until today, our brain shapes and functions evolved.

Archaeological research has further shown that East Africa was a region inhabited by a variety of Stone Age hunter and gathering populations. A range of pebble tools have been found in places like modern day Kenya and Tanzania. Some of these tools have been dated back to over 2 mya. The different types of tools found, give clues as to the kinds of hominins that may have been able to use such (at the time). This has made East Africa an important area for evolutionary human study.

Climate change

The planet has been constantly going through changes in climate, from its foundation millions of years ago. An understanding of climate change and its implications is not just important for life today — it is also an important way of understanding how hominins lived all those years ago. The climate would have affected early human development and behavior, similar to the way that it does today.

For example, today, regions of extreme heat or cold are lightly populated — if at all. This is likely to have also held true in the past. Hominins would have migrated from places with unfavorable living conditions, to more favorable ones (taking their languages and/or know-how with them). Any species that couldn't survive and adapt would go extinct. This was not just true for human-like species, but also for plants and other animals. This is especially important when it comes to African history, given the size of the continent and the range of different physical regions throughout.

During earth's long existence, there have been times of extreme cold (ice ages) and times of extreme heat. Extremes sometimes lasted thousands of years — greatly impacting the geography of the world at the time. In Africa, deserts would expand, and rainforests contract. And towards the other extreme, Africa would experience much greater rainfall, resulting in an expansion of rainforests and allowing rivers to flow — where they could normally not. It is thanks to these very phenomena, that the Sahara Desert was once lush and green.

Humans and the move out of Africa

The first of our ancestors to migrate out of Africa, Homo erectus, did so around 2 mya. This ancestor of ours had human-like body proportions, with shorter arms and longer legs (relative to the torso). They had also developed sufficient intelligence, technologies and diets — all of which enabled them to migrate and survive outside of the continent.

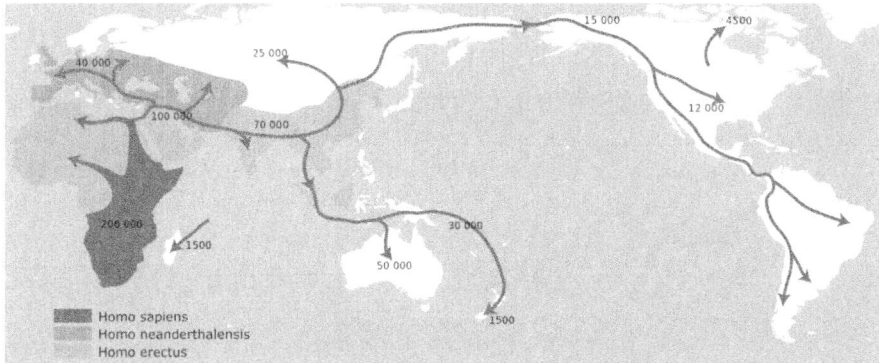

Map 9. Migration of Homo sapiens out of Africa. Source: Wikimedia Commons/Public Domain (Author: NordNordWest).

By around c. 110,000 BP modern-humans, from our humble beginnings, could be found all over Africa. Although there were migrations out of Africa prior to this, the first big migration is said to have occurred almost 70,000 years ago — into Western Asia. At the time, Africa was in somewhat of a dry period, and human population levels were quite low. Scientists have proposed a few routes, from which these early humans left Africa.

One of these routes is via modern Egypt and the Sinai Peninsula, and then on into the Middle East. The other route is crossing from modern Djibouti/Eritrea, across the Red Sea (the straits of Bab-el-Mandeb), into modern Yemen. A route via the Straits of Gibraltar into Southern Iberia (Spain/Portugal) has also recently been proposed — in relation to humans populating Europe. Either way, once outside Africa, humans spread in all directions — peopling the rest of the world in the process. From current evidence, it appears that humans populated the Americas last, with human entry beginning c. 15,000 BP.

As to the "color" of the first humans — they were almost certainly what is considered dark-skinned or "black" today. That would be the only way for them to have survived the subtropical climatic conditions of Africa. Humans adapting to changes in climate, diet and environment, as they slowly spread worldwide, is the reason why we have differences in skin color today.

Humans living in cooler climates developed paler or whiter skin, to help absorb sunlight (and increase the production of Vitamin D). Those that stayed in Africa's hot tropical areas developed even darker skin — protecting them from harmful rays of sunlight. It has been suggested that these changes in complexion are relatively recent, possibly as "late" as 10,000 years ago. If you think about it, 10,000 years is not so long ago, especially if you take into account that the first (anatomically modern) humans are said to have lived over 300,000 years ago.

Going back to the earlier section on "who was and is an African" we again now see why the varied geography and climate of Africa, is the main reason why you have so much diversity within the continent itself. Despite these differences, all human beings, African or not, belong to the same species (Homo sapiens).

3. The Stone Ages in Africa

The making of tools, is perhaps what made humans distinct from other species. This manufacturing of tools first occurred during the "Stone Ages" — a prehistoric period of time that historians estimate to have lasted around 3 million years (up until the widespread use of metals). We now know that this move towards metal use only took place c. 6000 BP — simultaneously with the rise of the first civilizations in the world.

We can periodize the Stone Ages into three — early, middle and late. These time periods relate to changes in the tools used by the earliest humans and their ancestors. And it reflects changes in lifestyles.

Early Stone Age (ESA)

Throughout this Early Stone Age period, hand axe tools, scrapers, cleavers, knives and throwing stones were all used by some of our first ancestors. The oldest of such tools are dated as far back as c. 2.6 million years ago. Even older stone tools have been unearthed. However, it is not known whether they were used by a "Homo" species, as no Homo fossils have been found for around that date yet. Therefore, this could potentially mean that toolmaking predates the Homo genus entirely. This is important as the ability to deliberately make tools, was thought to be a uniquely Homo (human) characteristic.

The tools used between c. 2.6 and 1.7 mya, are known as "Oldowan" tools or the Oldowan industry. The term Oldowan is taken from the gorge (Olduvai), in Tanzania, where the first such tools were discovered. These tools were made by removing flakes from stone cores (pebbles), creating a sharpened edge in the process. The final product was then used for cutting, chopping, and scraping — animals, plants and wood. The initial structure of the pebble in question mainly determined the final shape of a given tool.

Figure 1. Stone Age tools found in Fauresmith, South Africa. Source: Wikimedia Commons/CC BY-SA 4.0 (Author: John stonetool hunter).

Following on from this you had "Acheulean" tools, used from c. 1.7 mya to 200 kya. They are named Acheulean after the Saint Acheul site in France, where they were first discovered in the 19th century. These tools were much more sophisticated stone implements — featuring both sharper and straighter edges. It is for such reasons that the production of Acheulean tools is seen as one of the major transitions in human evolution.

Not only was the making of Acheulean tools a major breakthrough, for the earliest humans, it was also important for our understanding of man's beginnings. Acheulean remains are what first clearly demonstrated that human history goes back well before the first civilizations (resulting in the theory of human evolution itself). At the time, this would have been back tens of thousands of years, but today we can trace back to millions of years ago.

Although the first discovery was made in France, the vast majority of Acheulean tools have been subsequently found in Africa. In addition, the oldest Acheulean tools have also all been found on the continent — with such tools found in Europe and Asia being younger. For example, the oldest Acheulean tools found in Europe are only c. 900 kya — coinciding with the movement of a human ancestor (Homo erectus) out of Africa. It goes without saying, that this also provides evidence for the movement of human-like beings, out of Africa, well before anatomically modern humans (Homo sapiens) arrived on the scene.

Acheulean technology is best known for its very distinctive stone hand axes. These hand axes were often pear or teardrop shaped i.e. they were deliberately chipped on both sides and shaped to be pointy. Finds have shown significant variations in size and quality of craftsmanship. Some of the discovered hand axes have been beautifully made, suggesting hours of skilled labor had gone into their production.

It is important to note that archaeologists also speculate that wooden tools, and other highly perishable materials, may have also been used in this time period. However, there is little direct evidence for this, due to the very nature of these materials. For example, wood decays relatively quickly.

Hunter-gatherers and rock art

Throughout most of the Stone Age, humans (Homo) lived off the land. This simply meant that the humans of the age lived on whatever food they could obtain by hunting and/or gathering. Humans of this time did not produce their own food, as we do today, farming was non-existent and animals were still yet to be domesticated.

Such humans would hunt animals, fish, gather wild vegetables and scavenge what they could. Stone tools, and any other natural materials they could find, aided in their ability to process the food resources acquired. Tools would be used to specifically skin animals, break bones, grind plant material and more. The skinning of animals was particularly important, as their skins (once dried and softened) could be used for things like clothing and making bags. Further, animal bones could be used to make bone tools, and a variety of ornaments (jewelry).

In these early times, humans are thought to have lived in small groups, moving from one place to another — looking for food, or moving because of seasonal/climatic changes. They would have likely stayed near lakes, streams and rivers — due to the availability of fresh water (for drinking etc.) and edible plant material. As a result, these humans would have stayed away from heavily forested areas.

Evidence for such lifestyle mainly comes from the archaeological record. However, as mentioned earlier, some materials are not as well-preserved as others. And so, easily perishable materials (precisely organic matter) rarely show in the archaeological record (going back over very long periods). What this means is that the use of certain materials can sometimes only be assumed.

Having said this, there have been discoveries of particularly well-preserved (Late) Stone Age sites — in the southern half of Africa. An example of such sites is the "Gwisho hot-springs", in Lochinvar National Park (Zambia). Here vegetable matter, bone, stone and human skeletons have all been unearthed (with the site dating to c. 2000 BCE). Sites such as this enable us to get an idea of how life would have been for early hunter-gatherers.

As well as scientific and archaeological evidence, for such hunter gathering lifestyles, there is also evidence in the form of "rock art". This art is simply paintings and engravings, found on the walls of the caves and shelters — in which the earliest humans lived. Such art can be found across the drier regions of Africa — both to the north and south of the continent. These paintings represent a number of things including humans, animals and the general landscape. Some appear to show events such as hunting, fishing or dancing. While others show more abstract things, that may be inspired by life, death and religious belief. And so, just as modern humans put pen (ideas) to paper, hunter-gatherers put pen to "rock".

Tassili n'Ajjer is often seen as one of the best prehistoric open-air museums in the world. It sits in the Sahara Desert in South East Algeria. Here you will find a large number of paintings and engravings, showing scenes of climate change, animal migration and human evolution. To date, over 15,000 such images have been identified. Some of the art has been dated at over 12,000 years old. This provides artistic evidence that the Sahara was once a habitable savanna or grassland, rather than the current desert it is.

Before humans got to rock painting, they would have first learned to draw. And so, the oldest known drawing, by (assumed) human hands has also been found in Africa — this time far to the south of the continent, at Blombos Cave, South Africa. A rock was found featuring a criss-crossed pattern, dating to c. 73,000 BP. Although it is almost impossible to know what it meant, it demonstrates the ability of such early humans to produce graphic designs on a variety of different mediums (using different techniques).

Figure 2. Saharan rock art. Source: Wikimedia Commons/CC BY-SA 2.0 (Author: Patrick Gruban from Munich, Germany).

Middle Stone Age (MSA)

The Middle Stone Age is said to have started c. 250,000 years ago and is mainly associated with anatomically modern or almost modern humans. During these times there were significant changes in the stone tools used, and by extension, the lifestyles of the humans of the time. And it is also during this period that some modern humans, started to leave Africa — to populate parts of Asia (and a bit later on Europe).

The humans that left were already exhibiting what is called "modern human behavior", characterized by abstract thinking, the ability to plan and strategize, "behavioral, economic and technological innovativeness," and symbolic behavior. Evidence of such comes up in the archaeological record of Africa. So it is in Africa that you will find the earliest evidence for things like the newest stone technologies, bone tools, increased geographic range (surviving in different, previously unoccupied, environments e.g. deserts, forests, marine etc.), specialized hunting, the use of aquatic resources, long distance trade networks, processing and use of pigment (ink), and artwork.

Linked to this "modern human behavior" are specialist tools. Tools at this time showed significant local variation, depending on the geography of the region in question. Where humans lived in open, less wooded areas they would likely have hunted animals — evidenced by finding tools related to hunting. Where humans lived in wetter more forest-like regions, fruit gathering and fishing were more likely to have occurred — evidenced by tools related to fishing and woodworking. Therefore, in this period, we can say that humans started to specifically adapt to the environments they lived in, utilizing the tools needed to make full use of the resources available to them. This contrasts with the Early Stone Ages where stone technologies, regardless of location, were quite similar or homogenous.

Early fire making

Making tools was the first great discovery that humans made. The second great discovery was how to make fire (artificially from scratch). Despite the dangers that fire can pose, controlled use of it has been very important to human life.

Fire allowed man to make ceramics and metals, and bricks to construct buildings with. It then enabled us to invent the steam engine, the internal combustion engine (vehicles, boats, ships, airplanes, and trains) and much more. The eventual uses of fire to help produce both pottery (ceramics) and metal tools (rather than stone) are pivotal moments or eras in ancient history. As we will see later, it was specifically off the back of these two manufacturing processes, that the first civilizations rose — the first civilizations to who the modern world owes a great deal to.

Prior to being able to create fires, early Homo likely learnt to control or make use of naturally occurring fires e.g. bush or wild fires. These natural bushfires are often highly visible, even from afar, meaning there would have been some awareness of fire very early on. Wildfires can occur when lightning strikes and ignites dry plants and trees. From pure observation, humans quickly learnt when natural ignitions from lightning would happen (wet seasons in Africa), and planned to make use of the resulting wildfires (which could last for weeks).

Being able to artificially "create fire" was a game changer, as it enabled humans to greatly improve Stone Age life. The most important of all these lifestyle changes, was fire allowing humans to cook and warm themselves. The consumption of cooked food is thought to have changed the physical characteristics of humans. For example, cooked foods are often softer than their raw equivalents — allowing humans to eat food with smaller teeth and weaker jaws. Further, cooking generally increases the digestibility of foods (like meat), kills bacteria and allows more calories to be extracted (from said foods).

The benefits of cooking — all link to the increased brain sizes of modern-humans. During the slow evolution of Homo, brain sizes ultimately increased. Given the bigger brains, more calories were needed to feed it (even while resting). And so cooking was a way to get the required brain energy or power.

Fire would have also made it easier to travel from place to place, transporting key fire making items along the way. Additionally, fire enabled humans to live in dark caves, to live in harsher climates, to "gather" around a fire place, to frighten away dangerous animals and much more.

Recognizing the first fires to have been started by humans is difficult. In open fields it is pretty much impossible to tell the difference between a natural wildfire, and one that has been started artificially. And so archaeologists tend to concentrate on sites of human activity i.e. where humans stayed or lived at for extended periods of time.

Taking this into account, Africa provides the earliest sites that preserve traces of fire, in one form or another. The two earliest finds are in Kenya, one near Lake Turkana and the other near Lake Baringo, with both dating to c. 1.5 mya. These are termed "open sites". Other early sites can be found in South Africa at Swartkrans and Wonderwerk, which are both "cave sites" (c. 1 mya).

Kalambo Falls is another Southern African site, which demonstrates early fire use. This site provides almost certain evidence for artificial human fire-creation. Here charred wood has been found, as well as artifacts — that would have been made with the help of fire. Moreover, a possible hearth (fireplace) was unearthed. The finds at Kalambo Falls are dated at 500 kya.

By the Middle Stone Ages fire use was widespread. Consequently, definite hearths (demonstrating repeated fire-use) begin to appear in the archaeological record.

Human creativity, beads, jewelry and other body ornaments

Most humans today are concerned with appearance — some to more degree than others. Consequently we wear clothes, not just to keep us warm, but to also make us look good. It is for such reasons that we also decorate ourselves with pigments (makeup) and wear jewelry. The use of such beads and pendants mark a key turning point in human behavior. The earliest known traditions of personal ornamentation can be traced all the way back to the Middle Stone Age in Africa. Evidence for such appears later in European and Asian archaeological records.

Put another way, the capacity for the brain to create (and learn/retain) art, and likely the creation of art itself, was established before modern-humans migrated out of Africa. This links to our prior discussion on "modern human behavior" — with art forming part of the "symbolic behavior" component of such modern human behavior. Any stylistic differences (in the art produced) may have already been established (within departing groups) or developed on journeys to final destinations. It is such cognitive ability, or brain power if you like, that allowed humans to adapt to, or "conquer", all corners of the globe.

As briefly mentioned earlier, the Blombos Caves of South Africa are an important archaeological site. Apart from the earliest known decorative patterns (separate from the body) finds here also include the oldest beads currently known (c. 100,000 BP). These beads were made from deliberately pierced marine shells (seashells).

Moving further back in time, to another archaeological site, Pinnacle Point (also in South Africa), humans there may have been the first to color or decorate their bodies with ochre (c. 164,000 BP). Ochre is a natural clay earth pigment (colors range from yellow to deep orange/brown), still in use today for things like body painting and as sunscreen. Incidentally, this same archaeological site also presents us with the earliest evidence of human use of marine resources i.e. adaptations to be able to acquire and eat food from the sea.

Other early artistic African finds include the Tan-Tan (Morocco) figurine or doll-like artifact (c. 400,000 BP). Although this rock-figure or sculpture is mostly natural, there are signs of deliberate modification, and that it may have also been deliberately colored (red). The oldest known examples of art created on a flat surface date from c. 30,000 BP. An example of this is the stone slabs found at "Apollo 11 Cave" in Namibia. On these detached slabs are paintings of animals, much in the same fashion as the better known (and more recent) South African rock art.

Body ornaments can be seen as mediums or technologies for communication — especially when it comes to conveying socially-relevant information (symbolism). Without using words, a single body modification can tell you a great deal about an individual. So things like background, beliefs, experience, religion, status and more. Therefore the wide scale adoption of body art, beads and similar ornaments, in the Middle Stone Ages, suggests that human societies had gotten more "complex". These adoptions would have likely been a means for humans to network and integrate with people of similar mindsets.

The appearance of such artistic creativity also coincides with archaeological and genetic evidence, for relatively large increases in human population levels (due to both technological improvements and favorable climatic conditions). Scholars have suggested that these populations, although all human, had started to become more internally differentiated. Or, in other words, you had the beginnings of contrasting cultures and/or organized tribes.

Late Stone Age (LSA)

The Late Stone Age marks the years just before some humans switched from purely hunter gathering lifestyles, to establishing more semi-permanent settlements — where they eventually farmed and herded animals. The move to the Late Stone Age is said to have started roughly 50,000 years ago. As this period of time is more recent, archaeologists know much more about the Late Stone Ages than previous eras. For example, it is from this period, that most of the surviving rock art comes from.

Although this section is called the "Late Stone Age", fundamentally, this age is not much different to the Middle Stone Age. Recent research has given archaeologists a clearer picture of the last 300,000 years in Africa, to the point where they have been unable to pinpoint sharp divides between the MSA and the LSA. In other words, you pretty much have continuity between the two eras, with any distinctions being merely arbitrary in nature.

Prior to this relatively recent research, scholars had mainly associated the LSA with characteristics of modern human behavior. As seen in the prior section on the MSA, these characteristics predate the LSA quite significantly.

Despite the inexact definition(s) of what constitutes the Late Stone Age, it can be said that there were significant improvements in the human ability, to produce a wide range of specialist tools. Further, the stone stools found in the LSA appear to be much reduced in size. These tiny or micro tools (microliths) were often fixed to separate material, for example a handle/shaft, producing what are termed "composite tools". Although the techniques for joining wood and stone were in use during the MSA, there was more reliance on such composite tools in the LSA.

Such microlithic technologies made more efficient use of available rock materials, such as flint. Of course, to produce such small flakes of rock — skilled specialists were required. Whereas before tools were made using either wood or stone exclusively, attaching small sharp rock flakes to wood or bone handles, gave humans greater leverage — when making use of the end-product. Needless to say, it also offered the user greater protection against the sharp stone i.e. it was much more comfortable to hold a wooden or bone handle.

An especially important composite tool was the bow and arrow. The bow and arrow greatly expanded human hunting abilities, allowing us to shoot and kill from far. This would have increased survival rates, and enabled populations to grow significantly. It also demonstrates particularly high levels of perception and awareness, both of which are requirements to be able to think of and create such a weapon.

The oldest known evidence of arrows comes from Africa, specifically the Southern African site of Sibudu Cave. Here, bone and stone points dating to c. 60,000 BP have been found. Recent studies also suggest that by the start of the LSA, poisoned arrows may have also been developed. Poisoned arrows would have made it somewhat easier to hunt and kill particularly large animals like the hippopotamus (hippo), remains of which can be found in the African archaeological record.

Of course, the bow and arrow may have been in use much earlier than 60,000 BP, but it is difficult to tell. As we already know, the organic parts of the weapon (wood, bone, cord and feathers), rarely survive (going so far back in time). Therefore, any early bow and arrow use, is inferred by archaeologists (given site contexts).

During this LSA period humans were everywhere, in different regions of Africa and around the world. And they continued to specialize, making the stone tools that allowed them to fully exploit the environments in which they lived — be it arid, open, wooded or coastal areas.

Towards the end of the LSA (c. 10,000 BP), as we shall see later, the so-called "Aqualithic" or "Aquatic" civilization made an appearance — across the then green and wet Sahara. The way of life of this civilization, was linked to bodies of water, and the subsequent exploitation of marine resources.

Burials, cemeteries and mummies

Burials are an extremely important aspect of archaeology, particularly when it comes to studying ancient civilizations. As writing was only invented c. 6000 BP, a great deal of knowledge prior to this comes from burial archaeology. Burials enable scholars to study how ancients disposed of, and celebrated the dead — a practice that is still fundamental to most human cultures today.

And so the funerary practices, of past societies, enable interpretations of religious beliefs, rituals, symbolism, social status and much more. These interpretations are derived from multiple sources of evidence including skeletal remains, grave furnishings (goods), burial forms, standing structures and landscapes. When available, integrating this with historical records, allows for pretty accurate descriptions of how people lived in the past (their social systems) and how they died. Having said this, there are alternatives to (ground) burials, such as cremation, that typically will not show up in the archaeological record.

A little under 15,000 years ago there were groups of Africans living in a cave called "Grotte des Pigeons" near Taforalt in Morocco. They were not the first people to live in or visit this cave, nor were they the last. Others before them left behind traces of their stay stretching back to well over 100,000 years. However, it appears that the more recent visitors did things that the others did not. One of which was using the back of the cave as a deliberate burial site, making it the oldest known cemetery in the world (c. 13,000 BCE). Scientists also managed to recover DNA from bone remains at the site. This DNA evidence, demonstrates the fairly fluid movement of people into, and out of Africa at the time. This fluid movement is inferred from genetic studies, showing that the dead were related to both modern Africans and Middle Easterners.

To round off this section on burials, the highlighting of the case of the oldest known African "mummy" is appropriate. This child mummy was found in the Fezzan (Libyan Sahara), at a place called *Uan Muhuggiag*. This discovery is important because prior to this, it was mainly thought that the Ancient Egyptians "invented" African mummification. However, with this Libyan find, which dates to c. 5600 BP, the origins of mummification can be said to ultimately lie elsewhere (probably in the Sahara). What was most remarkable about this recovery was the sophistication of the child's mummification, suggesting that the art of mummification itself had been perfected over a long period of time. The archaeological site, a rock shelter, was occupied by Saharan pastoralists, in the mid Holocene (just after the Sahara's green period).

Late Stone Age African societies

The people that lived in the Late Stone Ages were already technologically advanced. At this point in time, humans would have accumulated significant "retained" knowledge — throughout the early stone ages (c. 3 mya) up until this point (c. 50,000 BP). You can liken this to how a baby accumulates knowledge over (a much shorter period of) time — learning its left from its right and what is and isn't dangerous etc. This retained knowledge would have formed the foundations of the societies in which humans lived, and would go on to live in — with the rise of the earliest civilizations.

By then, these humans would likely have organized themselves into groups — on a family by family basis. Where food was more plentiful (wetter regions) larger groups would probably have lived together, where food was more scarce (drier regions) groups would have been smaller.

There was no centralized leadership structure or leaders/rulers per say, as is mainly the case today. That is to say, everyone was more or less equal — nobody had to do anything (if they didn't want to), and major decisions were made together (by consensus). Clear distinctions founded on power, wealth, prestige and rank, would come later, as groups got even larger — first with chiefdoms and then state-level polities.

During this period, cooperative labor and communal effort would likely have been firmly established. For example, hunting the large animals required, to feed relatively large populations, could only be effectively done with the help of others. There was probably also a division of labor, the men would go out and hunt/fish — bringing the food back to be shared by all. And the women would care for the children, gather plants and look after the camps in which they lived. Manmade living shelters would have also been constructed, to a much greater degree than before. These huts or tents, not only offered an alternative to cave life, but they greatly increased the living space available to man.

A lot of this described behavior is still seen in surviving hunter-gathering groups — some of who can be found in Africa today. By observing such modern hunter-gatherers, anthropologists have been able to draw conclusions as to how Late Stone Age hunter-gathering societies worked. Based on the technologies available to such LSA people, they would have needed relatively large amounts of land to sustain their communities. It goes without saying, the more fertile or resource rich the land, the less of it would be needed. Regardless of the potential productivity of such lands, using it for hunter-gathering purposes is generally far less efficient, than the modern-ways in which land is used — to sustain the much larger population levels of today.

As populations grew, societies would grow larger. Limitations in available resources, would then force people to expand to other parts of the continent (or to seek to dominate others). Of course, different parts of Africa would have had different environmental factors for people to deal with. And so, not only would people's ways have needed adapting, but so too their phenotypes (what they looked like) and their languages.

4. People and languages of Africa

A valuable way of understanding Africa is through its languages. This information is particularly useful to the historian. Through study of modern and ancient languages, linguists are able to get a better understanding of where people came from, how people lived and how civilizations developed over time.

Human language is said to be unique, when compared to any other form of animal communication. This uniqueness stems from its compositional nature — humans can express an infinite number of thoughts (and ideas). As a result, language (and writing after that) is a pillar upon which humans have been able to transmit information from one generation to the next (retained knowledge) — a pillar upon which almost all subsequent technological innovations are based on. Some scholars believe that no other species had language (like we know it) except ours (Homo sapiens).

African origins of human language?

Like the African origin for man, it has also been suggested that Africa may also have been the origin of human language. Put differently, like human genes, human speech originated just once — somewhere in Africa. If this was the case, then human language would have pre-dated the out-of-Africa migrations from c. 70,000 BP. Accordingly, some scholars argue that language was an essential cultural innovation, which underpinned man's ability to venture outside the continent, and successfully colonize the world. This theory fits in well with that which says modern human behavior, was developed before man left Africa (discussed in prior sections).

This theory of the purely African origin of human language is inferred, and although there is no consensus on the "hows", "whys", "whens" and "wheres" — many are in agreement. When it comes to the origins of language, by nature of language itself, it is hard to tell —

given the much less direct or empirical evidence available. More plainly, (unwritten) words do not really leave traces in the archaeological record. And so scholars use a combination of archaeology, modern language diversity, language acquisition studies and more — to try and paint a picture of language evolution.

Given the lack of empirical evidence, there are many other theories as to the origins of human language — particularly in relation to the timing of complex language development. An alternative to the one briefly highlighted above, is the theory that suggests that complex language ability developed much earlier. That is to say, well before both the coming of anatomically modern humans (Homo sapiens) and the (subsequent) development of modern human behavior. This implies that the special properties of language evolved in stages (over time), rather than suddenly appearing as "one package" — perhaps starting with Homo erectus (c. 2 mya), or even predating the Homo genus altogether.

Languages are constantly changing

Languages are constantly evolving and changing (albeit relatively slowly). The English language of today is not the same as that of yesterday. In fact, most modern English speakers would barely be able to understand any form of "Old English" (the earliest recorded form of the English language). And prior Old English speakers would hardly be able to understand modern English — with its many loanwords (from other languages) and all the new technical terms of today.

The same way English has adapted to suit its users, is the same way African languages have also adapted. The earliest Africans would have tailored their languages, to suit the varied environments in which they found themselves in. In other words, the languages they carried with them, as they spread across all corners of the continent, needed to reflect their changing lives, experiences and cultures. Over time, these Africans would also have needed their languages to accommodate new ideas, inventions and technologies — borrowing from other languages when necessary.

As time went on, differences between languages widened greatly. As an example, in two relatively isolated populations, both initially speaking the same language, most new changes will not be shared (between the two groups). Consequently, each of these groups will slowly drift apart linguistically, until it reaches a point when they will be unable to understand each other. The end result of such differences is the approximately 2000 languages that are spoken in Africa today —

as part of four indigenous language families (or groups). There is also an additional language family (Austronesian) spoken in Madagascar, which has roots in South East Asia.

In linguistics, the concept of a language family relates to the idea that certain languages are somewhat similar to one another. This connection or relationship is said to come about via languages having a common ancestral or parental language — the "proto-language" of that family. It is from this proto-language, that all subsequent languages (within the family) are said to have evolved from.

When it comes to language families there are a few things to note. Firstly, not every language fits neatly into a language family, these languages are conveniently termed "isolates". Secondly, the actual concept of language families — if the family exists, how they are grouped, what languages go into what sub-family etc. are still disputed (especially when it comes to African languages). Thirdly, language families do not necessarily imply any "racial" link.

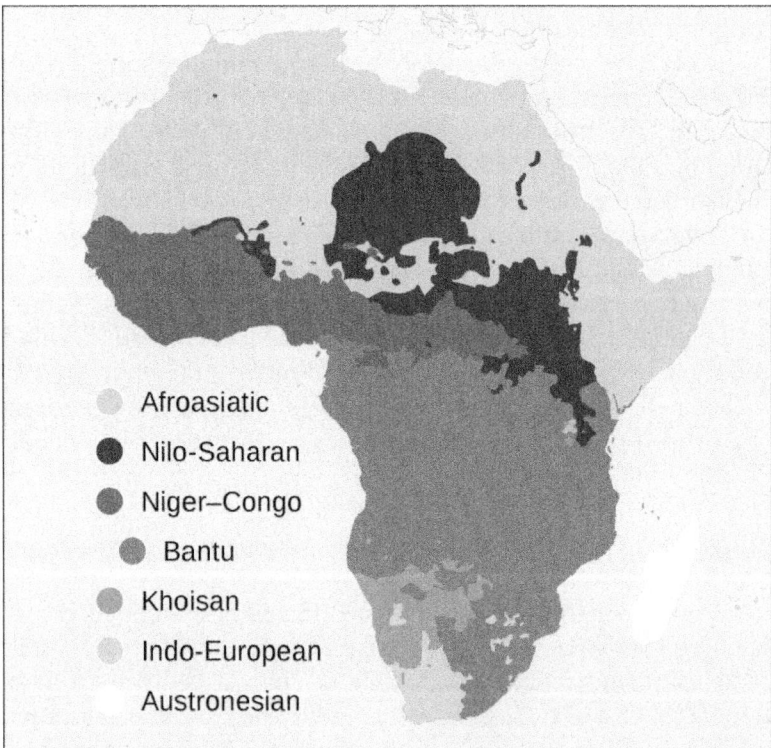

Map 10. African language families. Source: Wikimedia Commons/CC BY-SA 4.0 (Author: User:SUM1).

Genetics and the four continental language families of Africa

A widely used classification system, for African languages, is that initially proposed by American linguist Joseph Greenberg. Greenberg classified almost all African languages as Niger-Congo, Afroasiatic, Nilo-Saharan or Khoesan.

Nilo-Saharan, although accepted by some linguists, is still disputed. Khoesan has not been accepted as a valid language family, with the term being used more as a "convenient" grouping of specific languages. Niger-Congo and Afroasiatic are more widely accepted, although both do have their critics.

A combination of both genetic and linguistic studies, as well as archaeological evidence, enables researchers to suggest how and when languages split from each other. Having said this, the precise dates and locations of these splits, cannot be said with absolute certainty. And some theories are more disputed than others. For example, how old is Proto-Afroasiatic, and does its origins lie in Africa or the Levant? Lastly, it is important to note that scholars have made attempts to link events in prehistory, to each one of these language families, with these events leading on to the subsequent spread of the resulting "sister" languages.

Niger-Congo languages

Niger-Congo (or Niger-Kordofanian) is the largest language family in Africa — in terms of both the number of distinct languages (c. 1000) and the number of speakers (c. 700 million). The majority of Niger-Congo languages are tonal, with the same word potentially meaning different things (depending on the pitch or tone). The most widely spoken (native) Niger-Congo languages are Fula, Igbo, Yoruba and Zulu. If you're looking at the total number of speakers, however, Kiswahili (Swahili) is number one — primarily due to its use as a lingua franca in much of Eastern and South Eastern Africa.

As of yet, no words relating to "cultivation" (agriculture) have been (securely) reconstructed to the proposed Proto-Niger-Congo language. Therefore researchers think that any split in the languages likely occurred prior to the coming of agriculture. Accordingly, the origins of Niger-Congo probably go back to at least the early Holocene (c. 10,000 BP).

Around this time hunters, using bow and arrow, moved south from Northern Africa — into the greener Sahara. These hunters were part of the so-called "Ounanian" culture, marked by Ounanian arrow-points. By around 10,000 BP, these arrow-points start to appear in the West African archaeological record. And so, some researchers argue that, those of the Ounanian culture may have spoken Niger-Congo languages, giving Proto-Niger-Congo a potentially Saharan homeland. There is evidence of early Niger-Congo speakers having the bow and arrow i.e. being able to reconstruct "bow" and "arrow" (back to the Proto-Niger-Congo language). This potential Saharan homeland, could also explain the close relationship between Nilo-Saharan languages and Niger-Congo languages (the merger of the two as "Kongo-Saharan" has been proposed before).

There are a number of other proposed homelands for the original Proto-Niger-Congo language including the Inner Niger Delta (modern day Mali) and the Guinea Highlands. From either of these two initial locations, Niger-Congo speakers would spread across West Africa, following riverine routes, before eventually going south — beyond the equatorial rainforests of Central Africa. This movement into the central rainforests is known as the "Bantu Expansion". Although it has its critics, this theory may explain how Bantu languages (a sub-family of Niger-Congo) spread across most of the central, southern and eastern parts of the continent.

Nilo-Saharan languages

Nilo-Saharan is a proposed language family of around 200 distinct languages. In total, these languages amount to over 50 million speakers. The Nilo-Saharan languages have a wide geographic spread (found in 17 nations). As suggested by its hyphenated name — Nilo-Saharan languages stretch across the Eastern Sahara, the upper Nile Valley, and the areas surrounding Lake Victoria. The Nilo-Saharan languages with the most speakers include Kanuri, Kalenjin, Luo (Dholuo), Dinka, Zarma, Maasai and the Nubian Languages.

It is proposed that Nilo-Saharan populations migrated from an initial homeland in and around the border areas of Sudan, Chad and the Central African Republic. Some scholars have specifically proposed Central-East Sudan, south of the confluence of the Blue and White Nile, as the homeland — which somewhat fits in with the genetic, archaeological and linguistic data. Initial migrations then went northward towards the Eastern Sahara, westward to the Lake Chad area and southeastward to parts of East Africa (Kenya and Tanzania). Like with Niger-Congo speakers, these migrations were likely due in part to climate change (in the early Holocene), and the subsequent introduction of pastoralism.

It has been suggested that Nilo-Saharan speakers created or are linked to the so-called Aquatic Civilization of the Sahara-Sahel — given that the geographical spread of its languages somewhat matches the archaeological evidence for this Aquatic civilization (more on this later).

Afroasiatic languages

Afroasiatic or Afrasian (previously Hamito-Semitic), along with Niger-Congo, is one of the six largest language families in the world. Spread across some 250 languages, are its over 300 million speakers. These speakers are found throughout the Middle East, North Africa, the Horn of Africa and parts of the Sahel. Afroasiatic languages include Arabic, Hausa, Oromo, Amharic, Somali, Hebrew, and a variety of Berber languages. Several very well-known and very old languages are also said to be Afroasiatic namely Ancient Egyptian, Akkadian, Biblical Hebrew and Old Aramaic.

A great deal of research has been undertaken on some of these languages due to their religious connections — Judaism (Hebrew), Christianity (Aramaic) and Islam (Arabic). Interest also stems from the fact that a lot of what is termed "Western civilization" has its roots in Afroasiatic cultures.

There are six defined branches in the family Berber, Chadic, Cushitic, Egyptian, Omotic and Semitic. Although many scholars agree with these six branches, there is no agreement on the actual internal relationships between individual branches i.e subfamily classifications. Moreover, the inclusion of Omotic, as part of Afroasiatic, is still debated.

Ancient Egyptian provides the earliest written evidence for an Afroasiatic language — dating to c. 5000 BP. The second oldest (written) Afroasiatic language is Akkadian (Semitic). As Ancient Egyptian was already much different to Akkadian, it is thought that significant time must have passed between their split (from Proto-Afroasiatic). Accordingly, some have estimated that Proto-Afroasiatic goes back to at least 15,000 BP. This would make Proto-Afroasiatic by far the oldest, somewhat reconstructable, proto-language in the world. To put this in context, Proto-Indo-European (with subsequent languages now spoken in most of Europe and parts of South Asia) only dates to c. 7000 BP.

The original homeland of Proto-Afroasiatic is yet to be agreed on, and has proven to be a very controversial topic. Scholars have made arguments for both a Levantine (Middle East) origin and an African one.

Seeing as five of the six branches of the Afroasiatic family are (only) found on the continent, many have argued for an African origin (particularly linguists). But even within Africa there is no consensus on exactly where the proto-language originates. The Horn of Africa (Ethiopia/Eritrea) is sometimes cited, due to the area being home to a variety of Afroasiatic languages, all in close proximity to each other. Other scholars look towards the South Eastern Sahara/Sahel for the homeland, somewhere in and around Sudan. An African origin for Proto-Afroasiatic probably means that subsequent splits (into sister branches/languages) occurred before the coming of agriculture i.e. before the beginnings of food production in Africa.

Those in favor of a Levantine origin cite a variety of reasons, including some languages sharing distant relationships with Indo-European languages, and other Near Eastern languages (which can only be explained by ancient geographical proximity). Here the proto-language is proposed to have taken two paths into Africa. The first path is via Arabia and the straits of Bab-el-Mandeb (Red Sea), into Ethiopia/Eritrea. The second route is via the Sinai Peninsula, first into Egypt, before spreading to the rest of North Africa and the Sahel.

Khoesan languages

The Khoesan (Khoisan) family is formed by a unique set of languages, mainly spoken in parts of South Western Africa. There are also a few East African languages that (traditionally) belong to the Khoesan family. Many of these languages are endangered — some to more degree than others. The number of speakers of specific languages do not exceed more than a few thousand, while for others, the figure drops to only a few hundred.

The term Khoesan is a compound one, made up of the words for two ethnic groups — Khoekhoe and San. These two peoples were hunter-gatherers, with some of their members later becoming herders. Khoesan languages have the distinctive linguistic feature of the extensive use of "click consonants" (also found in certain Bantu and Cushitic languages). An example of a click consonant (familiar to English-speakers) is "Tsk! Tsk!" — an expression used to show disapproval or annoyance.

Khoesan languages do not form part of a universally accepted language family. Although there is some uniformity in their use of clicks, there are a lot of differences (word formation, sentence structure and vocabulary) from language to language. As a result, Khoesan is mainly a loose term to refer to languages that use clicks, and that cannot seemingly fit into the three main language groups of Africa.

Genetic and linguistic evidence points to an East African (Rift Valley) origin for some Khoesan-language speakers. Later migrations of Bantu and Nilo-Saharan speaking peoples, into Eastern and Southern Africa, displaced most of the Khoesan languages, leaving the limited presence of such to the Kalahari Desert (Namibia and Botswana), and to the Tanzanian part of the Rift Valley.

Genetics

The oldest known genetic lineage in living people can be found in the DNA of Khoesan speakers. This "Haplogroup" (gene) "L0" (mtDNA) — dates to c. 200,000 BP (which roughly agrees with the archaeological data for the first modern humans). mtDNA passes from mother to both son and daughter, while Y-DNA only passes from father to son. The genetic (mtDNA) makeup of all living humans can be traced back to origins in Africa — back to haplogroup "L". L0 and L1–6 are two sub-groups of the original L. It is L1–6 that is associated with the migration of humans out of Africa, from where the DNA has gone on to mutate into the several unique forms we see today. These unique gene "identifiers" have allowed researchers to chart potential migration routes out of, and back into Africa. This again highlights the diversity of the continent, given that only some groups of Africans actually left the continent (in the first place).

As a result of this genetic diversity, Africans have a number of genetic adaptations that have come about in response to varied geographic conditions (e.g. sickle cell disease). And so like with archaeology and linguistics, genetics too play an important role in understanding African history. Although the data, on African genetic material, has increased somewhat, there is still a significant lack of such — compared with non-African populations. This is particularly the case for very ancient DNA — where skeletal remains found in Africa have yielded very little of such DNA. More data will enable researchers to gain a greater understanding of human evolutionary history (as well as human biology and diseases).

5. The First Agricultural Revolution

It is said that, for us humans, the first great discovery was how to make tools. The second was how to make fire. And the third was how to produce food. Seeing as the first two have already been covered, here we can talk about the beginnings of both farming and the raising of livestock i.e. the beginnings of agriculture.

This Neolithic or First Agricultural Revolution, was essentially humans recognizing that they could plant (crops) today and harvest tomorrow, as well as rear (livestock) today for tomorrow's consumption. However, this revolution was not one specific event. Rather, the agricultural revolution was a more gradual or learned process. Due to this gradual nature, and despite extensive studies on the subject, scholars are still not in agreement on both the precise origins of agriculture, and the reasons for its coming. Consequently, there are many competing theories.

Perhaps unsurprisingly, the beginnings of agriculture, specifically in relation to Africa, are particularly contentious. In fact, the origins of African agriculture, presents almost the perfect case study for why assuming what works in one place, must work in another, can lead to "false" conclusions. And thus, this highlights the importance of judging each case on its own merits.

Although there is debate, and depending on what exactly can be classed as agriculture, many scholars agree that it probably first began in the Middle East (c. 11,000 BP). As a result of this, much of early research has been somewhat "tinted" with a Middle Eastern bias. To explain, in scholarship you may sometimes hear the term "Neolithic package" — referring to the material culture associated with the development of agriculture in the Middle East. Parts of this "package" are said to include animal domestication, farming, pottery and settled lifestyles. In Middle Eastern sites these aspects often do truly appear as one package i.e. where there was evidence for pottery, you would also find evidence for agriculture and settled life.

Therefore you have a Near Eastern shift from hunter-gathering to agriculture, story of — people settling in villages, cultivating crops, raising livestock and then producing pottery to store such food. This new model or way of life, then quickly found its way to Europe and parts of Asia.

This contrasts with Africa, where you would often only find parts of the package. For example, animal domestication without crop cultivation, or pottery without signs of any agriculture. Although this could potentially be attributed to archaeological site preservation, and data recovery issues — it also suggests that the story of the African move to food production, differs from that of the Middle East. Subsequent research has pretty much proven this to be true, in that the African food production story is indeed a unique one.

Domestication process

Going back to the origins of agriculture, its rise coincides with the end of the last Ice Age and the beginnings of the early Holocene (c. 11,000 BP). During the last Ice Age it would have been almost impossible to develop agriculture, given the much colder climatic conditions, in large parts of the world. And so with the coming of the Holocene, came the arrival of more stable and warmer weather conditions — favorable to plant growth and raising livestock.

Initially plants would have grown naturally, in the wild. Humans were then able to study how these wild plants grew, under what conditions, and their growth cycles. They would have realized that this process could be manipulated for more favorable outcomes (domestication). This manipulation would have first come in the form of protection and weeding, saving seed, and resowing of wild grains and root crops. Later, fertilizer and irrigation were added to the mix. And from there, only the best plant seeds would have been selected for resowing next year. Over time, this would have resulted in bigger and better harvests.

If you think about it, farming hasn't really changed much over the years. The basic concepts remain as true as ever — choose the right time, break up the soil, see to its fertility and moisture, hoe early and harvest early. The only difference between us and the earliest farmers is us being able to manipulate this process (using better technology) to a much greater extent — giving us the ability to produce much more food per acre of land. Of course, being able to produce much more food is a necessity, without which we would be unable to support the much larger global population of the day. Like the earliest farmers, however, we still remain at the mercy of Mother Nature (weather, climate, geography etc.) for the most part.

Figure 3. Cattle being herded in Angola. Source: Wikimedia Commons/CC BY-SA 4.0 (Author: Edward Middleton).

A similar thing occurred with animals of the time. Humans first learned what animals best suited their needs, and what those animals needed to eat (to grow). Those needs mainly fell into three categories — companionship (cats and dogs), food (cows, pigs, sheep, turkeys etc.) and working animals (camels, donkeys, horses etc.). Knowing this, humans would then protect these animals from predators, moving them from one safe zone to another, making sure the animals had enough to eat. Over generations, and with the help of selective breeding, positive characteristics would increase, and any negative characteristics reduce.

However, not all animals could be (easily) domesticated. And so desirable traits would have included fast growth rates, hardiness, ability to be raised in groups (herds), low aggression, predictability, low fear and more. Not many wild animals in Africa had all these desirable traits — particularly low aggression and predictably. And so for example, domesticating animals like hippos, rhinos and zebras, was practically impossible.

How agriculture changed their and our lives

People domesticating animals, and learning to cultivate crops, such as wheat, barley, sorghum and millet, was a huge leap forward — in that it enabled the beginnings of intensive food production. This ability to produce food meant that people were now able to live settled lives, without roaming from place to place — looking for what to eat. From living in small isolated villages, society slowly became more complex. More permanent homes were constructed, often made out of reeds or mud bricks.

With more (food) stability, came rapid increases in population — on a scale never seen before. This population boom came about because of both more productive subsistence systems, and because women were able to bear more children — in increasingly safe, stable and secure environments. More children meant more hands were available to help with agricultural production. And so the cycle continued. With each cycle, more knowledge was retained. Soon enough, specialized agricultural techniques or activities were introduced.

By modifying the natural environment, with activities like irrigation and deforestation, people were then able to produce far more food than they needed. In other words, they were able to generate a surplus (of food). This surplus could be kept as "insurance" for hard times, perhaps when the rains did not come, or it could be traded for other things. For example, raw materials or clothing — not found in given communities. This ability to generate surpluses meant that not everyone needed to be directly involved in producing food; some could specialize in other non-food-generating activities. For example, you could have expert blacksmiths, builders, carpenters, shoemakers, tailors and much more.

The ability to accumulate or amass a food surplus, may have also introduced the notion of "private property". Whereas before, plants and animals were "wild" resources, cultivated crops and domesticated animals were not — they were the "fruits" of one's labor if you like. And these fruits needed to be defended. This is in stark contrast to prior hunter-gathering groups, who worked more on the basis of open access to group resources and communal sharing.

Although direct evidence for having private property rights is hard to come by, prior to the emergence of writing, this may be inferred by looking at the archaeological record. Some historians have argued that some elements of private property rights, may have even been in place before the permanent shift to agriculture, with certain areas becoming naturally productive enough (in the Holocene) to sustain semi-permanent and then permanent settlement. Others still, have argued that the development of private property rights, is what allowed farming to take place i.e. it gave people the incentive to undertake the investments (field preparation, housing, storage etc.) needed to farm (without having to share).

The development of farming meant that society needed to change (social evolution). It needed more and more cooperation, organization and planning — as the number of people increased. This was the basis for developing centralized administration and political structures (states). It also encouraged the development of writing, law, warfare, urban planning and architecture, specialization, division of labor, trade, marketplaces and much more. Linked to the notion of private property or ownership, and in particular the desire to acquire luxury goods, is the concept of social class or division — the rich and the poor. Or put another way, the elite who had the political power and the masses that did not.

The culmination of this agricultural revolution (or evolution) is the birth of the first two civilizations in the world — Ancient Egypt and Sumer (Southern Mesopotamia or Iraq). There is still debate as to whether Egypt or Sumer came first, with dates for both going back to at least c. 5000 BP. Who came first very much depends on what you define as a "civilization" (more on this later). In addition, opinions are likely to change based on whether you ask an Egyptologist, or a scholar of Sumerian history.

Agricultural revolution(s) in Africa

The term "Agricultural revolutions" is far more appropriate than the singular "revolution". The reason for this is simply that there was no one revolution. Agriculture emerged at different times, in different parts of the continent. If we take Africa as a whole, pastoralism (specifically cattle-herding) was the earliest form of food production (c. 9000 BP) — crop cultivation came later.

On the continent, there are places where agriculture is said to have developed independently, that is to say — the practice was not introduced from elsewhere. The Sahel, West Africa (tropical), the Ethiopian Highlands and the Nile Valley are said to be regions of such independent domestication. Locally domesticated crops and animals include millet, sorghum, African rice and guinea fowl (Sahel) — African yam, oil palm (Tropical West Africa) — coffee, teff (Ethiopia) — tigernut, sycamore fig, donkey and cat (Nile Valley). These crops and animals were initially domesticated in climatic regions most suitable for their growth.

By the way, it may not be so obvious, but the donkey was an extremely important work animal (or beast of burden) — that transformed ancient trade/transport systems in both Africa and Asia. Donkeys are sturdy desert-adapted animals that can carry heavy loads — meaning they aided mobile pastoralism and were crucial to the development of overland trade routes i.e. trade routes that did not utilize rivers. They were also extensively used to redistribute food from areas that generated a surplus; to those that focused on non-food generating activities i.e. they facilitated the development of specialized manufacturing hubs/towns. Donkeys were domesticated by at least 5000 BP, which is considerably earlier than another well-known work animal — the camel.

In contrast to cattle herding, evidence for the cultivation of domesticated African plants (stated above) appears much later in the archaeological record (from c. 4000 BP). However, before this time, crop cultivation was already well underway in the Nile Valley. This earlier cultivation (c. 7000 BP) was based on Middle Eastern crops, including barley, flax and wheat. It is thought that both sheep and goats were also introduced, from the Middle East, around the same time. This is primarily due to the fact that there were no wild sheep or goats, in the Sahara, from which domesticated varieties could be obtained.

This early agro-pastoralist based economy appears to have been restricted to the Nile Valley. Having said this, cattle herding expanded across the Sahara relatively quickly. As for the rest of Africa, the ways of agriculture spread later (c. 3000 BP), with the so-called Bantu Expansion, into Central, Southern and Eastern Africa. Around the same time, Khoesan people may have also taken sheep and cattle herding techniques, far to the south of the continent (from East Africa).

It is important to note that this agricultural revolution, by way of birthing the concepts of permanent marketplaces and specialized manufacturing hubs or towns, was an important factor in the spread of languages across the continent. Languages would have spread not just with the physical movement of people, but also along lines of communication.

Those that were not part of this new economic system (hunters in deep forests for example) would have been (initially at least) unaffected by language shift. As the concept of "ownership" grew more and more popular, those that remained as hunter-gatherers were pushed from prime (fertile) lands — to more unfavorable areas. Those that stayed were assimilated, embracing food production and gradually shifting both culture and language in the process.

Change is never easy — Africans becoming farmers & religion

Despite the "invention" of intensive food-production, in certain areas, it took time for this invention to spread throughout the world — including around Africa. Even though groups of people may have been aware of agricultural practices (and its benefits), like any new technology we have today, it took time for people to embrace and/or adapt to such new ways. This again highlights why the adoption of agriculture was a gradual process, rather than something taken up with immediate effect.

Despite its benefits, and as it is today, practicing agriculture may have not been suitable in large parts of Africa. This suitability would have been determined by environmental and geographic factors, the same environmental and geographic factors, which as we have already covered, led to widespread migrations within and from the continent. As the English saying goes "there is more than one way to skin a cat", in this context meaning farming was only one of the options available to prehistoric Africans. In other words, in certain circumstances, continuing with hunting, gathering or fishing was more productive.

Another factor when it came to embracing farming was as humans were already relatively well established in parts of Africa — they had already learned to live with the continent. If you compare this to the first humans that left Africa (c. 70,000 BP) they were quite new on the scene. This created its own problems, and where there are problems there are often pressing needs for change or innovation (i.e. agriculture).

Those that adopted and embraced farming early on would have had to deal with new challenges — one of which was Mother Nature. People would have learnt, with time, that in order to plant and grow certain crops — specific climatic conditions were required. This meant that rain and sunshine became ever so important to the earliest farmers.

This link between agriculture and Mother Nature is said to have had an impact on traditional African religions, or the spiritual world. This can be seen with Ancient Egyptian religion. For example you had RA — the god of the sun. RA was also known as the creator god, as the sun was seen to give life by controlling the ripening of crops. So with the adoption of agriculture came a more sedentary life, in which the spirits or gods were instrumental in ensuring adequate sunlight, adequate rain, fertile lands, and a subsequent good harvest.

Similar concepts held true in animal husbandry. To this day, cattle play a critical role in religion and mythology, both within and outside Africa (for example in Islam and Hinduism). This should come as no surprise, given the number of functions cattle served — working animal, meat provider, milk provider etc. In some way, you can think of cattle like the "oil" of the ancient day — possession of which meant great wealth (for the owner).

6. African geology, geography, climate and the rise of its civilizations

As already discussed, for the most part of history, humans have lived off the land — exclusively hunting wild animals, fishing and foraging. This was the case both within and outside Africa. As humans retained more and more knowledge, they became better and better at hunting and gathering. These same humans were also able to live with climate change, either adapting to changing conditions or migrating to more favorable lands. This story remained unchanged, until relatively recently, when some humans left their old lifestyles behind and embraced food production — either rearing livestock or cultivating crops. As of today, the vast majority of people eat food either directly produced by themselves, or produced on their behalf.

As we shall look into further, agriculture or the ability to produce food (or at the very least having a stable, predictable supply of such) was and still is an essential component of civilization, and subsequent developments in art, science and technology. Of course this ability to produce food is almost exclusively dependent on geological, geographic and climatic factors. And thus, we can state that these fields of science have historically played an integral role in the fortunes of nation states — in Africa or elsewhere.

What is a civilization?

Before we discuss how, where and when — the first civilizations started in Africa. And despite having already used the term somewhat, it is only right that we briefly go over what exactly can be described as a civilization. This is important because civilization is one of those terms that tend to be "thrown" about in lectures, films and books — with few fully understanding what is meant by it or acknowledging that it can mean different things to different people (mainly depending on context). Ultimately, what you define as civilization, determines the hows, wheres and whens of the first civilizations.

One can define a civilization as a "complex society" or even culture. A civilization may share common characteristics with other civilizations. Characteristics such as generating food surpluses, higher population densities (cities), division of people into social and economic classes, systems of taxation, divisions of labor, regular trade, and retained knowledge. Other characteristics may include administrative structures, state/religious ideology, development of writing, science, the appreciation of the arts and warfare. This of course is not an exhaustive list, societies that only have a few or some of these characteristics can still be defined as civilizations. Further, as civilizations "advanced", more and more of these individual characteristics would have become apparent.

Rather than debating what can and cannot be considered a civilization, what is far more important is making the distinction between the basic hunter-gathering lifestyles, that we modern humans have practiced for over 95% of our existence, and the new ways of life and societies built since we learned newer ways of doing things (c. 12,000 BP). Using the terms civilization or complex society or complex culture allows us to do just that.

In doing so it is important to acknowledge that no civilization, or way of life, was inherently better than another. This is because humans had to adapt to the environments they found themselves in. It is this concept of adaptation that remains key to understanding the history of not just Africa, but any other continent. As you have already read, man has only been practicing agriculture for the last 10,000 or so years. But, man's history goes back way further than this. It was the need to adapt to a "new normal" that brought in the agricultural revolution and all other (significant) advances since then. And in relation to this normal, some were "forced" to adapt much sooner than others. This ability to adapt is arguably a large part of what distinguishes Homo sapiens (humans).

Why early African civilizations started when and where they did

If you take a look at a world map, specifically looking at major cities, you may notice a pattern — they all tend to be located on or near rivers, lakes and coasts. Example cities include Baghdad, Budapest, Cairo, Khartoum, Lagos, London, Mumbai, New York City, Paris, Shanghai etc.

There are two primary reasons for this — sustainability and commerce. Sustainability is with respect to access to food to eat, and water to drink. Commerce is with respect to trade — water transportation was the fastest and cheapest means of transportation available (which is still true to a large extent today).

Locations near rivers and other sources of water are also where the first civilizations developed; this is true in terms of Africa and the planet as a whole. That is to say, where there was civilization (or life) there must have been water.

And so, the question to ask is — where exactly are Africa's rivers? Before we go into that, some understanding of geology is helpful. Or in other words, how was the African continent actually formed?

Formation of the African continent

If you look very closely at the shapes of the world's continents, you may notice something. As an example, take a look at the two land masses on opposite sides of the South Atlantic Ocean — more specifically Africa and South America. Notice how, if brought together, they seem to fit together — a bit like a jigsaw?

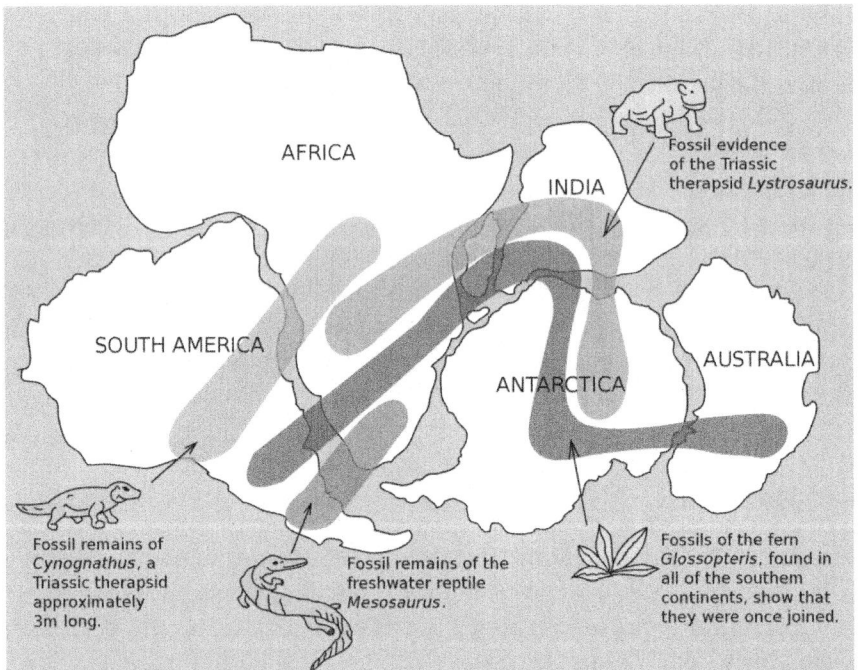

Map 11. Continental fossil patterns as evidence of the Pangaea. Source: Wikimedia Commons/Public Domain U.S. Geological Survey (Author: Osvaldocangaspadilla).

Around 300 or so million years ago, Africa was not its own continent. Instead, it formed part of a "supercontinent" the "Pangaea", with the Pangaea being surrounded by a single ocean known as "Superocean Panthalassa". A supercontinent is simply defined as an assembly of most, or all of the earth's cratons (stable pieces/parts of continents) to form a single large landmass.

This idea of the Pangaea was part of the theory of continental drifts, first proposed by Alfred Wegener — just over 100 years ago. In his theory, Wegener suggested that the world's continents once formed a single landmass, but with time, had floated apart. An analogy is how icebergs break from glaciers, and float freely in open water. Scientists have since found plenty of evidence for this, fossils of the same plant and animal species, found on the shores of different continents — matching geological trends (distribution of glaciers/ice) between the west coast of Africa, and the east coast of South America — and much more.

This Pangaea was not the first supercontinent on earth, in fact; supercontinents have assembled and dispersed multiple times in the (geologic) past. This kind of goes with the general theme of things moving in cycles — whether that's supercontinents, climates, and a whole host of other things (the four seasons, day and night, rise and fall of civilizations etc.)

Before the Pangaea, the "Pan-African orogeny" (an event that occurred c. 500 mya) is said to have brought together old cratons — forming the basis of the eventual shape of Africa as we know it today. Examples of these cratons include the West African, Congo, Kalahari, Tanzania and more. These cratons were all conveniently named in relation to what part of Africa they sit in now.

The end result of the Pan-African orogeny was the formation of an ancient supercontinent — "Gondwana". This supercontinent was made up of today's South America, Africa, Arabia, Madagascar, India, Australia and Antarctica. It was Gondwana, that merged with the minor supercontinent of "Euramerica" or "Laurussia" (North America, Europe and other parts of Asia), to form the Pangaea. And from this Pangaea (c. 200 mya), the continents slowly drifted apart to produce what we see today.

In between the Pangaea breaking up and today, the planet went through a few different "geological periods". During these periods, well before man himself, different life forms would come and go (become extinct). One such example are dinosaurs, who roamed earth in the

"Triassic", "Jurassic" and "Cretaceous" periods. As a whole, these periods are often referred to as the "Age of Reptiles" or the "Age of Dinosaurs". And more scientifically the "Mesozoic era".

During these geological periods, landmasses would have been constantly moving. And so, there were changes in landscape, which would have come with changes in climate and vegetation (food supplies). To make clear, as the continents drifted, what was once near the ice pole may now be near to the equator (and vice versa). This resulted in either large migrations taking place, or species adapting to changing habitats, just like humans were also eventually forced to do. Therefore, physical changes to earth by the way of continental drifting, also helps us to explain the evolution of man, fauna (animals) and flora (plants).

Africa is being torn apart!

To explain, we need to build on the model of the continental drift — using the (newer) scientific theory of plate tectonics.

The theory is quite simple. Earth is said to have seven large "plates", and several other smaller plates. These are plates made up of different parts of the earth's lithosphere (basically the land/continents and oceans). The outermost layer of each lithosphere is conveniently called continental crust and oceanic crust respectively (what we actually see). So in essence, plates can be made up of both continental (landmass) and oceanic (ocean) crust. Most plates do contain both. It is these tectonic plates that are constantly drifting apart and coming back together again. Where they meet is called a plate boundary (or fault). At these plate boundaries earthquakes, volcanic activity and mountain-building can all occur.

Now, the African continent is mainly made up of two plates — the "African" (or Nubian) plate and the "Somali" plate. The plate boundary, between the two, sits in East Africa, and is said to be divergent. This means that the two plates are sliding apart from each other, very slowly (by 6–7mm a year).

This splitting of plates is what created the resulting East African Rift Valley, a geological wonder of the world, roughly 4000 miles long and 30–40 miles wide (on average). All of the African Great Lakes (the source of the White Nile) were formed as a result of this rift, and most still lie within the rift valley (Western branch). On the Eastern branch, instead of forming lakes, you have greater volcanic activity — here you will find both Mount Kenya and Mount Kilimanjaro (the highest point in Africa).

Over time (millions of years) the Somali plate will eventually breakaway from the African plate — creating fresh ocean space between the two. This is similar to the way that the Arabian Peninsula split from Africa — creating the Red Sea in the process.

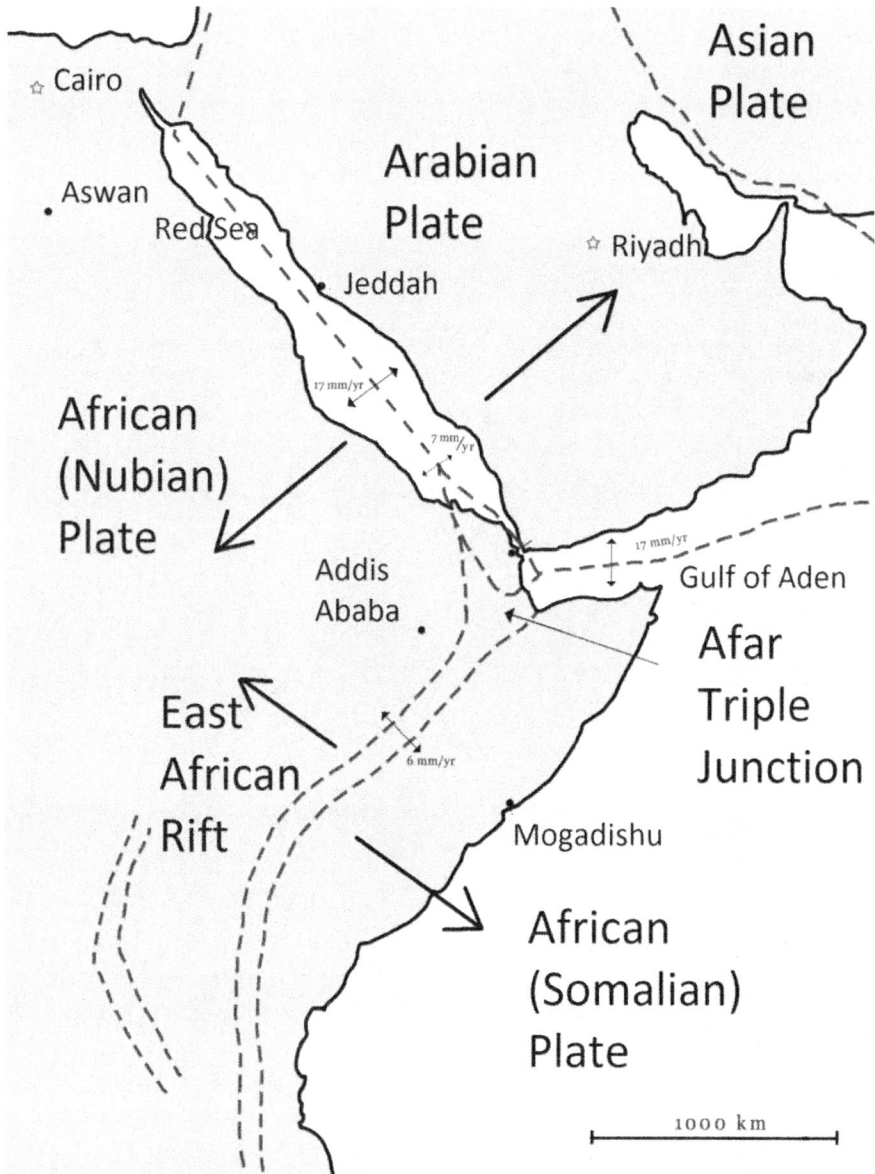

Map 12. East African Rift and plate boundaries. Source: Wikimedia Commons/CC BY 3.0 (Author: Razashah1).

What's in a map?

Africa is the second largest continent in the world, although it does (sometimes) look relatively small, if you compare it to say — Russia. This "distorted" view of Africa comes through the lenses of maps based on a "Mercator" projection, which is a common projection for maps in general use today. Like some flat (or 2D) maps, the Mercator projection actually distorts the sizes of countries, making some landmasses (as you move away from the equator) appear larger than they are in reality. You can see this "exaggeration" in size, not just with Russia, but with Europe, North America, Antarctica and Greenland.

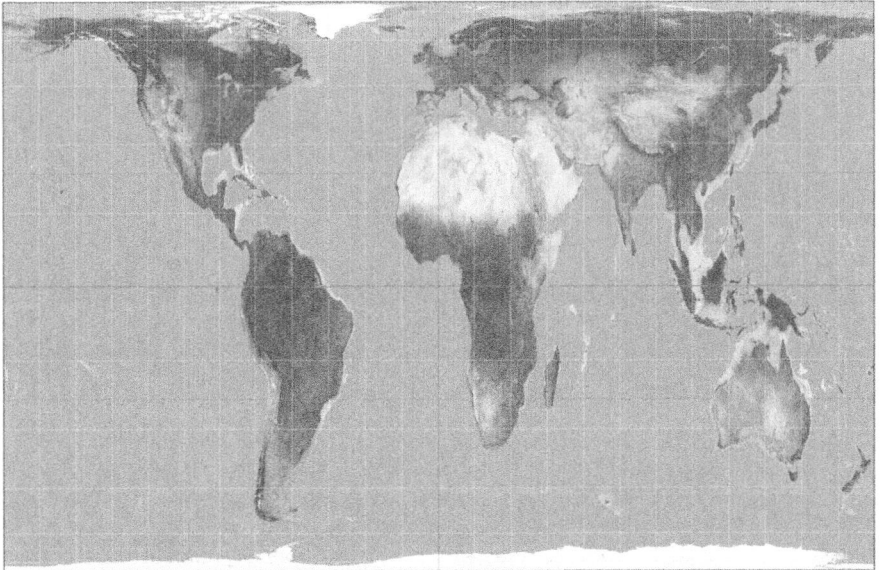

Map 13. Gall-Peters projection of the world map Source: Wikimedia Commons/CC BY-SA 3.0 (Author: Strebe).

Now if you look at Africa through the lenses of a "Gall-Peters" projection map — it looks much bigger. A Gall-Peters projection, maps all countries such that they all have the correct sizes relative to each other. But even this is a distorted view, as it doesn't give an accurate shape for such land masses.

And so Mercator — right directions/angles/shapes of countries, but wrong size (was good for helping ships navigate the seas)

Gall-Peters — right size of countries, but wrong shapes

There are many more map projections. But sadly, 2D maps can never be perfect, simply because the earth is much like a sphere — meaning that you cannot map it on a flat surface without errors in proportion. Put another way, to create the ideal 2D map, any projection would need to preserve angles, areas and distances — which is impossible.

With the aid of a Gall-Peters map, we can now see that Africa is a huge continent — much bigger than a lot of people think. The continent has a land area of 11.7 million square miles — which is more than enough land to fit in the United States, China, India, Mexico, Japan, United Kingdom and most other European nations (all at once). Judging by these numbers (or some maps), logistics, or more simply, movement in Africa, is and has always been challenging. In line with this challenge, are issues related to rivers, specifically waterborne transportation — which has played an important role in the history of the continent (more on this later).

General geography and climate of Africa

Africa is a land filled with incredible natural beauty and huge variety. Its landforms range from your standard mountains, hills, plateaus, and plains — to vast river basins and deep canyons. Surrounding the continent you have the Mediterranean Sea (North), Indian Ocean (East) and the Atlantic Ocean (West).

Africa straddles the equator, having a roughly equal south and north extent. Either side of the equator lie the tropics — the Tropic of Cancer (in the north) and the Tropic of Capricorn (in the south). Areas between the tropics generally get more direct exposure to sunlight, and are generally hotter and wetter, than elsewhere on the planet.

This straddling of the equator has the unique effect of making the climatic and physical conditions, in the northern and southern halves of Africa mirror themselves. As an example, you have conditions in the Mediterranean region (Northern Africa), being almost similar to the Cape area (Southern Africa). A further example, the Sahara Desert in the north — compared with the Kalahari Desert in the south.

In terms of elevation, generally, North and West Africa are low-lying, and so are the continent's coastal areas. On the other hand, East and Southern Africa tend to be hillier and mountainous (they sit on plateaus). To put this in figures, the lowland areas (north and west) have an average elevation of 320m, while the highland areas (east and south) have an average elevation of 1020m. This affects weather, river navigability (as we will see later) and more.

Although the climate does vary from region to region, the temperature is pretty much hot throughout — making Africa the most tropical continent in the world. Only where you have very high elevation, or on the continent's northern and southern fringes, do you have more temperate climates. Climate is far more variable by rainfall, than it is by temperature, with West and Central Africa, receiving more rainfall than anywhere else on the continent (hence the rainforests).

Africa can be grouped into nine major physical regions — Sahara, Sahel, Ethiopian Highlands, savanna, Swahili Coast, rainforest, African Great Lakes, Southern Africa and Mediterranean Coast. Each region influences how people live, and have lived, differently.

Sahara

Arguably one of the most known parts of the continent is the Sahara. It is likely also the most famous desert in the world. Most are aware of its vastness — some 3.3 million square miles. Despite this fact, it is actually not the largest (or the second largest) desert in the world. First and second place goes to Antarctica and the Arctic — both of which are termed "cold" deserts.

The Sahara is however, the largest hot desert in the world — by some distance. To give you a better idea, the Sahara is roughly the size of continental Europe or the United States. Making up around a quarter of Africa's entire landmass, the Sahara spans 10 countries and one disputed territory — Algeria, Chad, Egypt, Libya, Mali, Mauritania, Morocco, Niger, Sudan, Tunisia and Western Sahara (disputed).

Temperatures in the Sahara regularly exceed 40 °C. Having said this, it is not always so hot. Temperatures can drop dramatically at night, and snow can fall (albeit very rarely). As you might expect of a hot desert, the area receives very little rainfall — on average less than 1 inch of rain a year. This heat and lack of rainfall makes life tough (and in many cases impossible) for humans, animals and plants. Despite the challenges, an estimated 2.5 million people live in and around the Sahara, with some permanently living near water sources (oases), and others living more nomadic lifestyles (herding sheep, goats, camels etc.).

Apart from the Ancient Egyptians, the legendary Kingdom of Kush was also centered along the Nile Valley — the Nile being one of the two permanent rivers in the Sahara (the other being the Niger River). The Kushite heartland sat in an area called Nubia — which is today split between the countries of Egypt and Sudan. This Nubian region was an early cradle of civilization, producing a number of complex societies that engaged in trade and industry across Africa, Arabia and the

Mediterranean. The Kingdom of Kush flourished between c. 1070 BCE and 350 CE.

Sahel

The Sahel is a relatively narrow strip of land, which extends over 3000 miles eastward from Senegal to Sudan. Land in the Sahel is semi-arid, as it forms the transition zone between the Sahara Desert to the north, and the savanna to the south. Parts of the rivers Niger, Nile and Senegal run through the Sahel region. In terms of climate, the Sahel is generally hot, sunny and dry — though it does not get quite as hot as the Sahara. During the "Harmattan" season, in the Western Sahel, it can get significantly dusty and windy.

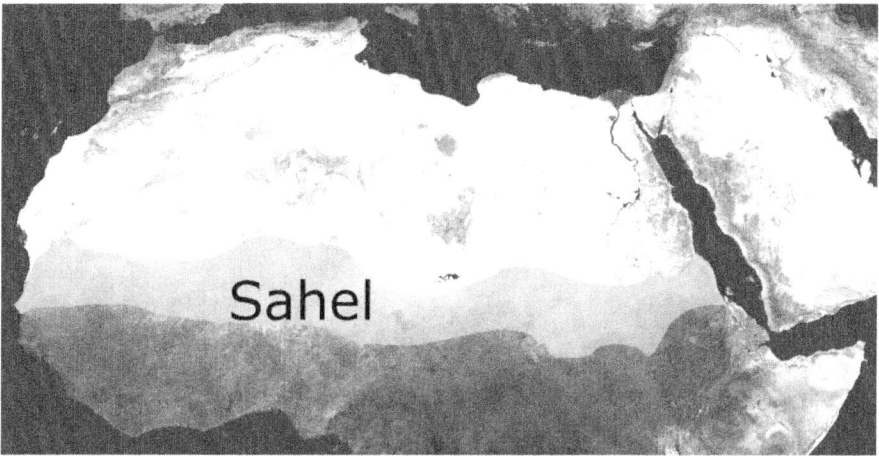

Map 14. The Sahel, with the Sahara directly to its north. Source: Wikimedia Commons/CC BY-SA 3.0 DE (Author: Flockedereisbaer).

Many hundreds of years ago, the Sahel used to be much bigger in size (its northern limits reaching further into the Sahara). But like the Sahara, it too is feeling the full effects of climate change, in this case desertification. As a result, the Sahel is also experiencing extreme temperatures, and erratic rainfall — which has led to both droughts and flooding in parts. This has had an impact on food security. It has also affected grazing patterns, sometimes resulting in conflicts between herders and farmers (as herders move further south in search of grazing land). The strategically important Lake Chad, sits in the central part of the Sahel, from where it provides water to millions of people in Chad, Cameroon, Niger, and Nigeria.

If you have ever heard of the Sahelian Kingdoms, the Sahel was their domain. These Sahelian Kingdoms were a series of states that existed between the 8th and 19th century. Over more than 1000 years, you had the Ghana Empire, the Mali Empire, the Songhai Empire, the Kanem-Bornu Empire, the Hausa Kingdoms and finally the Sokoto Caliphate. These Sahel states were all limited from expanding further south, into the forest lands of West Africa, primarily due to their heavy reliance on cavalry (in combat). Unsurprisingly, horses are not very mobile in dense forest cover.

Figure 4. View over Bani, Sahel region of Burkina Faso. Source: Wikimedia Commons/CC BY-SA 3.0 (Author: Adam Jones, Ph.D.).

Ethiopian Highlands

The Ethiopian Highlands are a rugged mass of mountains, positioned in North East Africa. Nowhere else on the continent, do you have such a large continuous area of elevation, and it is for such reasons that the area is often called the "Roof of Africa". Putting this in numbers, little of its surface falls below 1500 m — with summits reaching upwards of 4500 m.

The Ethiopian Rift Valley (part of the East African Rift) divides the highlands into two — the North Western and the South Eastern Highlands respectively. It is in the North Western Highlands that you will find Lake Tana, the largest lake in Ethiopia, and the source of the Blue Nile (or Abay River). Along with the White Nile, the Blue Nile is one of the major tributaries of the main river Nile.

This Blue Nile contributes over 50% of the long term river flow of the main river Nile — even more in rainy season (June-September). To explain, because of its high elevation, the highlands attract large amounts of rainfall (influenced by the southwest monsoon that also affects India). This heavy rainfall erodes a lot of fertile soil from the highlands, which makes its way downstream (as silt). This silt turns the water a murky brown, and it is eventually deposited along the banks of the main Nile (in Egypt). It is this silt that is said to have created the rich fertile soil, which sustained the Ancient Egyptians for a few thousand years.

Figure 5. Road to Simien Mountains National Park, Ethiopia. Source: Wikimedia Commons/CC BY 2.0 (Author: A. Davey - from Where I Live Now: Pacific Northwest).

Despite being close to the equator, thanks to the elevation, Ethiopia has a relatively cool, moderate climate. These climatic conditions make agriculture very favorable in parts. Depending on the elevation, different forms of agriculture are practiced in the region, which helps support a variety of different groups.

These highlands played host to the Great Kingdom of Aksum. The Aksumites facilitated trade, across the Red Sea, by minting their own coins (currency). According to the Prophet Mani (Manichaeism), at one time, Aksum was among the four great kingdoms in the world. That one time was a little under 2000 years ago (in the 3rd century). The three other competing kingdoms were Rome, Persia and China.

Savanna

The Savannas, or tropical grasslands of Africa, are found to the north and south of forest or woodland regions. Savanna covers almost half of the continent — some 5 million square miles. Much of West, East and South-Central Africa is savanna — with the notable exception of the Congo Rainforest belt (near the equator).

Figure 6. Elephants in Serengeti National Park, Tanzania. Source: Wikimedia Commons/CC BY-SA 3.0 (Author: Bjørn Christian Tørrissen).

Savanna areas feature two different seasons — dry and wet. There is little to no rain in the dry season. During the wet season, vegetation grows, and you get lush green areas. The further away you go from the equator, the less rainfall you get. Accordingly, the grasslands get drier and drier. As well as grass, this vegetation includes scrubs i.e. low woody plants and small scattered trees.

Perhaps the most important thing to understand, in relation to Africa's savannas, is that typically the soil or land is not very fertile. This is primarily due to climate and weathering. Given the high temperatures, nutrients and organic matter, found near the top of the soil, decay rapidly. Further, the soil tends to be very hard, which makes it difficult for plant roots to penetrate the subsoil — restricting vegetation growth in the process.

Arguably, the most famous of Africa's savanna regions is the Serengeti Plains, in Northern Tanzania and Southern Kenya. These plains, rich in wildlife, span over 12,000 square miles. You can find all sorts of animals here, from lions to hyenas to zebras, giraffes and elephants. Many of these animals are unique, in that they cannot be found anywhere else on the planet. The region also hosts one of the largest mammal migrations in the world — the "Great Wildebeest Migration". For all such reasons, it is a popular safari destination.

Between the 17th and 19th century, the Savanna woodlands played home to three multiethnic kingdoms — Luba, Lunda and Kuba. They were specifically centered on the Central African savanna, between the Congo Basin Rainforest and the Zambezi River. The introduction of new crops and technologies promoted strong and centralized governments, with new forms of leadership. This enabled the states to greatly expand their spheres of control — subduing neighboring chiefdoms, controlling trade routes, and increasing their wealth.

Swahili Coast

The Swahili Coast is a relatively flat and thin strip of land that stretches over 1000 miles — from Somalia to Mozambique. A few coastal islands are also conveniently included as part of the Swahili Coast, like Comoros. Specific areas of the coast, particularly in Kenya, have become an important part of the 21st Century Maritime Silk Road (part of the Chinese Belt and Road Initiative). The term "Swahili" is derived from an Arabic word meaning "people of the coasts". This is somewhat related to the term "Sahel" — which derives from the Arabic word for "coast" or "shore".

The East Coast of Africa experiences seasonally alternating Indian Ocean monsoon or "trade winds". In winter, the flow of these winds tend westward (i.e. it blows from the north east). In summer, the direction reverses, tending eastwards (i.e. it blows from the south west). This links to the rainfall experienced in the Ethiopian Highlands, in summer monsoon season (June to September), and the subsequent yearly flooding of the Nile. These monsoon winds also enabled the extensive East Africa-Arabia-India trade or maritime network (that began around the 1st millennium CE).

On the whole, the sandy Swahili Coast does not produce enough vegetation to sustain diverse (land) animal life. Just inland from the coastal sands begins the mainland interior, which is generally more fertile and suited for agricultural production. For example, for growing fruit trees and spices. Coconut palms can be grown in the more sandy areas. Fishing has been, and remains, an integral part of life for those living along the coast.

From the 8th to the 16th century a unique culture flourished off the coast of East Africa — the Swahili city-states or confederation. These city-states were an important part of the Indian Ocean trade network, at the time. Important trading cities included Mogadishu (Somalia), Mombasa (Kenya), the island of Zanzibar (Tanzania) and lastly Kilwa (Tanzania). This extensive trading system gave rise to Swahili culture, and also led the way to the Swahili language becoming an East African lingua franca.

Tropical Rainforest

The Congo Basin Rainforest is a prominent feature of the African continent, and as such, is often described as "the great green heart of Africa". It was even more prominent decades ago, before extensive deforestation — caused by development, agriculture, forestry and more. With the unique combination of ecological, climatic and human interactions — Africa's tropical rainforests have helped shape its past and present.

The tropical forests of Central and West Africa, known as the Guineo-Congolian region, is the second largest tropical forest region in the world. To put that in numbers, it is over 1.2 million square miles in size, and second only to the Amazon Rainforest region in Brazil. Given such numbers, the rainforests are comparable in size to the landmass of India. Over 90% of the African rainforest area can be found in this region, with the majority of this area being taken up by the Congo Rainforest. Africa's other rainforest patches can be found in East Africa and Madagascar.

The Congo Basin Rainforest is home to a rich variety of both plants and animals. For example, you have animals like African forest elephants, gorillas and chimpanzees. You also have a whole host of different bird and butterfly species. These rainforests are not just home to animals and plants; you also have humans living here. The rainforest residents are known as African Pygmies (the Mbenga, Mbuti and Twa) — called so because of their smaller stature (their heights are often less than 155 cm). Their phenotype has been explained as adaptations to the rainforest habitat.

Figure 7. River running through a rainforest in North Kivu, DRC. Source: Wikimedia Commons/CC BY-SA 2.0 (Author: MONUSCO Photos).

One of Africa's great rainforest kingdoms was that of the Kingdom of Benin. The Kingdom prospered between the 13th and 19th century, in what is now Southern Nigeria. Their capital Edo, now called Benin City, was a center of trade, controlled by a central figure — the King or "Oba". This trade network extended from Benin, to the shores of the Mediterranean Sea, via the Sahelian Kingdoms and the Sahara. Around the 15th century, trade links were directly established with the Portuguese. The Benin Kingdom is arguably most famous for its artworks, including its impressive brass sculptures, masks and plaques — some of which are displayed in European and American museums.

African Great Lakes

The African Great Lakes are a series of lakes that can be found in East Africa, specifically in and around the Great Rift Valley. These lakes are home to many of the largest and most ecologically diverse freshwater systems in the world. The three largest Great Lakes (Victoria, Tanganyika and Malawi) together hold more than 25% of the entire planet's total surface freshwater. As touched on earlier, these lakes all owe their very existence to the formation of the Rift Valley. Similar to the Ethiopian Highlands, the elevation in the Great Lakes region is notably high.

The availability of fresh water, means that the Great Lakes region supports a diverse mix of both aquatic and land animal life. It also supports a variety of agricultural activities including banana gardens, fisheries and cattle herding. Given the favorable living conditions, like with the Ethiopian Highlands, the human population density here is high. This contrasts with surrounding regions — tropical forests to the west (Congo basin), savanna to the east (Kenya and Tanzania), and a mix of dry/marshy land to the north (along the South Sudan border).

Lake Victoria is one of the sources of the Nile River (White). It was named (in 1858), by the English explorer John Hanning Speke, after the then Queen Victoria of Britain. To Europeans, the source of the Nile had remained a mystery for many hundreds of years — going back to the Greeks and Romans. It is said that the Romans even had a proverb — *quaere fonte Nili* — to look for the Nile's source was like "looking for a needle in a haystack". The fact that the source of the Nile was only discovered (by Europeans) less than 200 years ago, again demonstrates the sheer size of the continent and the challenges movement presents.

A "land of kings and lakes" — that was how Swahili traders spoke of the Great Lakes. It was such stories that got British merchants first interested in the region. Before you knew it, the first expeditions had been financed (in the mid-1800s), and with that came the first European eyewitness accounts of the Great Lakes Kingdoms. Some of these Kingdoms included Burundi (modern day Burundi), Bugunda (within modern day Uganda) and Rwanda (modern day Rwanda). Observers were said to have been fascinated by the sophistication of the monarchies they encountered, in particular, how they were able to control both large territories and populations.

Southern Africa

The Southern African region is extremely diverse — in terms of physical features, climate and vegetation. Here you can find everything from lush coastal plains, to snow-covered mountains, savanna high plateaus, and hot deserts. Tropical rainforests are the only things missing, in this part of the continent.

Through this region run several of Africa's most important rivers including the Zambezi, the Orange and the Limpopo. The Zambezi River is the fourth longest in Africa, flowing from North Western Zambia all the way to the Indian Ocean — off the sandy coasts of Mozambique. On this long, 1700 mile journey, the Zambezi passes through the stunning Victoria Falls — one of the largest waterfalls in the world.

The Kalahari Desert, lying primarily in Botswana, is an extensive inland desert region that features a semi-arid/sandy savanna landscape. The desert does experience rainfall, in parts, and when adequate enough, this brings the grasslands to life — providing grazing opportunities for wildlife. In contrast, the Namib Desert, found along the West Coast of Namibia, receives very little rainfall.

Most of the Southern African rainfall is experienced nearer to the eastern coast, and it is here that you will find the majority of the grassland, and some of Africa's most renowned nature reserves. The southern tip of the continent, in and around Cape Town, features a Mediterranean climate, appropriate for a range of agricultural activities — such as growing fruit orchards and winemaking.

Some 500 years ago, in what is now Northern Zimbabwe and Mozambique, a powerful local state dominated the area — the Mutapa Kingdom. This kingdom was very rich in gold, iron and ivory — which they first supplied to the Swahili city-states, and then eventually the Portuguese. In exchange, Mutapa imported luxury products, from as far as China. The specific products imported include cloth, glass beads and porcelain. Therefore, we can say that, the Mutapa Kingdom was an important player in the Indian Ocean trade network (of the Middle Ages).

Mediterranean Coast

Africa is bound by the Mediterranean Sea to the north, which separates the continent from Europe. To the west of the Mediterranean, lie the straits of Gibraltar, which connects the Mediterranean to the Atlantic Ocean, and separates Spain from Morocco. The Mediterranean Coast is the coastal strip that runs from Morocco (via Algeria, Tunisia and Libya) to Egypt. It is one of the most densely populated regions in Africa.

The coast has a climate similar to that experienced in the Western Cape region of South Africa. This Mediterranean climate features mild, rainy winters, and hot, dry summers. In terms of food production — barley, wheat and other cereals can be grown without irrigation. Other agricultural produce includes olives, citrus fruits, grapes, strawberries and tomatoes. Like you may expect, nowhere else in Africa can you "naturally" grow such, in any significant volumes (apart from the Cape Coast and a couple other places). There is also significant fishing activity in the region.

The eastern half of the coast generally gets less rainfall than the western half. Further, although Egypt is part of the Mediterranean Coast, only a small fraction of its coastline actually has the typical Mediterranean climate. The western half of the coastal strip (Morocco, Algeria, and Tunisia) is bounded to the south, by the famous Atlas Mountains. And so here, the mountains separate the coast from the Sahara Desert. Some of the mountain's peaks actually experience fairly regular snowfall in the winter months (January and February).

The Mediterranean Coast, and by extension the sea, has been a historic trading center — upon which many great civilizations have been built. An example of such great civilizations is the Carthaginian Empire. At its height, around the 3rd century BCE, Carthage ruled significant parts of the coast, and its capital was one of the wealthiest cities of the time. The empire's power lay with its strategic position — that provided it with access to fertile lands, and major trade routes it could control.

Natural barriers

As briefly touched on before, one of Africa's natural barriers is the East African Rift Valley, with its various mountains (and highlands). However, mountains are not the only natural or geographic barriers in Africa. There are also deserts and rainforests. We can use these barriers, together with savanna, to more simply describe the influence of geography on the rise of African civilizations. Therefore we have North Africa — desert, West Africa — savanna, Central Africa — rainforest, East Africa — mountains, and Southern African — desert/savanna. Of course, you also have oceans and seas as natural barriers.

Moving through natural barriers like deserts, mountains and rainforests is difficult. Add to the mix the actual size of Africa, and movement becomes very difficult — virtually impossible in some cases. These natural geographic barriers restricted or limited the movement of not just people, but culture, goods and ideas. And so we can say there was "isolation" in many parts of the continent, which also implies little to no direct competition for resources — food or otherwise (more on this later).

Seas or oceans were also obstacles, initially at least, with this in mind; we can differentiate Africa's eastern and western coasts. As highlighted earlier, thanks to the Indian Ocean monsoon winds, and very early on (at least c. 2000 BP), Eastern Africa formed part of a widespread maritime network. Ships could "hug" the coast lines, slowly making their way from East Africa all the way to China — via Arabia and India.

Maritime trade networks on Africa's Western coast developed much later, around 500 years ago, as direct trade began with the Europeans. Prior to this time, and the coming of the "caravel" (ships that could sail "into the wind"), strong winds and tidal currents had made ocean travel very difficult. Hence the reliance on caravan trade routes, via the Sahara, before this time. As you will see examples of, later on, trade goes together with the ability to acquire resources, and thus the ability to develop and maintain civilizations or states.

Barriers were not just physical; however, disease was also a factor. Parts of Africa were infested by the "tsetse fly", which caused "sleeping sickness" — a potentially fatal disease. Tsetse flies tended to lurk in bushy/woody areas, and moist low-lying valleys — making it hard for cattle and other animals to live or pass through such places. Consequently, the Sahel and the drier open savanna regions of Northern Africa are where specialized pastoralism developed first. The movement of herders, into the southern half of the continent, came later — with the opening of "tsetse free" corridors (linked to climate change).

Where there were fewer natural barriers, and where there was access to water, is where the earliest African civilizations emerged — namely in parts of North, East and West Africa. By nature of geography, Central and Southern Africa moved to intensive food production later, and so too did its civilizations rise later. This essentially split the continent in two, roughly at the line of the equator. Perhaps more accurately, the "dividing line" may be drawn just above the Congo Rainforest, extending eastwards to pass above the African Great Lakes region. As commented on earlier, this (imaginary) horizontal line, above the Congo Rainforest, was arguably a bigger barrier to movement in Africa than the Sahara Desert ever was.

Despite some drawbacks, natural barriers were not all bad — they did have their advantages. Deserts, mountains, rivers, plateaus and seas provided natural defenses, at the cost of movement and trade. Like many of today's modern nation states, Ancient Egypt had many of such barriers, keeping the state relatively stable, by protecting it from foreign invasions. Apart from protecting states, Africa's natural barriers enabled indigenous cultures and societies to survive for hundreds of years — without interruption or external influence. This links to the idea of natural barriers being part of the reason why, it took so long to map the interior parts of the continent.

Africa's major rivers

As the earliest hunter-gatherers found out, and the farmers came to know even more — water is the lifeblood of man. Where there is water, there is life, and there is civilization. And where there is not, life dies out, and so too does civilization. A classic example of this is the once green and lush Sahara Desert, which used to flow with rivers and streams. Now that those streams have mostly dried up, the Sahara is a shadow of its former self. Incidentally, there are still huge amounts of groundwater beneath the Sahara; it is such ancient water that underpins the Great Man-Made River, financed by the government of the late Libyan leader Muammar Gaddafi, it is the world's largest irrigation project/system.

Technically, there are still two rivers running through the Sahara. One runs from south to north, the famous river Nile, or as some like to call it — the "river of rivers". The other is the river Niger, running from west to east, which by chance, the Tuareg people also call the "river of rivers". The five other major rivers are the Congo, Zambezi, Senegal, Orange and Limpopo. Looking at a geographical map of Africa, you will find three of these rivers in the northern half of the continent, namely the Nile, Niger and Senegal. The four other rivers are in the southern half of Africa.

The importance of rivers is not only applicable to Africa. The three places, apart from the Nile, where humans first began farming (and permanently settling) were all near major bodies of water — in the Near East, along the Tigris and Euphrates rivers; in the Indian subcontinent, along the Indus River; and in China, along the Yangtze and Yellow rivers. This river settling phenomena continued throughout history, with rivers increasingly finding other uses, apart from farming, like transportation (trade) and power generation.

We can look at the United States as an example. Its biggest cities, most of which are relatively new, have one thing in common — they are either port cities or cities with easy access to water. New York became the biggest, and perhaps the wealthiest city in the world, with the help of rivers. For one, New York's harbor, at the mouth of the Hudson River, is one of the deepest and most extensive natural harbors in the world, which allowed ships to dock directly next to the city. And two, the Hudson River, a major waterway for trade and commerce, passed straight through the city. Other competing cities — Boston,

Philadelphia, Baltimore etc. simply did not enjoy the same geographic advantages that New York did.

Where you do not have natural rivers, you build canals (artificial waterways) — Suez Canal, Panama Canal, Erie Canal and more. The Suez Canal almost halved the time from London to the Arabian Sea; the Panama Canal handles 5% of global trade, while the Erie Canal accelerated New York's growth even more — by giving it unrivaled access to the American West. The importance of water to man is easily forgotten, especially by those of us that live in urban environments (where water is simply piped into the home).

Navigable rivers and what is your destination?

Rivers and waterways are not just beneficial for agriculture. They also provide travel routes for exploration, commerce and recreation. This is of course, if the river is navigable, and if it takes you somewhere useful.

Again, looking at a map of Africa, how many rivers connect to the Mediterranean Sea? Alternatively, how many significant rivers connect you to the Nile? And where are they found? To answer — there aren't many.

These questions are important because the very first civilizations were developed in and around the Mediterranean. Those with better connections to this area enjoyed better opportunities for trade, commerce and the subsequent development of civilization. Easy contact with each other meant easy exchange of ideas, and eventually an early case of "keeping up with the Joneses" occurred i.e. trying to copy or not be outdone by one's neighbors. This is why, for a couple thousand years at least, all the civilizations around the "Joneses" (Mediterranean) were (technologically) far "ahead" of their Northern European counterparts, or their counterparts across the Atlantic (in the Americas) or those closer to the southern tip of Africa. Whether it was an African (Aksum, Carthage, Egypt, Nubia etc.), Asian (Hittites, Persia) or Southern European (Greece, Rome) civilization — it didn't matter — the story was the same. This was until the tech and ideas started to slowly spread, to areas relatively far away from this "ancient highway" i.e. the Mediterranean Sea.

As to the navigability, some rivers happen to be naturally navigable, while some are not. To put it another way, not all rivers are ones that boats can easily travel on. The need for (more) waterways, suitable for navigation, led to the development of canals, which are simply man-made rivers built to carry goods from one place to another (by boat).

Canal building was a major feature of the industrial revolution in
Britain, in the 18th and 19th century. The following single paragraph
(Rees, A. 1806 "Canals". The Cyclopaedia. Vol 6.) perhaps best highlights
the benefits of navigable waterways or canals:

> The advantages resulting from canals, as they open an easy and
> cheap communication between distant parts of a country, will be
> ultimately experienced by persons of various descriptions: and more
> especially by the manufacturer, the occupier or owner of land, and
> the merchant. The manufacturer will thus be enabled to collect his
> materials, his fuel, and the means of subsistence, from remote
> districts, with less labour and expense; and to convey his goods to a
> profitable market. As canals multiply, old manufactures revive and
> flourish, new ones are established, and the adjoining country is
> rendered populous and productive.

Before canals became a thing, man had to make do with the natural
rivers he could find — natural rivers that could provide many of the
same benefits that the canals were built for.

So what makes rivers navigable? Rivers, canals, lakes and other
bodies of water, are said to be navigable if they are deep, wide and slow
enough for vessels to pass. In addition, the fewer obstacles in the way,
the better — that is no rocks, trees, ice etc. However, it is important to
understand that navigability is in relation to context. What may be
navigable by a small boat may not be navigable by a large ship. Finally,
thanks to improvements in technology, we have been able to make
shallow rivers more navigable by installing locks or dredging — both of
which increase water depth (allowing larger ships to pass). Incidentally,
there is evidence that the practice of dredging (harbors) began with the
Ancients.

This brings us back to the question of Africa and its major
(navigable) rivers. To start with, and once again, the northern half of
the continent has the "advantage" when it comes to river navigability.
We can see this with both the Nile and Niger rivers. The Congo River is
also navigable to an extent, generally more so than its southern
counterparts.

Looking at the Nile, it is fairly navigable by ocean-going vessels. In
other words, vessels can enter the Nile directly from its mouth at the
Mediterranean Sea, and travel all the way to Aswan (and vice versa). At
Aswan, the navigability of the river declines, due to cataracts or rapids
(rocky terrain). At these cataracts there are little to no flood plains,

limiting agricultural development and subsequently population levels. This is true today, and was true in the days of the pharaohs. It is for such reasons that the historic border between Ancient Egypt to the north, and what was Ancient Nubia to the south, was around the first cataract at Aswan.

The three other largest rivers the Niger, Congo and Zambezi, along with most other African rivers, are only navigable in (limited) parts. This is due to a combination of reasons, which may or may not apply to each specific case.

The first reason is due to rapids and/or waterfalls — caused by rivers going from plateaus (mainly south of the equator) to lower-lying land (mainly along the coasts). The second is particularly shallow rivers, which cannot accommodate larger vessels — limiting what can be carried. The third is seasonal rivers, which do not have stable flows — too shallow in dry season and/or flowing too fast in rainy season. The fourth is rivers that are not relatively straight i.e. they twist and turn a lot (meandering). The fifth is sandbanks or shoals (ridges that are submerged in water) near river mouths. And finally the sixth is swampy rivers (forest wetland).

Expanding on the sixth reason, one of the largest freshwater ecosystems in the world can be found in South Sudan — The Sudd Wetlands or Swamp. This wetland, almost the size of the United Kingdom, is sustained by the flow of the White Nile from Lake Victoria. It was one of the barriers to finding the source of the Nile, for both Roman explorers, and a whole host of other explorers after that.

Problems with navigating the Zambezi can also be commented on. 1878 was the year that the British company — The African Lakes Company (ALC) was formed. Its purpose was to navigate:

> the rivers and lakes of Central Africa, and especially of those rivers and lakes which communicate with the Indian Ocean by the River Zambezi and the River Zambezi itself, with a view to develop the trade and resources of the country, and to encourage legitimate traffic amongst the natives (Wilkie, 2020).

But the ALC soon saw, first-hand, that the rivers of the Zambezi were not constant and predictable — like many of those found back-home in Britain. Frederick Moir, one of the company's agents, noted at first:

> The banks of the river were covered in beautiful green trees and shrubs ... We seemed to be in a tropical paradise

This quickly turned to:

> What a change when the tide had ebbed! A stretch of several hundred feet of slimy mud lay before the town (Moir, 1923 cited in Wilkie, 2020).

This of course eventually led to substantial financial losses for the company.

We can compare African rivers to those found around the world. And in doing so we find that, in direct contrast to Asia, Europe and North America, Africa has very few navigable rivers. That's not to say that African rivers are completely unnavigable. It's more to say that the navigability is limited, when compared to other rivers found globally. Despite this, Africans still had to make use of their rivers — where and when they could. After all, they were still important avenues of communication, trade and travel — like anywhere else in the world.

I leave this discussion, of Africa's geography in relation to the rise of its civilizations, with this direct quote from Samuel Whittemore Boggs — a former Geographer of the US Department of State.

> NOTHING in the annals of geographic discovery seems stranger than the belatedness of African exploration. Although ancient civilizations flourished in Mediterranean Africa, it is only within the lifetime of men still among us that the elementary geography of the interior of the continent became known. The great rivers and lakes of North and South America were better known within two centuries of Columbus' voyages than were the Nile, the Niger, the Congo, and the Zambezi and the great African lakes a hundred years ago. By 1850 even the exploration of the Arctic and Antarctic left problems perhaps no more baffling than those of central Africa. This apparent anomaly in geographic exploration is not a historical accident, however, but due in large part to the character of Africa's coasts and ocean currents, its topography, climate and vegetation—factors that affect Africa's future as certainly as they have influenced its past. (Boggs, 1943).

7. Age of Metals — Copper, Bronze and Iron Ages

For the sake of completeness and before we individually look at the earliest African civilizations, a general discussion on the impact of metals is important. This nicely follows on from the earlier section on the Stone Age. Accordingly, we first have the "Bronze Age", which is then followed by the "Iron Age". These three ages — stone, bronze and iron — make up the "Three Age System".

Metals and materials in general (bone, clay, wood etc.) ultimately determine what man can and cannot do. That is to say, the use and exploitation of materials has been an integral part of technological developments throughout history. The simple fact of the matter is — everything is made from something. Imagine, slowly, removing some of our common material things — first concrete, then glass, next metals, textiles and so on. As we remove each material, one by one, it'll feel like slowly going back in time, and before we know it, we'll be back in the Stone Age (hunting and gathering once again).

In the ancient world only seven metals were known to man — copper, gold, iron, lead, mercury, silver and tin — the metals of antiquity. Of these seven metals, only two can be found in a (native) form pure enough to be of immediate use — copper and gold. As a result, these were likely the first two metals discovered by man. The other metals all had to be "produced", essentially from their corresponding ores (rocks that contain the metal).This process of extracting metal from ore is known as smelting — smelting itself being a form of metallurgy. The term, metallurgy, also applies to modifying or mixing metals.

Ancient peoples soon learnt how to combine one metal with another, to produce a better or final product. This likely would have happened through trial and error, or perhaps an early form of science. Bronze (copper and tin) and electrum (gold and silver) were particularly important alloys (mixes) of metal. The ability to refine and work significant quantities of iron came later, as the technology to do so evolved.

Copper

Copper, a shiny reddish-brownish metal, was an extremely important metal in ancient times. So much so that archaeologists have also given it an "age" i.e. the Copper Age or Chalcolithic Age. This age (c. 5th to 4th millennium BCE) is seen as more of a transitional period, between the First Agricultural Revolution and the beginnings of the Bronze Age. The start of this Copper Age relates to the development of the technologies needed, to process or work copper into desired shapes. Remember, as mentioned above, copper can be found "natively", although only in small amounts. Therefore, native copper would have been worked first, once native deposits had been exhausted, smelting was employed to extract copper from rock.

As for the beneficial properties of copper, it was easily hammered into shape and it held a sharp edge. This meant that it could readily be made into a range of tools, ornaments, and weapons — much more easily than stone ever could. However, and arguably, the most important use of copper was it being one part of the "equation" needed to form bronze. Add a small bit of tin, to a lot more of copper and you get bronze — the all-important metal alloy of the earliest civilizations.

In the book *Red Gold of Africa*, Eugenia W. Herbert argues that copper was actually perceived as more valuable than gold — in certain parts of Africa. She stresses that, the increased value of gold only came about as a result of strong demand, and perceptions, from overseas. Herbert shows that copper served many of the same functions as gold had (in non-African societies). It was the basis of money, was used in art, had a role in religion and was a symbol of status, power and wealth. This was the case in a number of different precolonial African societies.

Bronze Age

North Africa

The Bronze Age represents the period of time that follows on from the Stone Age (and/or the Copper Age). This period of time lasts from roughly 3300 to 1200 BCE. Although it is the alloying or mixing of tin and copper, to form bronze, that gives rise to the term Bronze Age — there were other significant happenings or defining events. To give you an example, it is during the Bronze Age that writing was first developed in Africa (Ancient Egypt) and the Near East (Sumer civilization). With writing came literacy. And with literacy came the ability for humans to record things. It is these recordings, together with archaeology, linguistics, science etc., that help us study ancient history.

Therefore, this age could equally be termed the "Age of Literacy". It probably isn't for two reasons. One, this coming of writing, only applies to the relatively few civilizations that managed to develop such (during this time frame). And two, the Age of Literacy doesn't quite fit in as nicely in the Three Age System — Stone, Bronze and Iron Ages. As this age was the beginnings of what is termed "recorded human history", it is also traditionally seen to be the beginnings of ancient history — with everything before this being known as prehistory.

This period of history is both an interesting one and a crucial developmental phase in African history. It starts at a time when small-scale agricultural communities, were transformed into more centralized or administrative states. It was also in these times that somewhat of a global trade network began to form. You had the movement of valuable goods between parts of Africa, Asia and Europe — with the eastern half of the Mediterranean (North East Africa and the Middle East) being the center of this trade.

As tin was only found in select places, civilizations needed to produce and trade something — in order to obtain this "precious metal". Copper was relatively more wide spread. With the two, you could make more advanced (bronze) weapons. And with more advanced weapons, you had the ability to project power. Or to put it more simply, you could engage rival civilizations in warfare, both attacking and defending when necessary.

Of course, none of this trade could have happened without a system being in place. A system, where everyone knew their role, and who they answered to — a hierarchy. If everyone did their job properly, there would be order and prosperity for all. And on the contrary, where there was failure in any one part of the system — anarchy was on the cards. This system could only be achieved by some form of government, a state of some sort, which had enough food resources to sustain a populace, in which not everyone worked the fields. This enabled specialized non-food production — with surpluses being available for export (i.e. trade).

The end of the Bronze Age, and the end of the trade network, came about due to what is now termed as the "Late Bronze Age Collapse".

Early Mediterranean civilizations, such as the Hittites and Mycenaeans, all ended abruptly — almost simultaneously. Ancient Egypt was one of the few civilizations that survived this sudden collapse (although its power was much reduced). Several explanations for this sudden collapse have been made. However there is no consensus. Explanations include developments in military weapons and tactics, barbarian invasions, drying up of tin supplies, climate change and more. Some historians have argued that it was simply a combination of all these factors, that happened to occur at the same time (c. 1200 BCE), rather than one specific factor.

Rest of Africa and the origins of metallurgy

Apart from the Nile Valley (Egypt and Nubia), there is very little evidence for much of a Bronze Age in the rest of Africa. Instead, and in most cases, copper and iron smelting appeared around the same time. This lack of chronology in African metalworking has made the issue hotly debated in scholarship. Unlike the established Near Eastern chronology, of first copper being worked, followed by bronze and then iron — African metallurgy appears to go against this "norm". And so we have the question:

How can iron smelting be invented, without at least some prior knowledge of copper or bronze working?

It is this going against the norm that has scholars unable to reach an agreement, on the complete history of African metalworking. This may of course also be in small part to, the relative lack of archaeological excavations undertaken on the continent.

The traditional explanation, before the advent of radiocarbon dating (around 50 years ago), had been that knowledge of metalworking either came via the Nubians in North East Africa or the Carthaginians in the North West (by the way of some form of early Trans-Saharan trading). However, there was very little concrete evidence for such — if any at all.

Despite this lack of evidence, copper metallurgy seems to have come before iron metallurgy in Nubia. Here, evidence for the technology needed to smelt copper dates to c. 2300 BCE, with a furnace for bronze casting having been found in Kerma (modern Sudan). There is also evidence of early copper using traditions emerging in Akjoujt (Mauritania) and Agadez (Niger).

Arguably, more actual evidence points to an indigenous African invention of metallurgy. Scholars that back this argument cite the diversity of metal production technology, techniques, and installations

— which can all be found in the archaeological record. This relates to the geographic diversity of the African continent. Given such geographic diversity, there clearly was a need for the variety of iron bloomery furnaces used across the continent. With this in mind, Africa can be compared to Europe, where there were far more limited variants of the bloomery furnace.

Africans that lived in areas with fewer trees developed efficient furnaces that wasted little charcoal. Those Africans that lived in regions with access to plenty of charcoal, had no need for such, and thus their furnaces were very much what you could call "charcoal consumers". These charcoal consumers, or more properly, these natural draft furnaces, were more labor efficient and they also tended to produce a higher quality end-product. Moreover, furnaces were also adapted to the range of iron ores found on the continent. Not every furnace could smelt every ore, given the fact that ores did not purely contain iron — some contained other elements that had to be considered (e.g. iron-titanium ores).

Another example of African ingenuity, when it came to metalworking, is the development of smelting furnaces capable of directly producing carbon steel — going back c. 2000 BP. These furnaces relied on (the invention of) a complex process of "preheating" — which enabled temperatures inside the furnace to reach consistently high levels. As such, both productivity and efficiency was increased. Evidence of this has been found in North Western Tanzania, on the western side of Lake Victoria — the home of the "Haya" people. These preheating techniques predate similar innovations found in Europe by close to 2000 years. Slightly related, is the idea of the Lake Victoria area being an important "stepping stone" for the eventual spread of ironworking (and agricultural know-how) — throughout Africa south of the equator i.e. the proposed Bantu Expansion (discussed later).

Like has been highlighted before, the human ability to adapt to a wide variety of circumstances, is what allowed us to conquer the planet — so to speak. And so what we can say for certain, regardless of whether or not Africans invented metallurgy, is that they were no less inventive in the use of it (than anyone else).

Iron Age

North Africa
The Iron Age is the period of history that follows on from the Bronze Age. Incidentally, the effects of the spread of iron-based metallurgy

have been cited as a potential reason for the Bronze Age collapse — that ushered in this subsequent Iron Age. Depending on the specific region in question, this segment of history lasts for approximately 700 years. That is between c. 1200 and 500 BCE (in North Africa).

Although the people and civilizations of the Bronze Age likely knew about iron, they did not come to realize its superior qualities to bronze. They also didn't have much incentive to innovate in relation to iron metallurgy, as copper and bronze seemed to be doing a more than adequate job. With the Bronze Age Collapse however, things changed almost instantly. With the fall of several civilizations came the loss of old and treasured trade routes. Trade routes that sought to bring in the much needed tin — to smelt with copper — to make bronze.

Civilizations needed a replacement. And they found this in the form of iron. Iron was a metal that was much more common than both copper and tin. The problem was, in order to smelt it, you needed much higher temperatures. This was simply because iron has a higher melting point than copper. The tech to effectively produce iron was beyond the capacity of civilizations in the Bronze Age. Due to the unavailability of tin, civilizations were somewhat forced to learn the ways of effective iron production. It was either that, or be faced with shortages of metal — which would in effect be like going back to the Stone Age. This "forced" innovation meant that rapid advances in ironworking were made, which soon became widespread.

Now if you take a bronze weapon and an iron weapon, comparing their usefulness in terms of strength, they are about equal. The main difference is iron weapons can be made with one substance, while bronze requires two. There is one other advantage of iron, add just the right amount of carbon to it and you get steel (which is much stronger than both bronze and pure iron). It must be noted, however, that it took hundreds of years to develop the tech and skills needed, to consistently craft good steel weapons.

If the materials required to make bronze (tin and copper), were conveniently located in the same place, this would somewhat lessen iron's advantage. But, they rarely were found in the same place. What this meant was that in order to make bronze weapons, you needed to control separate territories, which had the required raw materials. This was done by either controlling the trade routes or governing the land directly. Not directly controlling the sources of these two metals meant that you could be cut off from trade networks, making your civilization vulnerable to conquest. This is pretty much what happened in the Bronze Age collapse, resulting in the move to the Iron Age.

In fact, it can be argued that the need to stabilize trade in the ancient world was why the Bronze Age was more peaceful (and so lasted longer). This peaceful nature was in contrast to the Iron Age, with its cheap and abundant sources of iron. Abundant sources of iron meant that quality weapons could be made — in much larger quantities than ever before (enabling the equipping of larger armies). Thus civilizations moved from a time where most interactions, between one another, were peaceful (Bronze Age), to a time where civilizations sought to dominate one another (Iron Age).

Of course, the effects of iron were not just felt on the battlefield, it also allowed societies to be far more productive, with the introduction of "mass produced" iron tools. Although bronze tools, were available before, they were simply more "expensive" to acquire (via trade). This meant that stone implements were in simultaneous use (in the Bronze Age and to a lesser extent in the Iron Age).

The Ancient Egyptian civilization fell for good around this period, as did Carthage (which rose and fell in the same time frame) — both ultimately falling to the Roman Empire (towards the end of the 1st millennium BCE). Despite a number of battles between the two, Nubia (Kush) was never dominated by the Romans. In fact, the Nubians went on the offensive on a number of occasions. As a result, the Roman presence in Africa remained, more or less, limited to the Mediterranean Coast and Egypt.

Rest of Africa

There is plenty of evidence for early ironworking in the rest of Africa. Some of this evidence dates back to much earlier periods in time than others. For example, recent excavations have produced radiocarbon dates for ironworking that stretch back to c. 2000 BCE. If the results are accepted, this would make the site of "Oboui", in the Central African Republic, among the oldest known ironworking sites in the world (if not the oldest).

Clearly, these dates throw the "conventional" chronology of African metallurgy up into the air. And so, you will find debates on dating techniques, site integrity etc. The assessment of radiocarbon dates can be complicated, and dates produced for some past archaeological sites, have eventually proven to be incorrect. Ultimately, much more archaeological work needs to be done in cases like this, before more scholars can move from the position of "not being sure". For this, more funding (and expertise) is required to carry out more extensive excavations, not just near this site, but throughout the continent.

Iron smelting and forging techniques are said to have also existed in West Africa, as early as the 6th century BCE, as part of the "Nok culture". This knowledge of ironworking is seen as one of the things that led to the growth and development of more centralized kingdoms in West Africa. And so you had kingdoms such as Dahomey, Benin, and the Yoruba Kingdoms (Ife and Oyo). Iron tools allowed for more organized agriculture, more efficient hunting, and the ability to engage in warfare successfully.

As for the southern and eastern parts of the continent, the spread of ironworking techniques has been linked to the "Bantu Expansion". There are a number of theories regarding this expansion. These can be boiled down to theories that argue that significant physical migrations of Bantu people took place, and those that argue that there were no (or limited) physical migrations — rather there was a movement of ideas/knowledge/language.

Archaeological evidence for the Bantu Expansion comes in the form of ceramics (pottery) and settlement patterns. This goes with the linguistic evidence in that the Bantu languages, spoken in large parts of Southern and Eastern Africa, descend from a common language spoken in Western Africa. Lastly, there is also some genetic evidence. However, none of this evidence is conclusive enough to say — that this is exactly what happened either way (more on this later).

8. Ancient Egypt

Ancient Egypt is considered by many to be the very first "nation state" in the world. A nation state is simply a state where a great majority shares the same culture. Today there are many such nation states — Bangladesh, Japan, Portugal etc. In order to fully understand the roots of the concept of the nation state, one needs to have an appreciation of the Ancient Egyptians. This is partly what has given rise to a whole field of study called "Egyptology".

Technically it could also be called "Kmtology" or "Kemetology". This is because; the Egyptians knew their land as *KMT* or *Kemet*. KMT is the original spelling (without vowels), and it means "the black land" or "land of the blacks". There are differing opinions on whether this refers to the color of the people (of Egypt), or if it refers to the color of the fertile soils, either side of the Nile (resulting from the silt that comes down from the Ethiopian Highlands).

Given we have over 3000 years of Ancient Egyptian history, it is almost impossible to cover it all — within the confines of this book. Having said this, we can touch on the basics. The traditional way of covering Ancient Egyptian history is chronologically. In other words, starting from the very beginning and going all the way to the end. Although this framework is convenient, it can be quite boring to read and difficult to understand. A thematic discussion (social, trade, government, science, arts etc.) provides a much more enjoyable read, while retaining most of the important information.

Egyptology and deciphering the Ancient Egyptian language

Compared to many other African civilizations, we know a great deal more about the Ancient Egyptians. This is primarily due to the fact that they kept records of their happenings (writing). It is these records that historians have been able to study. If you combine this with archaeology and science, we get somewhat of a first-hand view of the

Egyptian civilization. That's not to say that other African civilizations did not develop writing, or that there are no records of them — far from it. There are African scripts which have not been deciphered (so cannot be translated), as too have many scripts been destroyed or simply lost over time.

Going back to Egyptology, until relatively recently, the meanings of those mysterious but beautiful Egyptian "hieroglyphs" (Greek for "sacred carvings") were unknown. Many great minds had tried and tried again, to decipher the language, without success. Deciphering hieroglyphic scripts was a problem, as too was deciphering its sister scripts — "hieratic" and "demotic". These two other scripts can be thought of as simplified versions of hieroglyphics. Hieratic is nearly as old as hieroglyphics (c. 3000 BCE), while demotic is much newer (c. 600 BCE).

All three scripts were either forgotten or no longer understood by c. 400 CE, with them being replaced by the Coptic alphabet. The Coptic language is the latest stage of the Egyptian language, and its alphabet is an adaptation of the Greek alphabet — with the addition of a couple of letters to signify sounds not found in Greek. Coptic was spoken for a few hundred years, but has now been replaced by Egyptian Arabic (although it is still used in the Coptic Church as a "holy" language).

This inability to understand the Ancient Egyptian scripts did not happen overnight — it was a slow process. It came about during the rise of Christianity in Egypt. And with the coming of Christianity, there was no more space for the "pagan" Egyptian religion, as Christian priests, bishops and monks spread throughout Roman Egypt.

In the following centuries, various scholars (Islamic and European) had tried to interpret hieroglyphs — with progress being slow due to a false assumption. This assumption was that hieroglyphs simply represented pictures or ideas. In other words, they thought hieroglyphs were purely picture writing, and not, how we have come to learn, that they actually also represented sounds (phonetics). Further progress would only be made, when a famous Frenchman came onto the scene.

This Frenchman was not a historian, or an archaeologist, or a scientist. He was just a military general that went by the name of — Napoleon Bonaparte. The same Napoleon Bonaparte that would later become the Emperor of France, and who would conquer much of Europe in the early 19th century.

As an unintended consequence of the French campaign against Ottoman Egypt (1798), a rare stone was unearthed by a group of soldiers — the Rosetta Stone. Written on this stone was parallel text in hieroglyphs, demotic and Ancient Greek. Now, at the time, nobody could read hieroglyphic or demotic scripts — but they sure could read and understand Ancient Greek. And so, it was hoped that from this understanding of Greek, and with knowledge of Coptic, the Egyptian written language could be "decoded".

The Ancient Greek was quickly translated, revealing that the Rosetta Stone contained a decree from the general council of Egyptian priests, issued in Memphis, Egypt (196 BCE). This was but one hurdle. Other hurdles remained. All related to the fact that there had not been anyone that could actually speak "Ancient Egyptian", going back hundreds of years. What this meant was that nobody knew how the language really sounded. This made it very difficult to work out the "sounds" of the hieroglyphs.

An English physicist, by the name of Thomas Young, was the first to demonstrate that parts of the Egyptian scripts corresponded to a royal name — specifically that of King Ptolemy V. By 1822, Jean-François Champollion, a French scholar, proved that some hieroglyphs represented sounds, and that multiple hieroglyphs could form a word. From there on, it only took a few decades until Ancient Egyptian texts could be fully translated. This birthed the modern discipline of Egyptology, as we know it today.

This ability to understand hieroglyphics, and other Egyptian scripts, has allowed us to uncover much of the history, culture and achievements of Egypt's ancient past. More than just the history of the Egyptians, it has also enabled us to access the earliest stages of recorded human history. Without such, much of this history would have been lost in time, and subject to speculation, particularly where science cannot provide definitive answers. Much is owed to the discovery of the Rosetta Stone. Today it is housed in the British Museum, with it being the single most-visited object.

Origins of Ancient Egypt

Some 10,000 years ago, the Sahara Desert was a landscape covered with grasslands, scattered with trees, dotted with several lakes and criss-crossed by rivers. The dramatic desertification or drying of the Sahara (c. 6000 BP), drove the inhabitants of this vast desert, to more stable water sources — one of which was the river Nile. This movement of people to (scarce) river sources was a major contributing factor to the birth of civilization in Egypt. Put another way, the appearance of these populations, on the banks of the Nile, marked the beginnings of

urban and socially stratified pharaonic (Egyptian) culture. And all that
subsequently came with it e.g. the Great Pyramids.

There is evidence that these Saharan Africans already had the
knowledge required for food production, subsequently allowing them
to permanently settle the Nile Valley. That is knowledge of both animal
husbandry and crop cultivation. Recent research shows that Saharans
cultivated and stored wild grains, going back to at least 10,000 BP. And
as already mentioned — evidence for domesticated cattle also goes
back to around the same time period.

Predynastic Egypt

The predynastic period spans the time before the development of
writing, from the first settlements — to the early dynastic period (c.
3100 BCE). During this time a number of "cultural phases" flourished
along the banks of the Nile, with each phase referring to places where
specific Egyptian settlements have been found (by archaeologists). The
majority of known predynastic cultures are found in Upper Egypt.
Arguably, the most important of which is the so-called "Naqada
culture". This Naqada culture can best be described as the "earliest face
of Ancient Egypt". Emerging around 4000 BCE, this culture directly
leads onto the unification of Egypt, and the subsequent first dynasty.

To make clear, "Lower Egypt" is technically Northern Egypt (as we
know it today), while "Upper Egypt" is Southern Egypt. This just derives
from the fact that the river Nile flows from the south (Great Lakes and
Ethiopian Highlands) northwards — into the Mediterranean Sea.

Life before the pyramids

Vertically cutting across the Sahara, the river Nile too was affected
by its drying. Before conditions got dryer, like other parts of the Sahara,
the Nile was a marshy place. To quote the Boston Museum of Fine Arts:

> The first settlers found the valley very different in appearance from
> what it is today. The annual inundation flooded a great portion of the
> land on each side of the river and after the water had receded
> swampy pools were left along the edge of the desert. Endless
> thickets of papyrus and reeds covered these marshy regions, and
> grew even more widely amongst the lagoons of the Delta. Land for
> cultivation had to be cleared little by little and the wild beasts that
> inhabited the swamps destroyed. Not only were there snakes and
> crocodiles to be feared, but the hippopotamus and elephant were
> still commonly met with. It is not surprising that formidable natural
> obstructions as well as diversity of origin should at first have

isolated the tribes which settled in different places along the valley. (Smith, 1960).

As it became dryer and dryer, people relied less and less on hunting and fishing. Further, river beds either side of the Nile, became considerably less marshy than before — encouraging farming in the process.

As already pointed out, in order to farm effectively, some form of social organization was required. Communities needed to work together to exploit the land, for example irrigating canals, clearing the grounds, filling in the swamps etc. Once organized, they could go about cultivating a range of crops (wheat, barley etc.) — subsequently allocating the proceeds.

As more and more people came, more and more organization was required. Clearly the ways of organization that worked before, could not remain the same. Innovation was needed, as the only way for success was large-scale coordination of work, and specialization (in a range of crafts). This is what the Egyptians mastered before anyone else, the ability to coordinate a large group of people, to produce desired outcomes i.e. a functioning state.

With more organization, inevitably came greater uniformity. In Egypt there was now a way of doing things — a proven template that worked. With this template came administrative, commercial and cultural structures, which further tied people together — across relatively distant Nile Valley settlements or "Nomes" (provinces). The very heart of this template was the Nile, for Egypt greatly depended on this natural highway. This natural highway that both efficiently and effectively transported resources, workers and administrators from a to b. The Nile was Egypt's heart and soul. This dependence would soon transform to an early form of state religion.

Unification of Upper and Lower Egypt

Before (and after) unification there was somewhat of a distinction between Upper and Lower Egypt. In times of internal turmoil (intermediate periods) the Egyptian state would often split back into its two constituent halves i.e. back into Upper and Lower Egypt. As such, and throughout Egypt's history, it was kind of a royal obligation to keep the two lands united. By doing so, order was kept and the state prospered.

It was a king from Upper Egypt who unified the Egyptian state c. 3000 BCE — a king by the name of Narmer (or Menes). This meant that it was the southern kingdom that gained dominance over the whole state, and Pharaoh Narmer was the supreme leader of this new state. As a result, Narmer wore the crowns of both Upper and Lower Egypt — a white crown for Upper Egypt, and a red one for Lower Egypt.

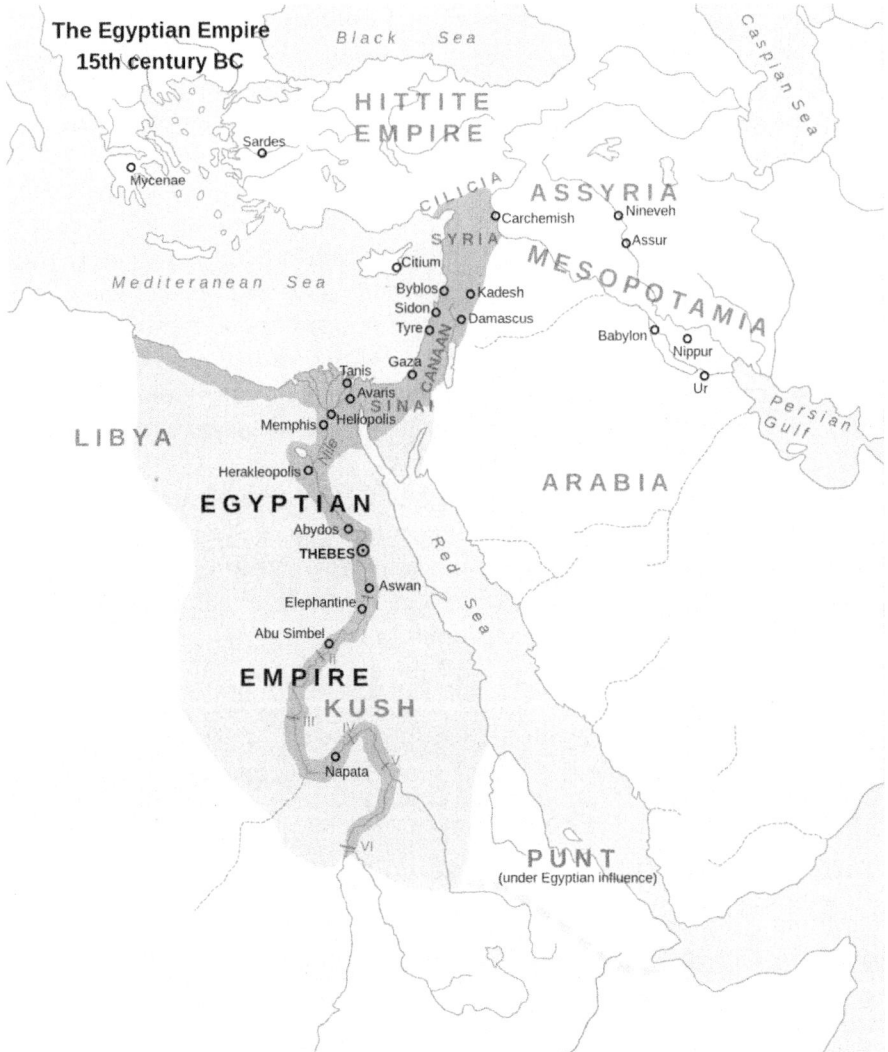

Map 15. Egyptian Empire or New Kingdom. Nubian Kush, Punt and Canaan also shown. Roman numerals mark the river Nile's cataracts. Source: Wikimedia Commons/CC BY-SA 3.0 (Author: Andrei Nacu, Jeff Dahl).

This unification of Egypt, by Narmer, was historic. It gave Egypt stability, trade and agriculture became even more organized, and record keeping (writing) was fully developed. There were a number of other customs and ideas that came from unification. For example art and architecture were elevated in importance, and a unified Egyptian religion spread throughout the Nile Valley.

Narmer's victory palette, a ceremonial engraving, can today be found in the Egyptian Museum (Cairo). The palette shows King Narmer defeating his enemies, and uniting the two lands. As it contains some of the earliest hieroglyphic inscriptions on record, it can be thought of as one of, if not, the first, historical document in the world.

Governance and administration — the social order of the state

Despite King Narmer's successful conquest, and unification of the two lands, a major problem presented itself — one of governance. This was a problem which King Narmer, and his successors in the first dynasty, would have to deal with.

How do you keep the lands united? What structures need to be put in place? How would the king defend the lands?

These were but a few questions that needed answers. The earliest kings had nothing to refer to, no books, no experts, nothing. And so, all the rules needed to be created from "scratch". They did have some experience managing individual provinces, but nothing on this grand scale i.e. at a state level. Egypt was a big place. The population, after unification, has been estimated to have been around 1 million, spread over the length of the Egyptian Nile. That is to say, from the first cataract in Upper Egypt, all the way to the shores of the Mediterranean in Lower Egypt — a distance of some 850km.

The initial capital was at a place called *Thinis*, but it was soon moved. The new capital of Memphis, a few miles south of modern Cairo, was deliberately chosen to be in Lower Egypt. This was where the Southern King's power was weakest. And being a strategic location, just before the Nile Delta, it was where commerce/trade, along the length of the Nile, could more easily be controlled. To guard the southern border with Ancient Nubia, a fort was constructed, on an island in the middle of the Nile (near the first cataract). This fort was known as Elephantine. It was both a great defensive position, and a cargo transfer point for river trade.

With Egypt's borders now secure, the pharaohs could turn their heads to bureaucracy i.e. managing internal affairs. Although the king was technically in charge of everything — military, priesthood, government, farming etc. — the job was clearly too much for two hands. The kings needed help.

Egypt was soon divided into 42 nomes. Each nome was ruled by a "nomarch" (provincial governor). And each nomarch was appointed by the pharaoh. There were 22 nomes in Upper Egypt and 20 in Lower Egypt. And with this you had the first nation state in the world. At the time (c. 3000 BCE), most other "urban" societies were either city-states, or a loose coalition of states. However in Egypt, everybody answered to the king.

The vast majority of people were peasant farmers, who lived in small mud houses near the banks of the Nile. They lived a subsistence life, off the food they were able to grow, produce and/or barter for.

Beer, bread, fish and onions were all commonly consumed. Like in predynastic times, the crops grown included wheat, barley and flax, as these were the crops most suitable for the (Egyptian) Nile Valley. Vegetables and fruits, such as figs and grapes, were also grown. Cattle, goats and sheep were raised. And people fished and hunted wild birds, in the Nile's marshes. Peasants that produced a big surplus were able to barter for other goods — clothes, shoes, ceramics etc. These "extras" would have either been locally produced, by expert craftsmen, or brought in from foreign lands (by merchants or traders).

You then had the civil servants. Most of these would have been scribes and/or tax collectors. Essentially, they enforced state policy on a local level. For example, they collected the required amount of taxable grain from the peasants. Some of these civil servants were engaged in other tasks, such as supervision of projects. Projects like the building of boats, pyramids and palaces. Other projects were the digging of canals and the draining of marshes.

Given the size of the state, administration of it greatly relied on record keeping — made possible thanks to the development of writing. A record of yearly events was critical — the size of harvest, the amount of rain (and when it came), how many soldiers were in the army, the number of workers etc. This of course required people who could read and write (scribes). But unlike today, it was only a select few who could actually read and write. The vast majority of Egyptian citizens were not literate — those who were literate, belonged to a higher social class — the priests, nomarchs and nobles of the day.

Soldiers too were fairly well regarded. They fought in the armies, in times of war, and would have helped supervise the peasants and "slaves" working on public construction projects. The issue of whether or not the Egyptians actually used slaves, in the literal sense, is debated.

All in all, you had a social hierarchy or social pyramid. The pharaoh (and the gods) at the top, then his most senior advisors, followed by the nomarchs, nobles and priests. The scribes, soldiers and artisans were next — with the peasants and slaves forming the lowest class.

Unlike today, there was limited social mobility in Ancient Egypt. The order of the state was seen as essential for its survival. And in order for the state to survive, the people had to believe in the system and its pharaoh.

This is linked to the notion of *Maat*, in Ancient Egyptian religion, the idea of truth, balance, order, harmony, law, morality, and justice. Where there was Maat, there was order and prosperity for all. The ideological opposite of Maat was *Isfet* — disunity, disorder, chaos, injustice, violence etc. It was the king's role to ensure the state of Maat, by destroying Isfet. In a way, the social hierarchy of Egypt can be seen as reflecting the principles of Maat.

Religious & mythological order

Ancient Egyptian religion was a complex system of polytheistic beliefs. That is to say, the Egyptians believed in multiple deities or gods (and goddesses). These beliefs were an integral part of the Egyptian society, kingship and by extension the state. Egyptian religion and mythology left behind many writings and monuments. It has also gone on to influence both ancient and modern cultures, within and outside Africa.

Along with the belief in Maat, an important central belief was that Egypt was god's land — the center of the world. Consequently, and by default, foreign lands and foreigners were seen as inferior to anything Egyptian — for foreigners lived in a land of chaos (Isfet). This strong belief in the superiority of Egypt, is a key reason why the state managed to survive for so long — despite the many setbacks. To put it more plainly, religion helped to give Egypt stability.

The pharaohs were the focus of formal religious practice. They were seen to possess divine powers, due to their position as kings of Egypt. The pharaohs acted as intermediaries between the people and their gods. As mentioned above, they needed to maintain Maat, and to do so, they offered sacrifices and performed rituals to sustain and please the gods. And so, the state dedicated vast amounts of resources towards these efforts, as well as efforts of glorifying the king's throne.

Maat was required not just at the state level, but also at an individual level. Egyptians depended on each other, and so were required to act with honor and truth in their daily lives. This was something that they were to be judged for, in the *Duat* i.e. the realm of the dead (underworld).

Egyptians believed there was life after death, for which one needed to prepare for. This belief is evident in the great efforts taken in terms of funeral practices. These practices were seen to be important, in ensuring the survival of their *Ka* (soul/spirit) after death. The temples, tombs, pyramids, mummification, grave goods etc. were all part of preparation for the afterlife. And so you have mummification to preserve the body, and grave goods to provide material comforts in the Duat.

Those who honored the principles of Maat were aligned with the gods, and the forces of good against evil — assuring themselves of a kind judgment by Osiris (the lord of the dead). Unsurprisingly, those that did not do "good", in life, did not get such favorable judgments from Osiris.

The roots of Egyptian religion can be traced back to the predynastic period, where evidence has been found of early religious practice, which continued on in pharaonic Egypt. Religion in pharaonic Egypt, with the help of centralized power, worship and rituals, was simply practiced on a much grander scale. Despite this, it is important to note that, religious beliefs did not remain exactly the same. Egyptian beliefs changed over time, adapting to the circumstances the state found itself in. Gods could evolve from minor deities into major ones, or be combined to form newer deities. This all meant that the importance of specific gods rose and fell over time.

Hundreds of gods and goddesses are said to have been worshipped over time. Very important gods included Ra (sun god), Osiris, Thoth (god of writing/wisdom), Anubis (god of mummification and afterlife), Isis (mother goddess), Horus (god of the sky and kingship) and Hapi (god of the annual flooding of the Nile).

Art, architecture and the pyramids

A great deal of what we know about the Ancient Egyptians comes from their art — their paintings, sculptures, carvings, scripts, and more. Art has allowed us to get a glimpse of what life was like going back c. 5000 BP. Art tells us what the Egyptians looked like, the clothes they wore, the jobs they worked, and what was most important to them. Much of this art remained consistent during the c. 3000 years of

Egyptian civilization. Therefore, artists followed in the artistic styles, which had already been laid down. Architecture, however, saw more significant changes — as wealth accumulated and engineering design improved.

In order to understand Ancient Egyptian art, one needs to have an appreciation of what it was fundamentally created for. And like with many other subjects and ideas from long ago, it is important that one understands Egyptian art from their point of view (not ours). Ancient Egyptian artworks and by extension architecture, served an almost essential purpose — a purpose that was bound with Egyptian religion and ideology. It gave subjects (people, kings, gods etc.) permanence. And so, even after death, their art would remain. Egyptians did have a sense of beauty/aesthetics, but their art was primarily intended to be a functional part of religion. In other words, art was typically not made for art's sake — rather it was for the gods and goddesses of the time.

Those amazing treasures, dug up from the tombs of pharaohs like Tutankhamen, were not intended to be seen by us, they were solely for the benefit of the divine and/or the departed. These very tombs can almost be thought of as secret art galleries, with the paintings and carvings on the wall, speaking only to the gods and goddesses of Egypt.

These paintings show the pharaohs as "larger than life" figures, to symbolize their divine powers. This is in direct contrast to their wives, children, slaves and animals, who were deliberately painted smaller — to show their lesser importance. Hieroglyphics, found within tombs, would often detail kings-lists, proving the king's ancestry or his/her link to past pharaohs (and gods).

This link between Egyptian art and religion is what gives rise to perhaps the earliest forms of what we now call architecture. Only a (religious) building of great importance would require such beauty, care and attention to detail — in short architectural excellence. This is in contrast to purely practical, far less elaborate forms of construction, used to satisfy the simple demands of the masses. For example, small mud huts with plain walls to live in.

The mud of the river Nile was the basic building material in Ancient Egypt. It would often be mixed with straw and other organic matter. Moulds would be used to help shape the bricks. And these bricks would be put out in the sun, to be hardened. Almost anything could be constructed from these bricks, which given the arid conditions in the Nile Valley, were extremely durable. The use of stone was mostly reserved for monumental building projects, such as constructing pyramids.

As religion was an integral part of kingship, and the Egyptian state as a whole, significant amounts of resources had to be dedicated to it. As such, much of the wealth of the first kings was directed towards the construction of ever increasingly "stylish" statues, monuments, tombs, temples and palaces. These were buildings that were unrivalled, in magnificence, at the time. The kings were of course divine figures, who maintained Maat for the state, and so with the construction of such buildings, they were to deservedly enjoy comfortable afterlives. King after king, dynasty after dynasty, religious buildings would often become more and more elaborate — leading up to the first pyramids.

Egypt's first large stone building was built in c. 2700 BCE, in the third dynasty, at a place called Saqqara (near Memphis). This pyramid was commissioned by Pharaoh Djoser, and designed by his architect Imhotep. Incidentally, this same Imhotep was one of the few non-royal Egyptians deified (made a god) after death.

The pyramid of Djoser was a step pyramid, built with small stone blocks. Its purpose, like with all the other pyramids to come, was to be the pharaoh's burial chamber. This step pyramid was but one part of the Saqqara "necropolis". The surrounding complex was vast, and included a funerary temple, courtyards, shrines, and living quarters. Other Egyptian royals and nobles came to be buried here, over a period of approximately 2500 years.

It was only a few decades later, and the Egyptians had mastered the full capabilities of building with stone, using blocks that weighed up to 10,000 kg. These blocks were employed in the building of the pyramids at Giza.

The Great Pyramid of Giza, built as a tomb for the fourth dynasty Egyptian Pharaoh Khufu, is today one of the seven wonders of the ancient world. In fact of the seven, only Khufu's pyramid still remains standing. At over 140 meters tall, it was the tallest man-made structure in the world — for almost 3900 years. What we see today is the core structure of the pyramid. Many years ago it would have been covered by fine white limestone, forming a smooth outer surface. Later pyramids would not reach the heights of the Great Pyramid. Native Egyptian royal pyramid building would stop (c. 1500 BCE) with the end of the reign of Pharaoh Ahmose I.

Figure 8. Step pyramid of Pharaoh Djoser in Saqqara. Source: Wikimedia Commons/CC BY-SA 3.0 (Author: Charles J. Sharp).

Egyptian art and architecture has gone on to influence later civilizations. Napoleon's expedition to Egypt, and the subsequent discovery of the Rosetta Stone, led to the concept of "Egyptian revival art" — in Europe and the United States. Here, Egyptian motifs were used in a wide variety of decorative objects and architecture, mainly in the 19th century continuing on into the early 20th.

Military and conquest

As part of the pharaoh's divine duty, he (or she) was required to defend Egypt from external threats (foreigners), and ensure the internal stability of the land. This was to be done through the militaristic control of trade routes, as and when required. Without a sizeable and well-trained army, the pharaoh's militaristic duties could not be fulfilled. Additionally, and apart from building imposing buildings, war was also a way for pharaohs to demonstrate their greatness. Evidence of such can still be found today, in the paintings they left behind on the walls of their tombs and temples.

Thanks to favorable geography, Egypt was positioned in a naturally defendable position. And so, Egypt could be described as "semi-isolationist", at least to begin with. The Nile Valley was shielded from potential invaders in all directions. To the north you had the Mediterranean Sea, and to the east you had both the Eastern Desert and the Red Sea. To the west you had vast desert land, which included Egypt's Western Desert, stretching all the way to the Atlantic Ocean. Finally, to the south you had the Nile's cataracts, as well as more desert and mountainous terrain. In short, directly invading Ancient Egypt was not easy — if not outright impossible. For the Egyptians, at the time, internal strife was likely a much bigger threat. These natural barriers were part of the reason why the Egyptian civilization lasted for so long.

As stated, the Egyptians were rather isolationist. In other words, they were not particularly expansionist — they were more focused on trade and internal affairs. When trade was not possible, or had broken down, Egypt did go on the offensive — to secure the supply lines. Although Egypt was blessed agriculturally, it did not have all the resources required to maintain the state. Some of these resources had to be obtained from foreign lands, be it by trade or by military means.

The actual military system of Egypt grew and developed over time. This was in line with the different circumstances the state found itself in. At first there seemed to be no large regular armies. Instead, soldiers were recruited from the general populace — from each of its 42 provinces. Those recruited would usually only serve for one specific campaign or purpose, before returning to civilian duties or normal life. By the Middle Kingdom (c. 2000 BCE), however, the army started to become significantly more organized, with a core group of professional soldiers at hand — supplemented by recruits and mercenaries. The actual number of troops available, during these early times, is unknown.

The earliest Egyptian armies would not have been very "sophisticated". In fact, there is little proof that suggests the Egyptian army held any technological advantage, or were in any way superior to that of its neighbors (in the Near East, Libya and Nubia). Bronze weapons were not mass produced, neither were horses or chariots deployed. Archers made up part of the army, and the infantry mostly used light weapons (spears, daggers, axes) — with little in the way of protective gear (armor, helmets etc.) being worn. To go with the ground troops, a royal flotilla or navy was eventually developed.

It has been suggested, that the early kings did not actually lead the troops in battle, with there being no scenes (artwork) that suggests otherwise. This had changed by the Egyptian Middle Kingdom, with the pharaoh either directly leading the army, or delegating to one of his sons.

Some form of military police had also been developed, by this time. The police were based at strategic forts, from where they patrolled the Nile, paying particular attention to the cataracts in the south i.e. the borders with Nubia. Towards the end of this period, the horse, and the chariot had been adopted. Many of the pharaohs that followed would have scenes commissioned of themselves as chariot warriors in battle.

By the New Kingdom (c. 1500 BCE), Egypt had adopted an almost complete Bronze Age culture. Together with their use of the horse and the newly introduced composite bow, the Egyptians had superiority — particularly against the Nubians in the south. Military philosophy was also changed; there was less reliance on the navy and more on the foot soldiers. The emphasis in battle continued to be speed and agility, rather than "brute force".

It was during this New Kingdom that Egypt expanded its borders, to its greatest extent — controlling large parts of Nubia and the Levant as a result. To control this larger empire, forts were constructed and garrisoned across the Levant and up the Nile. This enabled the pharaohs to better rule the newly conquered lands.

After this rise, came the fall. The Bronze Age Collapse, discussed earlier, laid waste to several competing civilizations. Old trade routes were lost and foreign invasions soon occurred. By around 340 BCE, the final native Egyptian dynasty had fallen.

Natural resources and trade

To build or make anything, including the grand temples, pyramids, statues, tools, weapons and jewelry — Egypt needed natural resources. Thanks to geography, it had some of the required resources, within its borders. However, Egypt did lack certain things, for which it would have to trade for.

The backbone of its economy was agriculture. The Nile, and the annual floods that revitalized the narrow flood plains either side of it, made farming relatively simple. And, as already covered, this was one of the reasons for people settling the Nile Valley in the first place (as the Sahara dried).

However, the Nile did not just make farming easy, it allowed Egypt to produce a surplus. A surplus which could be bagged, stockpiled and traded with others, for goods Egypt was in short supply of. As demonstrated by the magnificence of some of the architecture left behind, this Egyptian surplus must have been large. This agricultural wealth also meant that upon eventual Roman conquest, Egypt became the Roman Empire's main grain producer — its "breadbasket". This was in part thanks to the Nile enabling easy distribution of grain, all the way to Rome itself. Again, this shows why shipping by river/sea was cheaper (and often quicker) than equivalent transportation overland.

So in terms of agriculture, Egypt had the Nile, which thanks to farming gave it — wheat, barley, bread and beer. Add fruit to the mix and you get — grapes, wine, dates, figs, pomegranates, nuts, berries, melons and more. Also you had vegetables — beans, cabbage, chickpeas, cress, cucumbers, garlic, leeks, lentils, onions, peas and radish. In terms of oils there was — castor, flax, olive and sesame. A wide variety of herbs were produced as well, and papyrus (used to make paper and boats) was cultivated in the marshlands of the Nile Delta.

From this long list of agricultural products, it is clear that Egypt was more than self-sufficient in food. This food wealth was complimented, nicely, by the state's other natural resources. Limestone was easily available in the Nile Valley, as too was sandstone. Other stones like alabaster, diorite, granite and quartzite were also in close proximity. All of these resources could easily be ferried, via the Nile, to the construction sites in need of them.

In the Eastern Desert and the Sinai region, copper was available, together with a range of semi-precious stones (amethyst, turquoise etc). The copper ore, malachite, could also be found in these deserts, which was used for cosmetic purposes and painting. Natron is the name of a salt that the Egyptians used for hygiene, purification and mummification. This salt was found, in the appropriately named, Natron Valley (outskirts of Cairo).

Lastly, Egypt was rich in gold — very rich indeed. So rich that a Mesopotamian ruler, in c. 1340 BCE, remarked that "gold occurs in Egypt like sand on the roads" — when he sent a letter (asking for more gold) to Pharaoh Amenhotep III. This claim of gold wealth is backed up by a large number of gold production sites, identified by geologists and archaeologists, in South Eastern Egypt (and North Eastern Nubia).

Trade (imports and exports)

The Nile was not the only advantage Egypt enjoyed. As detailed already, the geographic position of the actual state was a big bonus, precisely being at the crossroads of the Middle East, Africa and Europe. In fact, had Egypt not been bound to the north by the Mediterranean Sea, and to the East by the Red Sea, its role in one of the world's first international trade networks would have been limited. This

Mediterranean trade network was one which Egypt controlled, for long periods of time, and grew rich off the back of.

One of the main goods which Egypt lacked significant quantities of, was wood. That's not to say that Egypt had no trees, rather, that the Nile Valley was not particularly wooded. Trees that grew in pharaonic times included acacia, sycamore-fig and the tamarisk — the woods of which would have been used in carpentry and joinery. Despite this, Egypt needed to import high-quality timber, in order to meet its demands. Other vital goods and luxuries on the wanted or import list included metals like tin (to make bronze), incense, spices, lapis lazuli, silver, ebony, ivory and olive oil.

These early trade networks were established with its closest foreign neighbors, namely the regions of the Levant, Libya and Nubia. Later, Egypt would add Punt (Eritrea/Somalia), Anatolia (Turkey), Crete and Greece as trading partners. Trade was conducted using both land and river/sea routes — more specifically across the Mediterranean, down the Red Sea, and overland routes via the deserts that bound the Nile.

Most trade agreements were established through peaceful means. However, at times, agreements were struck through military means — subjugating other societies in the process.

Nearly all of this trade was in the form of barter i.e. exchanging goods without using "money". The scenes of such barter can be seen in various Egyptian artworks. At first, there was no concept of cash or coinage in Ancient Egypt. It was not until the Persian and Greek invasions of Egypt, that there was a shift to a more coin based economy.

In the barter system, goods would be exchanged based on a standard value. By the New Kingdom, a notional unit of accounting, the *Deben*, was in use. If a day's labor was 1 Deben, and 5 loaves of bread was also 1 Deben — one could be fairly paid for a day's labor with 5 loaves of bread or the equivalent i.e. 1 Deben may also be equal to 1 bag of flour or 2 liters of wine etc.

Manetho and the periods and dynasties of Ancient Egypt

In establishing the chronology of the pharaohs of Egypt, scholars rely on both archaeology and a variety of written records. One such written record comes from an Egyptian priest/historian, who went by the name of Manetho. He authored a book, in Greek, entitled *Aegyptiaca* (the History of Egypt) — sometime in the 3rd century BCE. At this time, Egypt was under the control of the Hellenistic (Greek) state known as the Ptolemaic Kingdom. Manetho recorded the kings of Egypt right from the first, Pharoah Narmer (Menes), all the way to the last, Pharaoh Nectanebo II.

These dates only give a general idea of Egypt's chronology, as Manetho's original work has been lost in time. What we know of what Manetho wrote, we get from other ancient authors — that happened to reference his work. Despite the limitations, Manetho's Aegyptiaca is still widely used as a guide to the history of Ancient Egypt.

Modern scholars also periodize Egyptian history. This periodization is based on dynasties or "royal houses". Just like you have various dynasties in Europe, 30 dynasties were recorded by Mantheo, covering 3000 years of Ancient Egyptian history. These dynasties have been conveniently grouped into related periods. Periods where centralized government was strong are known as the three "Golden Ages" — the Old, Middle, and New Kingdoms. Periods known as "intermediate periods", are times when centralized control of Egypt broke down, whether through internal strife or foreign rule. And so we have:

Early Dynastic Period (3100 BCE)
Old Kingdom (2600 BCE)
First Intermediate Period (2180 BCE)
Middle Kingdom (2040 BCE)
Second Intermediate Period (1650 BCE)
New Kingdom (1550 BCE)
Third Intermediate Period (1070 BCE)
Late Period (660–332 BCE)

You should be aware that these dates are only approximations. Translating the dating system used by the Egyptians, into absolute BCE terms, has proven difficult, and is in fact a matter of debate — not helped by the sometimes contradictory evidence available.

We have already looked at the pre and early dynastic periods of Egypt, by both discussing the state's origins, as well as the unification of the two lands. Therefore, we will now begin our chronological overview, by first looking at the Egyptian Old Kingdom.

Old Kingdom

The Old Kingdom relates to the third, fourth, fifth and sixth Egyptian dynasties. It is also known as the "Age of the Pyramids". Even before the building of these pyramids, kings from the first and second dynasties had already started building elaborate burial grounds and tombs. These royal tombs were rectangular in shape, had inward-sloping sides, and were flat-roofed. Constructed out of mudbricks, the tombs were called *mastabas*. As trade links had already long been established with Libya, Nubia and lands in the Levant — these tombs were already being filled with various artifacts. These artifacts were of course things that the kings took with them into the afterlife.

Thanks to his architect, Imhotep, who doubled as many things including chief minister and doctor, 3rd dynasty Pharaoh Djoser took royal tomb building to the next level — with the very first step pyramid at Saqqara. The building of this pyramid demonstrates that the Egyptian state had reached a very high level of organization, by the Old Kingdom, owing to the fact that the logistics of building such a structure was complex.

It was this mastery of the supply chain — docks, mines, quarries, warehouses, workshops and labor force — that enabled the subsequent construction of the three Pyramids of Giza. The first was built by King Khufu, the second by his son King Khafre, and the third by his grandson King Menkaure. Each one of these gigantic structures was just a small part of a much larger pyramid complex, which included monuments, palaces and temples.

One of these monuments or sculptures was the Great Sphinx of Giza. It is both one of the oldest known monumental sculptures in Egypt, and one of the most recognizable. Having said this, the exact origins and history of the structure remains a matter of debate. The statue's body resembles that of a lion, lying down. The face is that of a man, who many believe to be Pharaoh Khafre. This colossal structure measures over 70 meters in length, 20 meters in height and 19 meters in width. Accordingly, and at the time, the Great Sphinx must have been a great symbol of pharaonic power.

The pyramids constructed by future kings were on a much smaller scale. This was perhaps due to the costs involved. Not just economic costs, but costs in terms of time. None of the pyramids were built in a day; it took many years of dedicated work.

The pharaohs of the fifth dynasty did build pyramids, but they focused more on developing larger temples — which were beautifully decorated. Particular attention was paid to the internal finishing of their burial chambers, where walls were covered in hieroglyphs of religious inscriptions. Known as "pyramid texts", these inscriptions are some of the oldest collections of "religious writing" in the world. Pharaoh Unas was the first to have such texts written in his pyramid. The texts were basically prayers and magical spells, written to help the pharaohs in their quests for good afterlives. It is said that the idea of these texts came about to reduce a pharaoh's dependence on living priests, who continued to offer prayers, even after a pharaohs death.

Old Kingdom pharaohs also sent out more state-sponsored expeditions. They moved into Nubia, up to the second cataract, and in the process gained direct control of the lucrative gold mines found in the area. These kings also strengthened their hold on the trade routes, specifically the Eastern, Western and the Sinai desert routes. Further, with Pharaoh Sahure, we have the earliest record of an expedition to the Land of Punt (Horn of Africa) — from where large amounts of myrrh, malachite and electrum were imported (among other things).

What followed, with the sixth dynasty, was a succession of relatively weak pharaohs, who ultimately were unable to hold onto centralized power. Foreign trade and expeditions had brought significant wealth to the lands of Egypt. Much of this wealth lay in the hands of provincial officials or nomarchs. These nomarchs sought to increase their authority over the regions they controlled. In around 2100 BCE, this led to the collapse of the Egyptian state, which King Narmer had unified almost 1000 years earlier.

Egypt was now divided. And internal strife was the result. This led to what can be described as a civil war. To make matters worse, for many years to come, Egypt no longer produced an agricultural surplus. In fact, Egypt could not feed itself; there was famine in the land. This was caused by a long period of drought, where the Nile stopped flooding as much as before.

Consequently, belief in the pharaohs was lost, as they could not maintain "Maat" (order). And so what Egypt now faced was "Isfet" (chaos). Scholars call this the "First Intermediate Period", a 150 year period or so, where local leaders paid little to no tribute to the pharaohs, and where several different rulers claimed the thrones of Upper and Lower Egypt. During this time, the Nubians reclaimed the land that they had lost — up to the first cataract.

Middle Kingdom

The fall of the Old Kingdom led to Egypt splitting, like before, into two separate kingdoms i.e. Upper and Lower Egypt. Upper Egypt's stronghold lay in the city of Thebes (modern-day Luxor), while Lower Egypt's power base was at Herakleopolis (100 km south of Cairo).

Following in the footsteps of Pharaoh Narmer, it was a king from Upper Egypt that would go on to unite the two lands (once again). This king, from Thebes, was called Mentuhotep II. He first conquered the provinces of the Middle Nile, before advancing north, and taking full control of the Nile Delta (Lower Egypt). And thus the Middle Kingdom had begun.

Mentuhotep II's reign lasted for around 50 years, in which he stabilized the country, returning it to some form of the prosperity it once enjoyed. Stabilization efforts involved purging the kingdom of old, disloyal nomarchs — replacing them with more loyal ones from Thebes. State level taxes were reintroduced, and security was beefed up.

Once stabilized, the pharaohs that followed looked outwards, regaining control of the desert routes and expanding south once again — into Nubia. In Nubia, fortified settlements were constructed — up to the second cataract. The end-result of all this was the reestablishment of old trading links. Like in the Old Kingdom, Egypt could once again import those luxury goods it so desired. Copper, gold and precious stones were all either mined at home, or brought in from overseas. Unsurprisingly, exports also grew. Egyptian objects, from the 12th dynasty, have been found in parts of Palestine and Syria.

Many of the imported products would again go into the building of grand structures and monuments — for the glory of the pharaoh, the country and the gods. The more "expensive" imports were allocated to the temples, while the pyramids were built with mudbricks, using cheaper construction techniques. Consequently, little remains of these royal pyramids.

Literature became a thing in the Middle Kingdom, and so this period is often seen as the "classical age" of Egyptian literature. Unlike before, where writing was mainly restricted to acts of worship, acts of praise or taxation — people began to record poems and stories. Hieroglyphs were also used to inscribe sacred texts, on the sides of wooden coffins (coffin texts). These were texts adapted from the pyramid texts of the Old Kingdom. Both of these texts would go on to become the basis for the "Book of the Dead" (used in the New Kingdom). The main difference between the pyramid and the coffin texts was that the coffin texts were open to all. That is, all that could afford a coffin upon death. And so, coffin texts were embraced by government officials, priests and some more "common" people.

In this Middle Kingdom, everyone had a right to an afterlife. And with that came the cult center of Osiris, based out of Abydos (500 km south of Cairo). It is here that individuals started to engage in the "rites of Osiris" — Osiris of course being the lord of the dead and rebirth. Being granted access to the Kingdom of Osiris, upon death, would mean a life of immortality. Therefore, with the festivals and ceremonies performed in the name of Osiris, Egyptians from all walks of life sought his blessings — pharaohs, civil servants, peasants and more. This made Osiris one of the main gods of Egypt.

Figure 9. Inside tomb (KV9) of Ramses V and Ramses VI. Valley of the Kings, Luxor. Source: Wikimedia Commons/CC BY 3.0 (Author: Tim Adams).

With the 13th dynasty, came much less stability and a resulting decline in fortunes. Unlike the 11th and 12th dynasties, there are not many records to go on. However, what is clear is that the pharaohs of the 13th dynasty did not last for long i.e. reigns were short. Further, it appears that many of these pharaohs were not actually related to each other, with the term "dynasty" being used more for convenience (in this instance). The decline in fortunes was not as sudden as that of the Old Kingdom. It was more of a gradual decline, in the face of separate political entities springing up (particularly in Lower Egypt). One of these entities was known as the "Hyksos", who eventually grew powerful enough to directly challenge the authority of the 13th dynasty kings — ushering in a second intermediate period in the process.

The Hyksos were immigrants from the Palestine-Syria area, who had earlier come to Northern Egypt. Some of them were engaged in farming, while others were engaged as menial or skilled laborers. Over time they culturally assimilated, and their influence increased, as dynasty 13's power weakened. Eventually, the Hyksos rebelled and seized control of Lower Egypt, ruling from the city of *Avaris* (Eastern Nile Delta). This effectively ended the Egyptian Middle Kingdom c. 1650 BCE. Incidentally, the Hyksos were technically the first "foreign" rulers of Egypt — although they retained Egyptian customs and ways of governance.

While power had been lost in Lower Egypt, and southern garrisons had been withdrawn from Lower Nubia, Upper Egypt remained under the control of native Egyptians — with their powerbase at Thebes. Once again, it was kings and leaders from Upper Egypt that rose and wrestled back control from the Hyksos, driving them out of Egypt a century later. This ended the Second Intermediate Period. With the expulsion of the Hyksos, Pharaoh Ahmose I proclaimed the 18th Dynasty, and with that came the start of the Egyptian New Kingdom (c. 1550 BCE).

New Kingdom

New Kingdom Egypt was more of an expansionist state — an imperial power if you like. It is during this period of time that Egypt conquered lands far away from its original borders, becoming richer than ever before. Many of the most famous Egyptian Pharaohs reigned in this period including Hatshepsut, Akhenaten and Tutankhamun. Scholars also have a much clearer picture of Egypt, in the New Kingdom, thanks to relatively detailed written records.

Egypt was now gone with the old ways, and in with the new. As a matter of state policy, Egypt wanted more control. Not just control of its own borders, but as much control as it could get — particularly over the desert and sea trade routes. Whereas prior kings had mainly been passive, and more content with simply trading with the inhabitants of both the Levant and Nubia, New Kingdom pharaohs wanted to call all the shots. Therefore, they acted accordingly. They built a larger, well equipped, professional army. And they also maintained a bigger police force. As part of this new police force, an elite group was introduced, the "Medjay", whose job it was to protect places of interest. Places of such interest included cities, royal cemeteries and Egypt's borders.

During the chaos of the Second Intermediate Period, the Nubians had recovered land that they had lost to the Egyptians. However, the Egyptians had always considered this land, up to the second cataract, to be Egyptian territory under foreign rule. Consequently, with their new found military power, the kings were able to quickly regain lost ground. With the initial reconquests, came the building of even bigger forts than before. But this time it was not just forts that were built, royal monuments and temples were too. In a way these large scale building programs, acted to stamp Egypt's authority on disputed land.

Part of the reason for Egyptian state expansion, was to create a buffer, that is to say — a buffer zone between the Egyptian heartland and Nubia (as well as the Levant). With this in mind, the kings of Egypt moved south, well past the second cataract — into the Nubian heartland i.e. Upper Nubia.

The pharaoh that began this push further south went by the name of Thutmose I. Thutmose penetrated the Nubian frontier, quickly taking the Nile island of *Sai* and advancing past the third cataract. A few years down the line and the king had taken the Nubian capital of Kerma, pushing past it all the way to *Kurgus*. Kurgus was positioned well beyond the 4th cataract, and thus it marked Egypt's new southern frontier. A frontier made known by the rock and boundary inscriptions of the pharaoh. And with that, most of Nubia had been conquered, and integrated into the "Egyptian Empire". As a result, the imports continued to flow.

The gold that came from Nubia was particularly important, for a number of reasons. All of which can be summed up as "maintenance". Egypt required the gold to maintain Maat (order) at home, and for the upkeep of its armies. These were armies that were sent to conquer lands in the Levant, more specifically land in Palestine and Syria. Once conquered, vassal states were created, who swore allegiance to the pharaoh, and also paid tribute. Army garrisons were established to protect these lands from the "Hittites", and other foreign threats. No gold from Nubia, meant no ability to maintain the state or its armies. This would of course lead to the outright collapse of the Egyptian political structure.

Rameses II, a 19th Dynasty Pharaoh, is often regarded as one of the greatest of them all. He reportedly built more monuments, and fathered more children, over his 66 year reign (c. 1279–1213 BCE), than any other Egyptian king. Rameses II also led several military expeditions. The result of one of these expeditions, to *Kadesh* (in the Levant), was the signing of the earliest known peace treaty in world history (c. 1259 BCE). This treaty is known as the Egyptian-Hittite peace treaty or the Treaty of Kadesh. At this time, the Hittites and the Egyptians were what you might call "superpowers" of the Mediterranean Basin.

Following this peace treaty, and more specifically after the death of Rameses II, things started to decline for the Egyptians. Internally, the ruling elite, in particular the high priests, had gotten especially wealthy and powerful. While externally, the heavy cost of foreign warfare had negatively impacted the state's treasury, thus contributing to the slow decline of Egypt's empire. Although Egypt managed to survive the Bronze Age collapse, it did so at great economic expense, leaving the state in a much weakened position. Due to this weakened position, Egypt was eventually forced to fully withdraw from most of the land that it had conquered, leaving behind the lucrative gold mines of Nubia. As a result, the prestige of the pharaohs declined. And Egypt was soon divided again. With this division came another period of Isfet (chaos) i.e. the Third Intermediate Period.

Late period and Ptolemaic rule

During the Third Intermediate Period (beginning c. 1070 BCE), along with the political instability, came times of conquest and rule by foreigners. Libyans, who had earlier been settling in the Western Nile Delta, grew increasingly autonomous, and eventually seized power in Lower Egypt. By exerting their control over the then "de facto" rulers of Upper Egypt, namely the priesthood, the Egyptian state was reunited. This reunification was short-lived, however, and infighting quickly resumed. The Nubian Kings in the south took full advantage of this, invading Egypt and establishing the 25th dynasty (c. 750 BCE).

The unity of this "United" Nubian-Egyptian Kingdom was soon threatened, by an ever expanding Assyrian Empire. By around 670 BCE, the Assyrians had succeeded in driving the Nubians out of Egypt proper — signaling the start of the "Late Period".

The Assyrians initially ruled by proxy, before a 26th dynasty Pharaoh, Psamtik I, declared Egypt's full independence. This, 26th dynasty, was one that would last less than 150 years, with the last of its pharaohs, Psamtik III, being defeated by the Persian King Cambyses II at the battle of Pelusium (Eastern Nile Delta) in 525 BCE.

Around 404 BCE Egypt did briefly regain independence, only for the country to be reconquered by the Persians c. 343 BCE. With this reconquest, the Persians had permanently ended native pharaonic rule i.e. the 30th dynasty was the last independent Egyptian one. The Persians too only ruled for a short while, before surrendering to Alexander the Great in 332 BCE.

With the permanent fall of Egypt, into foreign hands, came the beginnings of what historians call the Ptolemaic Dynasty. This was a period of significant change in Egypt, as the state became more "Hellenized" (Greek). Although the Ptolemies legitimized their rule, by embracing the Egyptian title pharaoh, Greek customs and ideals were slowly integrated into Egyptian society. Greek too would soon become the official language of the state, marking the start of the gradual decline of the Egyptian language.

The governmental bureaucracy was now mainly in the hands of the Greek ruling class. Any Egyptian that wanted to become part of this bureaucracy would typically need to Hellenize — starting of course with learning the Greek language. Despite this, local and religious institutions were still run by native Egyptians. For this reason, the Egyptian language managed to survive, with the priesthood, long after it was relegated from state, and eventually everyday use.

Some of the Greek rulers built new temples, restored older ones, and even participated in Egyptian religious life. The existing settlement of *Rhacotis* was also expanded, becoming Alexandria. As the capital of the Ptolemaic Kingdom, Alexandria grew quickly, becoming one of the leading cities on the Mediterranean. Egypt itself soon grew to become the wealthiest and most powerful Hellenistic state. This was before it too became weakened, due to internal dynastic strife and foreign wars. The Greek Ptolemaic Dynasty lasted for around 300 years, before the death of Queen Cleopatra and the subsequent coming of Roman rule (c. 30 BCE).

9. Ancient Nubia

Although you won't find a country called Nubia, on modern maps, it was home to some of the earliest known African civilizations. Nubia, with its own rich cultures, was also based in the Nile Valley — directly south of Ancient Egypt. While the borders of Nubia varied, it can be said to extend from the first cataract, close to Aswan, all the way to the sixth cataract, near to Khartoum. Therefore, around a quarter of Ancient Nubian land lies in modern-day Egypt. The proximity between Ancient Egypt and Nubia meant that relations between the two would fluctuate, from good to bad, as both sought control over key sections of the Nile. There were periods when Nubia was on top, and there were periods when it was not. This closeness would also inevitably lead to both civilizations influencing one another, in a number of different ways, as we shall see.

These days, there is more than enough evidence to suggest that the inhabitants of early Nubia developed a more "sophisticated" culture, much sooner than (what was to be) their Egyptian neighbors to the north. This early Nubian sophistication was also one of the sources for the initial pharaonic traditions of Egypt (e.g. burial practices). Some of this evidence comes in the form of pottery, with Nubian pottery (and much wider Sahelian African pottery) pre-dating anything found in Egypt proper.

Two large kingdoms or civilizations grew out of Ancient Nubia — Kerma and Kush. When looking at the Kingdom of Kush, scholars often divide its history into two periods — "Napatan" and "Meroitic". This simply refers to times when the capital was based out of Napata and Meroe (respectively). The Meroitic period stretches well into the Common Era, and so in this section, we will focus on Kerma and Napatan Kush.

The name Nubia (and Nubians)

The word Nubia can be a confusing one, especially with regards to what it actually means and who it refers to. The name only appears very late on in ancient texts, and its origins are still disputed. There are a number of theories, a popular one being its link with the Ancient Egyptian word *nebu* — meaning gold. This is plausible given the fact that Nubia was a rich source of gold — gold that the Egyptians so depended on. Another theory is the name deriving from a group of nomadic peoples known as the "Nobades", who moved into Northern Nubia (c. 400 CE).

Before the term "Nubia" came into use, there were other names. One of the earliest known Egyptian names for Nubia was *Ta-seti* — meaning "land of the bow" — demonstrating the Nubian expertise in archery. *Kush* was another term that referred to Ancient Nubia, appearing by the Egyptian Middle Kingdom (c. 2000 BCE).

Today, in general, what we refer to as Nubia or Nubian simply describes the geographic location, of a group of fairly related ancient peoples, rather than a single ethnic identity. There are still people who refer to themselves as Nubian, found in both Sudan and Egypt. Some of them speak a group of Nilo-Saharan languages known as the Nubian languages.

Written sources and archaeology

There are far fewer sources to work with, when it comes to Ancient Nubia, especially when compared to the range of documentation available on Ancient Egypt. There are also far fewer scholars that have taken an interest in studying Nubia itself (although things are changing). Consequently, not many people, in the general public, have even heard of the "Nubians". Those that have, will likely have only heard about Nubia through its association with Egypt i.e. rarely through the point of view of the Nubians.

To raise awareness, new exhibitions have been launched. For example, The Museum of Fine Arts, Boston (MFA) — recently launched an exhibition (2019) called "Ancient Nubia Now". Here the MFA, that holds the finest collection of antiquities from Ancient Nubia (outside of Egypt and Sudan), showcased some of its collection. The vast majority of these artifacts were collected during archaeological expeditions carried out in the early 20th century.

A great deal of what we know about Nubia, like with virtually all ancient civilizations, comes from archaeology. Scholars also refer to Ancient Egyptian texts, being neighbors, the Egyptians wrote about the

Nubians quite a lot (although not always in the best of light). This ha somewhat filled in for the lack of first-hand Nubian records.

The recent archaeological history of Nubia is of interest, particularly in relation to the dams that have been built on the Nile. Perhaps the most controversial of which, is the Aswan High Dam (modern Egypt). Its main objectives are to prevent destructive flooding, generate electricity and boost agricultural production. This came at a cost, however, specifically the flooding of parts of the Middle or Nubian Nile Valley.

This would have led to the certain loss of several ancient and archaeological sites. So, to prevent this, some temples and tombs were relocated as part of a United Nations Educational, Scientific and Cultural Organization (UNESCO) campaign, to save Nubian antiquities. Arguably, the most iconic of which, was the twin rock Temples of Abu Simbel, including its four massive statues of Ramses II. These were originally built to showcase the pharaoh's power, in what was then an Egyptian controlled Lower Nubia, and to commemorate his (disputed) victory at the Battle of Kadesh.

As well as relocating important monuments, major excavations of Nubia were undertaken. With these excavations came the unearthing of various rich artifacts, adding to scholarly knowledge of Nubia in the process. Despite the relocation efforts, the loss of untold antiquities and relics, under Lake Nasser, is a source of regret for archaeologists interested in Ancient Nubia.

Meroitic language

Although the Meroitic language was in use long before, it wasn't until c. 400 BCE that a written form of it was developed. It was written in two forms of the Meroitic script, namely Meroitic Cursive and Meroitic Hieroglyphic (both derived from Egyptian scripts). Much in the same way as the Egyptians, the former was used for general record-keeping, while the latter was used for religious/royal purposes. The Meroitic scripts fell into disuse, with the fall of Meroe (c. 350 CE).

As of today, although the scripts have been deciphered, little of the language is actually understood. This lack of comprehension partly stems from the fact that there are few existing, long-enough, bilingual texts, like the Rosetta Stone, from which the language can be fully "unlocked". This is also why the language remains unclassified — in terms of linguistics. Arguments for an Afroasiatic or Nilo-Saharan classification have been made. And so we have the "Meroitic Mystery" — so to speak.

d rise of Ancient Nubia

l to have lived in the Nubian region from at least c.
ly Stone Age. For an example of life in Nubia, during
..., ovocene or African Humid Period (AHP), we can look to
"Nabta Playa" c. 9000 BCE.

Nabta Playa can be found in the Nubian Desert, just north west of the second cataract. Back then, there was enough rainfall in the region to support a lake, to sustain some vegetation and people could engage in a number of activities (including cattle herding, hunting and gathering wild plants). Before long (c. 7500 BCE) people had permanently settled in the area, living in organized settlements, made up of small huts arranged in straight lines. Their permanent stay at Nabta was aided by their ability to dig deep wells, which would sustain them throughout the year. Local pottery was made, and (imported) sheep and goats soon appeared (c. 6000 BCE).

It is here, at Nabta Playa, that you will find the world's very first "astronomical site" — a stone calendar circle. Dating to at least c. 7000 BP, it is over 2000 years older than Stonehenge. Scholars believe that it was used to mark the "summer solstice" — a time that signaled the start of the summer or monsoon rains. Scholars also believe that Nabta eventually functioned as a ceremonial center, where groups of people would periodically gather. It has been suggested that this may have been part of a "cattle cult" (religion), something we see later on with the pharaonic Egyptians.

The so-called "Khartoum Mesolithic" was a well-established culture that lasted from c. 7000–5000 BCE. These people exhibited a semi-settled lifestyle, based on hunting, fishing and gathering. Wavy-line pottery was also a feature of this culture. And thus some of the oldest pottery in Africa can be found in Nubia. Ancients, including Nubians, typically used ceramics for domestic purposes (cooking, serving, storage etc.) and as an important part of funerary rituals. Unlike other materials (baskets, blankets, wooden tools, ropes, clothing etc.), ceramics can survive for thousands of years. Consequently, the study of ceramics allows archaeologists to get a glimpse of how people lived back then. And so, the dating of such also becomes crucial, for scholars looking to "connect the dots" — particularly with regards to the emergence of more organized societies.

As briefly stated in the introduction, Nubian pottery pre-dates anything found to its north i.e. found in Ancient Egypt proper. Whereas evidence of pottery in Sahelian Africa goes back to at least 10,000 BP, evidence of such along the Mediterranean Coast and in the Lower Nile Valley — appears much later. That is, specifically around 3000 years later (in the Lower Nile Valley). This is not to say that people were not living in those areas, rather it is to say that there is no current evidence for those inhabitants producing pottery. And it also suggests that, since they did not produce pottery, those living there led less settled lives than the Nubians did (in the same time period).

This evidence supports the idea of a northward shift in population i.e. from the south to the north, or from Nubia to Egypt. This links with the idea of King Narmer, eventually conquering Lower Egypt — from his southern base (Upper Egypt). And it forms part of a more than credible argument, as has been made by many, for a common origin for both Nubia and Egypt.

Rise of urban society

The move towards more settled Nubian cultures and the eventual rise of Nubian Kingdoms can be attributed to the end of the African Humid Period (c. 6000 BP). As with Ancient Egypt, the drying of the Sahara encouraged people to move closer to available water sources, of which the Nile was an obvious one. Proof of this changing climate comes from rock art — showing cattle in areas that has been desert for a few millennia. These rock paintings also provide evidence for the rising Saharan cattle culture, of the time. Groups of people, from all directions, would have been drawn to the Nile. And each of these groups came with their own knowledge. Be that knowledge in the form of cattle herding, farming, pottery, languages, and more. These people went on to build settlements across the Nile Valley, with increasingly high population densities.

Nubian societies became increasingly stratified. Put another way, society was divided into social classes, with an emergent elite class — headed by a chief. This elite class enjoyed social, economic and political privileges, as evidenced by their larger graves or burial sites. These were larger graves that featured an array of "grave-goods", like mace heads — which acted as symbols of authority. Evidence from their cemeteries also suggests that elite membership was hereditary, with elites enjoying funerary rights that "commoners" did not. Materials recovered from grave sites also show that trade networks had already been established, between Nubia and Egypt. In other words, we have trade that pre-dates the unification of the Egyptian state.

Given such evidence we can assume, with some certainty, that as the Neolithic era came to a close (c. 6000 BP), powerful chieftains had risen

— found scattered across the banks of the Nile Valley. Each chief would rule only a small area, and compete with other chiefs for resources and power.

A-Group Nubians

A-Group Nubia, called such as we have no actual records of its ancient name, was a culture that developed out of earlier Nile Valley ones. Here, chiefdoms grew larger and more powerful than ever before. Most of what is known about this group comes from archaeology — including artifacts, burials and cemeteries. These are to be found along the banks of the Nile, from the first to the second cataract i.e. the Lower Nubia region. A-Group culture lasted from c. 3800–3100 BCE.

The power and wealth enjoyed by A-Group Nubians primarily came from trade. Given Lower Nubia's excellent location, gold and carnelian were found in abundance — precisely in the deserts that surrounded the Nile. Moreover, they had easy access to exotic products, sourced from more southern areas. These were products such as ebony, incense and ivory. These luxury goods were traded with the Egyptians for products like beer, cereal, oil and wine — evidenced by the presence of large Egyptian-style storage vases (in Nubia). Copper weapons and Egyptian-made tools were also received. These grave-goods provide evidence of social hierarchy, among the A-Group, as do the royal cemeteries found at Qustul (Lake Nasser region).

This trading relationship also points to a period of strong cultural engagement, and easy lines of communication, between the A-Group Nubians and Upper Egyptian groups (Naqada culture). More distinctive identities arise later, closer to Egyptian unification. Proof of such close cultural ties is not only found in Nubia, but also Egypt itself. In fact, A-Group settlements have been found in (what was to be) "core" Egyptian territory, some almost 10 miles north of Aswan, at *Kubbaniya*. As such, it may come as no surprise that the so-called A-Group rulers — employed royal symbols that were also used by early Egyptian Pharaohs.

This trade network was soon to be abandoned, however, by c. 3100 BCE. Scholars are still unclear over exactly what happened. One explanation is that climate change caused parts of the Nile to dry up i.e. there were particularly low floods, which forced the Nubians to relocate (to Egypt or Upper Nubia) or simply to change lifestyle (becoming nomadic pastoralists). Another explanation suggests the aggressive expansion of Egyptian military activity, in the Lower Nubia region, due to Egypt's desire to directly control trade — forcing the prior "middlemen" (Nubians) out. Either way, the A-Group culture disappeared, and much of Lower Nubia was seemingly sparsely populated for centuries to come.

The gap that follows, between the A-Group and subsequent C-Group cultures of Nubia, comes about from the lack of much archaeological evidence. A lot of the available evidence comes from the Egyptian Old Kingdom fortified towns (as touched on before). To go with this physical or archaeological evidence, one can also refer to the Egyptian records. Of course, these records were somewhat biased — giving us only the Egyptian point of view. Nevertheless, these records suggest that during this gap, Nubia was still not a unified state — certainly not in the same way the Egyptians now were. Rather, the Egyptians who reported back from travels to Nubia, noted dealings with multiple different chiefs — ruling over different areas. Egyptian policy towards the Nubians also varied, going from aggressive, to commercial/peaceful, and back again.

As we know, from the section on Ancient Egypt, the Egyptians had so-called "intermediate periods" — when centralized state control was significantly weak. Just before the Old Egyptian Kingdom came to an end, and the First Intermediate Period commenced, C-Group Nubians started to resettle parts of Lower Nubia (c. 2300 BCE). This C-Group culture, in Lower Nubia, existed at the same time as Kerma culture in Upper Nubia.

Kingdom of Kerma and Bronze Age Nubia

By c. 2500 BCE a Nubian Bronze Age culture had started to form, one which was to last for almost a thousand years. The emergence of this Kerma Kingdom, was subsequent to the consolidation of various settlements in and around the Middle Nile Valley — specifically in the "Dongola Reach" area. These settlements all had similar material cultures, which enabled them to be readily united (politically).

This kingdom was centered on "Kerma", a town located just after the third cataract in Upper Nubia. This town was bigger than earlier settlements found in the region, suggesting that it must have served as the kingdom's capital. As expected, this capital was densely populated — while other areas of settlement were less so. The actual number of villages is also something to note, with a considerable number of such stretching along the banks of the Nubian Nile. Thanks to a rich and fertile Dongola Reach, people in these villages grew a variety of crops, and were engaged in animal husbandry. Barley, goats, sheep and cattle were all produced, and resulting taxes or tribute sent to the capital. Industries were also developed, like mining, metalworking, and pottery. And trade links, with the Egyptians, were strong.

The areas controlled by the Kerma Kingdom, cannot be established with certainty. Having said this, excavations (that show similar pottery and burial sites) suggest that Kerma's reach may have gone well past the fourth cataract. These cataracts were strategically important to both the Nubians and the Egyptians. With their capital at the third cataract, the Nubians could easily oversee all river trade — that moved goods both up and downstream. As highlighted earlier, these cataracts made the river Nile not navigable (in parts). Consequently, boats would have to unload their goods, and carry them past the cataracts overland. Once past the cataracts, journeys on the river could continue. Therefore, we can assume that these cataracts served as checkpoints — where cargo was taxed, stored and registered.

Agricultural surpluses and the ability to act as middlemen, between Egypt and more inner parts of Africa, made the ruling Nubian elite rich, and supported the development of Kerma town. The town was fortified with ditches, ramparts and big walls with towers. Shrines and palaces could also be found in Kerma, among other things.

One of the oldest and most impressive ancient monuments in Africa is the Western "Deffufa". This religious site (some have argued royal residence) was built out of mudbrick, and it stands at around 18 meters high — although it is much eroded today. Two other Deffufa (large mudbrick structures) can be found in and around Kerma.

A few miles east of Kerma, sits a large cemetery site. This cemetery hosts at least 20,000 graves or tombs. Within these tombs, one can find evidence for both animal and human sacrifice, both of which are symbols of royal power. Other symbols of wealth like jewelry, silver, gold and precious stones can also be found. Archaeologists have determined that burials got more and more elaborate with time. Accordingly, you had increasing inequalities in wealth, as suggested by "wealth markers" i.e. the actual artifacts or goods deposited in the graves.

The Kerma Kingdom coexisted with another Nubian culture, found further to the north, in Lower Nubia, where the A-Group once occupied. This culture is known as C-Group culture. These days, the C-Group is seen as more of an extension of Kerma culture. In other words, the heartland of the C-Group culture was nearer the Dongola Reach. And thus, the C-Group inhabitants of Lower Nubia came from the south.

Figure 10. C-Group pottery 2300–1600 BCE, British Museum. Source: Wikimedia Commons/CC BY-SA 2.0 (Author: Anthony Huan).

Initially, there was little difference between the Kerma and C-Group cultures. As time went on, differences widened, to the point that by c. 2000 BCE they differed greatly. Earlier cultural similarities are evidenced by pottery. Several forms of early Kerma pottery are pretty much identical to that found in early C-Group. The differences that eventually formed are likely to have come about, due to the resulting differences in their respective histories (somewhat shaped by proximity to Egypt).

Egyptian — Nubian hostilities

If we turn to Egyptian records, we get a picture of some of the social and political entities that emerged in Nubia — during this Kerma and C-Group period. These Nubian polities came under increasing pressure from the Middle Kingdom Egyptian state c. 2000 BCE. This pressure soon resulted in the conquest of Lower Nubia — the home of the C-Group culture. Subsequently, the Egyptians began building and expanding a series of forts, along the banks of the Nile. And these forts eventually became small towns, as more permanent settlers came. As already mentioned, the purpose of these forts was to gain greater control over the trade routes in Lower Nubia (particularly the gold).

Egypt's military frontier, around the second cataract, effectively split C-Group from Kerma culture.

The break down in power, during the Egyptian 13th dynasty (c. 1700 BCE), and just before the Second Intermediate Period, meant that Egypt's grip on Lower Nubia started to wane. Kerma Kingdom capitalized on this period of Egyptian weakness. It expanded north, capturing forts along the way, before seizing control of Lower Nubia in its entirety. Kerma went even as far as invading parts of Upper Egypt. These events occurred roughly at the same time as the Hyksos were establishing control in the Nile Delta. And so unsurprisingly, there were diplomatic relations between the Hyksos and the Nubians.

Like highlighted before, a re-unified New Kingdom Egypt (c. 1550 BCE) was able to reassert Egyptian control over Lower Nubia. However, this time the Egyptians went much further south than ever before. After several campaigns they were able to reach Kerma itself, and subdue the Nubian kingdom. And so, the Egyptians now controlled Nubian land, well past the fourth cataract at Kurgus — a good 800 miles upstream from Aswan and the first cataract. This was the beginning of a 500 year or so, Egyptian occupation of both Lower and Upper Nubia. For the Nubians, such a long period of "foreign" occupation, resulted in some "Egyptianization" of its cultures. Despite this, the Nubian masses did maintain somewhat distinct identities, backed by local languages and customs.

Kingdom of Kush

Five centuries of Egyptian control over Nubia was broken up, once again, by an intermediate period (the third). This enabled a Nubian revival, so that by around 800 BCE, a Kushite Kingdom had been firmly established in the Dongola Reach — this time centered on *Napata*. This kingdom was bigger than the previous one, eventually extending its influence both to the north and south.

Kushite elites may have decided to establish their capital at Napata, rather than reestablish it at Kerma, for a number of reasons. One such reason is geography. Napata sits in the middle of a large area where the Nile bends, just before the fourth cataract. This was somewhat more of a defensible position — that still allowed the Kushites to continue regulating the flow of trade between Central Africa and Egypt. Another reason is that Napata lies in the vicinity of the *Jebel Barkal*, which was an important landmark in this new Kushite cultural phase.

Jebel Barkal was considered as a "holy m
Egyptians and Nubians. Accordingly, several ter
including the Temple of Amun (c. 1300 BCE)
Amun (King of the Gods). The Nubian Pharoa}
the Temple of Mut in around 700 BCE — a
extended all the way to Lower Egypt. The Goddess Mu .
wife of Amun i.e a mother goddess. Other Kushite kings would gᴜ .
further develop the area into a cult or religious site, from where royal
power was gotten.

Although the exact details are sketchy, the Kushite kings were soon
to emerge as central figures in not just Africa, but the Near East as well
— with their invasion and subsequent control of Ancient Egypt. Alara is
thought of as the founder of the Napatan Kushite dynasty, which would
go on to conquer Egypt. Alara, ruling from c. 780–760 BCE, is said to
have consolidated the kingdom — from *Meroe* in the south, past Napata,
and up to the third cataract. As such, one can consider him as a kind of
Nubian King Narmer i.e. the unifier of the Nubian heartland or realm.
Like with Egyptian Pharaohs, Alara was required to demonstrate royal
power, through public works and architecture. And so he built temples,
including one dedicated to God Amun — who had given him divine right
to rule.

The successor to King Alara was Kashta. King Kashta at one point
gained enough power to take full control of Lower Nubia. Near Aswan,
precisely at Elephantine, a stela was found referring to Kashta as the
"King of Upper and Lower Egypt". This suggests that Kashta and the
Kushites already had some presence in Upper Egypt — a presence
which may have been achieved through diplomatic and political means.
Remember, during this time period c. 750 BCE, Egypt was not unified
under a strong central government. Like future kings after him, Kashta
too would dedicate significant resources to the worship of Amun, and
the development of the holy site of Jebel Barkal.

Kushite Empire / Twenty-fifth Dynasty of Egypt

Progress made into Egypt, by Kashta, was further advanced upon by
King Piankhy (Piye) — who went on to become the founder of the 25th
dynasty of Egypt. He ruled from c. 744–714 BCE. Piye often referred to
himself as the "Son of Amun", and so like other pharaohs before him, he
too became a "demigod". This status gave him the desire to fully
revitalize the Great Temple of Amun at Jebel Barkal — likely first built
by Thutmose III of the Egyptian New Kingdom. Stelae were also
commissioned dedicated to Amun of Thebes and Amun of Napata (Jebel

. These newer stelae sat next to an existing one, commissioned utmose III. This cemented the religious link between Nubia and pt, giving Piye legitimacy.

Piye peacefully took control of Thebes — the center of Upper Egyptian power. This peaceful takeover again suggests long-established diplomatic and religious links between Nubia and Upper Egypt — for Piye to have gained such acceptance with the Theban clergy or priesthood. This contrasts with the control of Lower Egypt, which was achieved militarily i.e. through conquest. To Piye this was not an invasion of foreign lands (Lower Egypt), seeing himself as the rightful ruler of all of Egypt, this was more of a quelling of rebellion.

Kushite conquest of Egypt

Some details of Piye's military campaigns, in Middle/Lower Egypt, were recorded on his "Victory Stela" — discovered at Jebel Barkal. At this time, the Nile Delta (Lower Egypt) was home to a number of princes. And so, a coalition was formed, with the aim of challenging the oncoming Nubian threat. This coalition was led by Tefnakht — Delta prince of the city of *Sais*. Piye marched northwards, from Thebes, towards Memphis — Lower Egypt's religious center and former capital. Some cities like *Hermopolis* were surrounded and besieged, while other cities like *Herakleopolis* remained loyal to Piye, and were taken without a fight.

Upon arrival at Memphis a battle commenced, in which Piye emerged victorious. And so the "god of creation", Ptah, whose major cult center lay in Memphis, recognized Piye as the legitimate ruler of Egypt. Soon, villages and towns near Memphis also capitulated. Tefnakht, was therefore left with little option, but to recognize Piye's supreme rule over all of Egypt.

As seen in the preserved texts, a clear link is maintained between Piye's campaign and religion. To explain, and going back to the notion of Maat, the opposition or coalition may have been seen as a threat to harmony or order (Maat). And so, Piye, as pharaoh, was obliged to conquer Lower Egypt and restore order. This emphasizes, as stated before, the "quelling of a rebellion" angle of Piye's campaign — rather than it being an invasion of Lower Egypt. Accordingly, throughout his reign, Piye was, at least publically, portrayed as a righteous and religious leader — who observed the ideals of kingship.

A now victorious Piye showed mercy. He forgave the rebels, and by doing so, avoided further hostilities. Piye even paid respects to the local gods of the cities he had captured. Subsequently, Piye returned first to Thebes, and then on to Napata.

There is limited evidence of how the now (almost) "United" or "Double" Kingdom of Egypt and Nubia was governed. Presumably, state administration would have followed the provincial or nome system traditionally used in Egypt — with provinces being run by members of the royal family, or elite members of Nubian (and loyal Egyptian) society.

Attempts to expand the new "Double Kingdom"

Piye did not consolidate the entire Nile Delta region, before returning home to Napata, and so there was some unrest. Eventual consolidation was left to successor Kushite Pharaohs Shebitqo and Shabaka, who both chose to reside in Egypt proper — rather than rule from Napata. The presence of the Kushite kings would have encouraged the migration of more Nubians to Egypt.

Figure 11. Kushite Kings including Taharqo and Tantamani. Source: Wikimedia Commons/CC BY-SA 4.0 (Author: Matthias Gehricke).

Egypt and Nubia now formed two halves of a United Kingdom, which stretched from the Nile Delta in the north — to well past the fifth cataract in the south. The Kushites ruled Egypt in a time of considerable uneasiness and turmoil — in the Near East. Remember, this was a time after the Late Bronze Age Collapse, which had destroyed many civilizations and disrupted trade routes.

With the control of Egypt, the Nubians controlled the flow of trade into and out of Africa. They were no longer middlemen, but now enjoyed a monopoly over goods. Luxury Egyptian items on offer included fine linen textiles, papyrus scrolls and finished goods (glass, ceramics etc.). This went with the inner African goods, which the Nubians could now directly export to the Levant (and beyond). Timber, in short supply, continued to be imported from Lebanon.

Egypt had already lost direct control of its former New Kingdom Levantine possessions. As a result, the Nubian Pharaohs did show some ambition, in wanting to regain control over parts of the Levant (to the east). However, the Assyrians had similar ideas, as they sought to expand westwards. Initially, diplomatic and trading links were established between the two kingdoms. Peaceful relations would not last long, however, and so by c. 674 BCE, war had broken out between the two kingdoms — Assyria and Kush.

This initial war resulted in a Kushite victory. But, a mere three years later, the reverse was the case — the Assyrians had defeated the Kushites. Esarhaddon, King of Assyria, annexed Memphis. The then Kushite King Taharqo, was forced to withdraw south (likely to Thebes). Although the king escaped, members of the royal family were captured and taken prisoner by the Assyrians.

Taharqo did manage to re-establish control over Memphis, and parts of the Delta. However, this was short-lived as Assurbanipal, the new Assyrian King, launched another campaign. The result of which was the recapture of Memphis, and a push to Thebes — pursuing Taharqo in the process. From written records it is not clear whether or not the Assyrians actually seized Thebes, and the rest of Upper Egypt. What is clear is that Taharqo managed to escape to Nubia, where he later died.

Taharqo was not buried at the elite graves of *El-Kurru*, as per old customs, with his predecessors. Rather, he became the first Nubian King to be buried at *Nuri* (north east of Jebel Barkal). Here, as a tomb, Taharqo built the largest pyramid ever erected in the Nubian heartland — standing at an estimated height of 55 meters. As well as being the largest, this was the first in a succession of pyramids built at Nuri (by

Nubian Kings). Although smaller than the Pyramids of Giza, the Pyramids of Nuri (and the surrounding sites of Jebel Barkal) are also on the UNESCO list of world cultural heritage sites.

Kushite permanent loss of Egypt

With the help of King Tantamani, the Kushites would go on to recapture Memphis one more time, but were again driven out by the Assyrians. Despite this, Kushite links with Upper Egypt would remain for a while longer. This was before a new native Egyptian dynasty rose from Sais, and with that, Kushite control of Upper Egypt was permanently lost. In around 593 BCE, an Egyptian army launched an invasion of Nubia itself, perhaps reaching as far as Napata in the process. Yet, the Egyptians appear to have retreated back to the first cataract, which continued to function as the de facto border between Egypt and Nubia.

In response to this growing threat from Egypt, the Kushites moved their capital further up the Nile — to Meroe. At Meroe, a resurgent Nubian civilization would flourish, one which used iron to take both construction and agricultural practices to the next level. This extensive use of iron was but one of the differences between Napatan and Meroitic culture (although there were many similarities between the two). With Egypt's eventual decline, came the establishment of direct trade links with new rising powers such as Greece, Rome, Persia and even India. Meroe would eventually fall to the Kingdom of Aksum, an East African civilization, in the 4th century CE.

10. Ancient Carthage

Before Rome — there was another African based power, on the shores of the Mediterranean. A power that would later challenge the full might of the Roman Republic. With their capital at Carthage, modern day Tunisia, the Carthaginian Empire flourished — at a time when the Egyptians were in terminal decline c. 500 BCE.

Initially founded as a trading post, of a group of people referred to as the "Phoenicians", Carthage soon became wealthy enough to gain outright independence from Phoenicia. The city of Carthage formed the backbone of the much larger Carthaginian Empire. This was an empire that dominated commercial and trade activity, in the Western Mediterranean, for over 300 years. Carthage was more than simply a commercial power, which came and went. Rather, just as other African civilizations before and after it, Carthage was a shaper of the Mediterranean world. Today, its legacy can be exampled with the initial development of many of the oldest and most important cities on the Mediterranean — Lisbon, Cadiz, Malaga, Tangier and more.

"Carthage must be destroyed" and written records

Unlike the Egyptians, there are very few first-hand records of the Carthaginians. This is primarily due to the fact that little of what they wrote survives. Apart from simply being lost over time, there are a number of reasons for this. One which is often claimed is that the Romans deliberately erased all records of the Carthaginians — when they defeated them for good and razed their capital (in the Third Punic War c. 146 BCE).

This idea is likely further fueled by a famous saying of a politician of the Roman Republic — "Cato the Censor". He was said to be among the most persistent advocates for the total destruction of Carthage, in debates held in the Roman Senate after the Second Punic War. This was following Cato's visit to Carthage. Cato is said to have been shocked by the wealth of Carthage, and the potential danger it still posed to Rome. Accordingly, upon his return to the Roman Senate, and after every speech he made, he would use the Latin phrase:

Ceterum autem censeo Carthaginem esse delendam

Translated to English as:

Furthermore, I consider that Carthage must be destroyed

This is often shortened to "Carthago delenda est" (Carthage must be destroyed). It is a phrase that still lives on today, typically used to refer to "total warfare"

How much of Carthaginian (Punic) literature got destroyed, whether deliberately or not, we'll likely never know. Having said this, some inscriptions do remain. Most of the existing accounts we have of Carthage come from Greek and Roman authors. Together with archaeological finds and the surviving Punic language inscriptions, we do know quite a lot about the Carthaginians. However, as with all history, questions do remain.

Phoenician and Punic languages

The Punic (Carthaginian) language, is an extinct variety or form of the Phoenician language. Phoenician has been classed, by linguists, as a Semitic language. As highlighted already, Semitic itself is a branch of the wider Afroasiatic language family — of which Egyptian is also a separate branch.

Phoenician is a historically important language. Why is such a little known language so important (you may ask)? Well the Greek, the Latin, and the English alphabets all ultimately derive from the Phoenician one.

So, Western literacy (reading and writing), and the formal establishment of various arts and sciences, like history and philosophy, is with thanks to the Phoenicians. And where does the Phoenician alphabet itself derive from? The answer is Ancient Egyptian hieroglyphs, by the way of a "Proto-Sinaitic" alphabet.

Archaeologists have found examples of this Proto-Sinaitic script at both Wadi el-Hol (near Luxor/Thebes — Upper Egypt) and the Sinai Peninsula. The discovery of the Wadi el-Hol inscriptions is more recent (1990s). Not only is this discovery more recent, but the inscriptions are dated to c. 1900 BCE — two or three centuries earlier than other discoveries. This strongly suggests that the script must have been initially developed in Egypt, before making its way into the Levant (via the Sinai).

From the Proto-Sinaitic alphabet comes the Proto-Canaanite alphabet, which is basically the Proto-Sinaitic script when found in Canaan (the Levant). Proto-Canaanite subsequently gave birth to the Phoenician (and later Hebrew) alphabet. As the Phoenicians traded and interacted across the Mediterranean Sea, their script followed — eventually being adopted by others throughout the region. One of such groups was the Greeks, who made a few changes and gave us the Greek script — upon which both Latin and English alphabets are based.

The now evolved Phoenician language soon made its way onto the shores of Northern Africa. As a result, we get the Punic language, spoken in Carthage. Punic, in contrast to Phoenician itself, became more and more influenced by African languages, especially Berber. The language survived the Roman conquest of North Africa, only going extinct c. 500 CE — just before the Arab/Muslim conquests began (c. 650 CE).

Phoenician origins of Carthage

The origins of the Carthaginians is a tale of two stories — one of the Phoenicians, and one of the Africans that they met when they arrived. Looking at the Phoenicians, there is significant debate among scholars, as to the question of — who they actually are?

The Phoenicians (a term from Ancient Greek) are said to have been a civilization centered along the Eastern Mediterranean Coast, in what is today Lebanon, Syria, Palestine and Israel. They came to prominence after the Late Bronze Age Collapse (c. 1200 BCE), that destroyed trade networks and prior civilizations in the region. Known for being excellent merchants, seafarers and explorers — they established a number of trading posts in the Mediterranean (Africa, Sardinia, Sicily and Spain). One of such trading posts was Carthage.

That is the common description, and it is also where the debate on their origins begins.

Ancient writers like Herodotus saw the Phoenicians as foreigners who migrated to the Eastern Mediterranean Coast, from the *Erythraean Sea* (Red Sea/Gulf of Aden area). Some archaeological evidence suggests that they were indigenous to the land. Another theory is that the term Phoenician did not refer to a group of related people per say, but rather

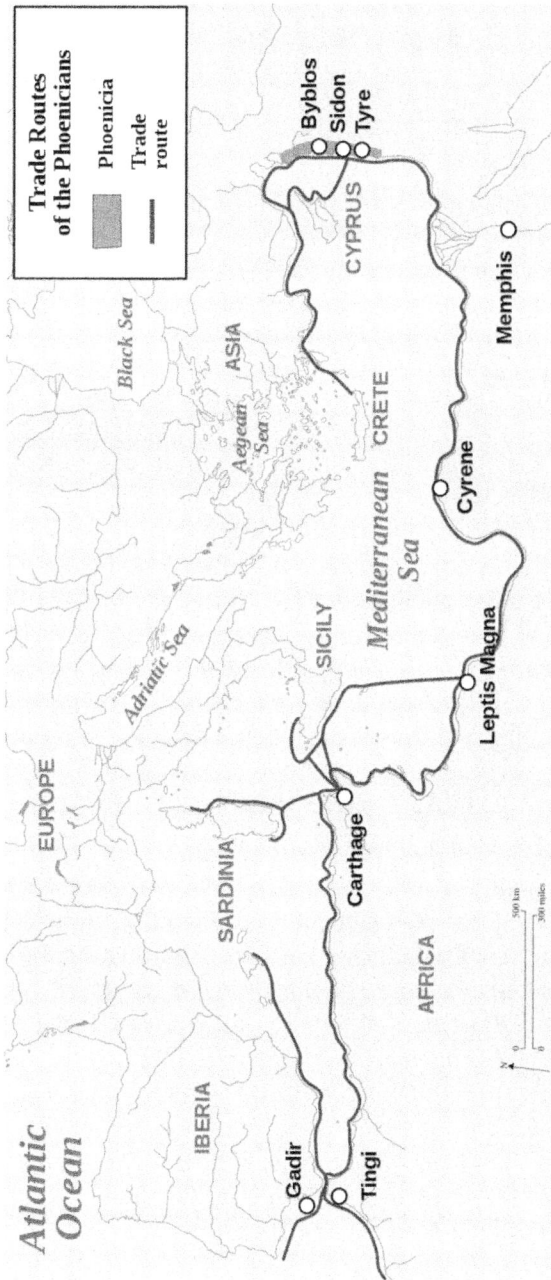

Map 16. Phoenician trade routes. Important Mediterranean cities also marked. Source: Wikimedia Commons/CC BY-SA 3.0 (Author: User:Rodrigo (es), User:Reedside (en)).

was a new economic/political model that emerged (following the Bronze Age Collapse). Others see the term Phoenician as being more of a "modern concept", since there were no people that actually identified as such (in antiquity).

Which of these theories is correct? Take your pick, since little has survived of Phoenician records. However, what is certain is the Levant's relationship to Egypt in the centuries before the Bronze Age Collapse. Most of the Levant, in the New Kingdom, was an Egyptian colony. In one of the "Amarna letters" (diplomatic correspondence between Egypt and the Near East) a Babylonian King says (to an Egyptian Pharaoh):

> The land of Canaan is your land and its kings are your servants

As already stated, Canaan refers to the Levant, in particular the Southern Levant — the same Levant out of which the Phoenicians rose. Undoubtedly, the Canaanites and the Phoenicians were influenced by both Egyptian culture and technology — as attested to by archaeological finds (and written records).

Following the Bronze Age Collapse, the Phoenicians emerged from Levantine port cities including Tyre, Sidon, Byblos and Beirut. These were a group of independent city-states — engaged in Mediterranean trade. They traded metal, ivory, glass, wood, textiles and powdered Tyrian purple (a purple dye used by the Greek elite to color garments). By c. 814 BCE, they had founded a trading post at Carthage.

Founding of Carthage, independence and administration

Qart-Hadasht or "New City" was Carthage's Punic name. It occupied a very strategic position, almost bang in the middle of the Mediterranean — from east to west — or from the Levant to Spain. This was the perfect location from which the lucrative Mediterranean trade network could be exploited. Further, this location, off the Mediterranean Coast, also meant that Carthage sat in the vicinity of large areas of both woodland and fertile agricultural land.

The Phoenicians that arrived at Carthage were not ethnically homogenous. That is to say, they were not "one group of people" — linking back to the prior discussion on Phoenician origins. Additionally, those Phoenicians that did arrive at Carthage would have met indigenous Africans already living there. In other words, the land was not uninhabited.

The city's founding myth says that exiled Queen Dido (also known as Elissa) actually leased the land from the Africans. In this myth, the local

Libyan King Hiarbas desired Dido's hand in marriage, which suggests that mixed marriages were common. Accordingly, this also suggests that Carthage city (and the eventual wider empire) was cosmopolitan. Further proof of this cosmopolitan nature, comes in the form of archaeological evidence, where studies have shown the presence of individuals from a variety of different backgrounds.

Due to the combination of favorable climate, fertile land and lucrative trade routes, Carthage grew rapidly — much more rapidly than the other Phoenician outposts in the Western Mediterranean (Cadiz, Lixus, Utica etc.). In a little under 200 years, a city that held upwards of 200,000 people had been developed. As a result, Carthage soon became one of the main commercial trading hubs in the entire Mediterranean Basin.

While this exceptional growth was taking place, in Carthage, fortunes in the Phoenician homeland were not so good. Phoenician power and influence had declined, due to hostilities with the Babylonians, Assyrians and eventually Persians. Carthage, being in North West Africa, was pretty much unaffected by such issues. Consequently, Carthage slowly started to assert itself more independently — assuming responsibility for the protection of the other (Phoenician) western settlements. By the 6th century BCE, Carthage was fully independent. And with that came the transition from city-state to more of an empire.

As for the administration of this new found "empire", Carthage most likely started off as some sort of monarchy — following in the footsteps of its mother city "Tyre". The tale of the city's founding, with Queen Dido, also seems to suggest a monarchy at first. To get an idea of how governance evolved, we can turn to Aristotle, an Ancient Greek philosopher. Aristotle (in *Politics*) writes:

> Carthage also appears to have a good constitution, with many outstanding features as compared with those of other nations, but most nearly resembling the Spartan in some points. For these three constitutions are in a way near to one another and are widely different from the others—the Cretan, the Spartan and, thirdly, that of Carthage. Many regulations at Carthage are good; and a proof of a well-regulated constitution is that the populace willingly remain faithful to the constitutional system, and that neither civil strife has arisen in any degree worth mentioning, nor yet a tyrant.

In essence, Carthage evolved from a monarchy (kingship) to a more inclusive republican form of government. With this republican system, you had two annually elected magistrates (one for the army and one for domestic affairs), a senate (composed of influential people) and an assembly of citizens. So you could say that there was some form of a "separation of powers" — specifically military from governance. Citizenship was not easily obtained, however, compared to say — Roman citizenship. This was the case even when Carthage expanded its borders. Due to its wealth, Carthage employed mercenaries extensively — who would fill in for the lack of "native" manpower (for wars).

Like almost all other ancient societies, the Carthaginians had their gods and goddesses — with each linked to specific themes or aspects of nature. The Carthaginians initially adopted the Phoenician polytheistic religion, before eventually developing their own more unique set of customs and forms of worship. Unsurprisingly, the gods were an important part of politics and people's lives, resulting in a thriving priesthood and tributes being paid by the citizenry.

As a side note, Ibiza, one of the Balearic or Mediterranean Islands which Carthage controlled, derives its name from the Ancient Egyptian (and Phoenician) deity Bes. This lion-faced dwarf god, with roots from Equatorial Africa, was the protector of households i.e. guardian of mothers and their children. Bes was regarded with such great respect, that he later featured on Punic artifacts — like coins.

Economy, trade and agriculture

Carthage was first, and foremost, a commercial maritime civilization. Its focus was on trade and acquiring wealth, not on conquest and aggressive expansion. All actions (and inactions) were primarily taken with profit in mind.

One of the best ways to get rich or wealthy is by having a monopoly. Carthage was fond of such monopolies. It would often seek to bar others (including the Romans) from sailing certain routes — only allowing them to call at specific ports. These restrictions enabled the Carthaginians to enjoy exclusivity on a variety of goods, which were of course marked-up significantly (when foreigners came to buy). When restrictions were ignored, or if Carthage felt that its trading monopoly was threatened, force was frequently used. For example, together with its allies, destroying newly found Greek colonies in Sicily and Libya. This willingness to use force inevitably led to conflict with the Roman Republic, in what is now called the Punic Wars.

Before then, the Carthaginians were the masters of the Western Mediterranean maritime network. Using their large fleet of merchant ships, they would call across major Mediterranean ports — exchanging all sorts of goods in the process. From the tin needed to make bronze, to a range of textiles, ceramics, and fine metalwork. This was similar to what the Phoenicians traded previously, but on a much larger scale.

Early Carthaginian trade did not specifically rely on coinage. In other words, there was no standardized currency (at first). The minting of coins would come later, sometime in the 5th century BCE. Prior to this, it was mainly a system of barter. Herodotus (*The Histories*) gives us an account of the system of barter used with various other Africans along the coast:

> Another story too is told by the Carchedonians (Carthaginians). There is a place, they say, where men dwell beyond the Pillars of Heracles (Straits of Gibraltar); to this they come and unload their cargo; then having laid it orderly by the waterline they go aboard their ships and light a smoking fire. The people of the country see the smoke, and coming to the sea they lay down gold to pay for the cargo and withdraw away from the wares. Then the Carchedonians disembark and examine the gold; if it seems to them a fair price for their cargo, they take it and go their ways; but if not, they go aboard again and wait, and the people come back and add more gold till the shipmen are satisfied. Herein neither party (it is said) defrauds the other; the Carchedonians do not lay hands on the gold till it matches the value of their cargo, nor do the people touch the cargo till the shipmen have taken the gold.

It is important to note that the Carthaginians did not only buy and sell — they actually manufactured products as well. They had a large number of artisans at hand, experts in working with glass, ivory, wood and metal. Hence, they were able to produce goods that were very valuable on the international market. This is what helped Carthage to become the wealthiest city in the whole of the Mediterranean (at one point).

Carthaginian trading activities were not just limited to the seas. Trade was also conducted across the Sahara Desert, as part of what you might call an early Trans-Saharan trade network. This early Saharan trade network relied on the Africans, living more inland from the Mediterranean Coast, who can be thought of as intermediaries or middlemen. People (or middlemen) known as the "Garamantes" were likely involved in such trading. Although the Sahara had mostly become desert, by the time of the Carthaginians, these Africans still maintained far-reaching links across it.

Goods from inner Africa would be passed from one desert oasis to another, until they reached the Mediterranean ports of Carthage. From there the goods would be exported. The reverse was also true — with the importation of goods into Africa. Goods that may have been traded include gold, copper, food and salt. Salt in these ancient times was super valuable. Hence you have the phrase "salt is as valuable as gold". In the time of no electric refrigeration, salt's value derived from its food preserving abilities — particularly when it came to preserving meat and fish. Consequently, you had high demand, with relatively low supply — hence the high prices (or value) of salt.

Even though trade was the "bread and butter" of the economy, the city of Carthage was positioned next to prime agricultural land. As we have already discussed, the coastal plains of North West Africa feature a Mediterranean climate. The soils are also rich, making coastal areas ideal for farming a variety of crops, fruits and vegetables.

Carthage started on a small strip of land, but the area under its control would expand — as the years went by. Soon enough, it developed a powerful agricultural center — in its countryside. Although records of Carthage's precise agricultural activities are scarce, there are some. One of the best descriptions of these practices, comes to us from an Ancient Greek historian — Diodorus Siculus (*The Library of History*), as part of a bigger piece (on a Greek invasion of Carthage) he wrote:

> The intervening country through which it was necessary for them to march was divided into gardens and plantations of every kind, since many streams of water were led in small channels and irrigated every part. There were also country houses one after another, constructed in luxurious fashion and covered with stucco, which gave evidence of the wealth of the people who possessed them. The farm buildings were filled with everything that was needful for enjoyment, seeing that the inhabitants in a long period of peace had stored up an abundant variety of products. Part of the land was planted with vines, and part yielded olives and was also planted thickly with other varieties of fruit-bearing trees. On each side herds of cattle and flocks of sheep pastured on the plain, and the neighboring meadows were filled with grazing horses. In general there was a manifold prosperity in the region, since the leading

Carthaginians had laid out there their private estates and with their wealth had beautified them for their enjoyment.

This pretty much sums up the wealth and beauty of the land called Carthage.

Military — army and navy

Carthage was mainly interested in trade and commerce. Having said this, it still needed to defend (and advance) its commercial and strategic interests (as and when necessary). Despite being primarily known for its activities on the seas, Carthage also had a more than capable army. In fact, as we shall see later on, one of history's best generals was a Carthaginian — by the name of Hannibal Barca.

As already touched on, Carthage had a small native population. This meant that it did not maintain a large standing army, and had a limited supply of native manpower — to fight its wars. To fill in this gap, mercenaries (foreign soldiers for hire) were extensively used. Given its large trade network, across the Mediterranean, Carthage was able to call upon a range of different mercenaries — from a variety of different sources. Only some of these mercenaries came from Africa, as over time — Celts, Balearics, and Iberians were all recruited. As you might expect, the generals that led the armies were almost always native Carthaginians.

Not all of the foreign troops, in the Carthaginian army, were mercenaries. This is a common misconception that people have with the Carthaginians — that they simply bought an army in times of need. This was only partly the case. The army's foreign contingent was also made up of allied troops and troops from client states. These alliances would often be cemented through political marriages. This shows that Carthage was more than just good at trading and fighting, but was learned in the art of diplomacy as well.

Heavy infantry fought in close formation, and were armed with long spears and shields. On the other hand, light infantry were equipped with javelins and used smaller shields. In terms of non-infantry troops, Carthage made significant use of cavalry. Numidian (African) light cavalry were small and very fast, and were typically used for light skirmishes. In other words — "hit and runs". They were said to be among the best on horseback, in the ancient world. And then you had the elephants, perhaps the unit that the Carthaginians are most remembered for. These were not just any elephants, but armored war elephants — specifically trained for battle. They had "drivers", and were primarily used to charge at the enemy — breaking their lines and instilling fear.

To control the sea trade, and in support of their land campaigns — the Carthaginians had a formidable navy. This was attested to by ancient writers, who saw Carthage as the "ruler of the seas". You have ancients like Dionysius of Halicarnassus (*Roman Antiquities*) making statements such as:

> the Carthaginians, whose maritime strength was superior to that of all others

Other ancients like Polybius (*The Histories*) give some reasoning to this fact with:

> The Carthaginians naturally are superior at sea both in efficiency and equipment, because seamanship has long been their national craft, and they busy themselves with the sea more than any other people

This proves that the Carthaginian navy was well respected — due to being strong and highly mobile.

Of course, there are two parts to a navy. One is of the actual ships, and the other is of the sailors that would man them. In terms of the ships, the Carthaginians were able to field not just technically superior ships, but field them in large number. This is with thanks to their ship building expertise and efficient production methods. As for their sailors, they too were well trained. Carthaginians were already very familiar with the seas, having travelled far and wide — for trade purposes. In fact, claims (on accounts from Herodotus *Histories*) have been made, that the Phoenicians before them, had already circumnavigated or rounded the entire coast of Africa:

> For Libya (Africa) shows clearly that it is encompassed by sea, save only where it borders on Asia; and this was proved first (as far as we know) by Necos king of Egypt. He, when he had made an end of digging the canal which leads from the Nile to the Arabian Gulf, sent Phoenicians in ships, charging them to sail on their return voyage past the Pillars of Heracles (Straits of Gibraltar) till they should come into the northern sea and so to Egypt. So the Phoenicians set out from the Red Sea and sailed the southern sea; whenever autumn came they would put in and sow the land, to whatever part of Libya they might come, and there await the harvest; then, having gathered in the crop, they sailed on, so that after two years had passed, it was

in the third that they rounded the Pillars of Heracles and came to Egypt. There they said (what some may believe, though I do not) that in sailing round Libya they had the sun on their right hand.

Herodotus, in the 5th century BCE, did not believe that the sun would be on the Phoenician's right, as they were rounding Africa. We now know that this would have indeed been the case. In other words, the sun would have been on the Phoenician's right. Therefore, this account perfectly describes what would have happened — sailing east to west (around South Africa). Replicas of Ancient Phoenician boats have been made, and used to successfully circumnavigate Africa in this modern day.

The idea that the Phoenicians rounded Africa, well before Vasco Da Gama and the Portuguese c. 1500 CE, definitely has some weight behind it. In any case, the sea power that the Carthaginians inherited from the Phoenicians — cannot be doubted.

Rise and fall of Carthage

We have already discussed the origins of the Carthaginians, the founding of their capital, and how they were able to dominate the Mediterranean (independently from Phoenicia). Now we can chronologically go over the rise and fall of Carthage.

By the 6th century BCE Carthage had to become more assertive, if it was to keep control of the lucrative trade network it had built up over the decades. The main issue was the growing threat from the Greeks. These Greeks were just as enterprising as the Carthaginians — with their own network of colonies in the Eastern Mediterranean. And so they sought to expand westwards, into Carthaginian territory. New Greek colonies were founded in and around places like Marseilles (Southern France) and Catalonia (North Eastern Spain). This caused friction, as Greek and Carthaginian colonies came into contact. Specific areas of dispute included Spain, Sicily, Corsica and a few other Mediterranean islands. This led to repeated conflicts, though initially on a small scale.

By around 550 BCE, Mago I had established a Carthaginian political dynasty — that of the Magnoid family. Only a few decades later, and Carthage had firmly imposed its control over the western half of the Mediterranean — precisely the North African coast, Andalusia, the Balearic Islands, Sardinia, Western Sicily, and Malta.

The Roman Republic was declared in c. 509 BCE, and that same year, a treaty was signed between the two states — that is Carthage and Rome. As mentioned already, the Carthaginians were mainly concerned with protecting their coastlines from foreign ships (commercial competition). With this treaty, the Carthaginians controlled the movement of Roman ships, and were better able to monitor Rome's commercial activities. As a result, Carthaginian ports were still largely reserved for Carthaginian merchants. For Rome, the treaty got them recognition, and independent access to some of the markets controlled by Carthage.

Wanting to put an end to the Sicilian ambitions of Gelon, ruler of Syracuse, and expand their position in Sicily — the Carthaginians launched an invasion in 480 BCE, led by Hamilcar. This was the first of the "Sicilian Wars". Traditional accounts put the Carthaginian army at 300,000 in number. Although this number may be inflated, it suggests that the Carthaginians were at considerable strength. Despite this strength, the Greeks won the-day at the Battle of Himera (in Sicily). The peace treaty allowed Carthage to keep its Western Sicilian bases, which were important for controlling east-west trade traffic. As part of this treaty, the Carthaginians were required to pay war reparations. In the aftermath, Carthage would renew focus on its African hinterland — both in terms of expansion and agricultural activities.

The next 70 or so years, were generally ones of peace, between Carthage and Greek Sicily. The inevitable return to hostilities occurred in around 410 BCE, partly for economic reasons (Greek Sicily had become very wealthy) and partly for want of Carthaginian revenge (for the defeat at Himera). And so there were renewed invasions of Sicily, first beginning with Magonid descendants Hannibal Mago and Himilco. These invasions started a 100 or so year period of sporadic wars against the Sicilian Greeks.

Towards the end of these Sicilian Wars, the then Tyrant Agathocles, of Syracuse, secretly invaded North Africa — while Carthage's main army besieged Syracuse itself. This forced the Carthaginians to suspend their siege and return home, to Africa, where they eventually forced Agathocles to withdraw. These wars, overall, resulted in little to no change in territory, as the Carthaginians remained in charge of the western half of the island (and the Greeks retained the eastern half).

Before the Punic Wars, Rome and Carthage actually entered into an alliance, during the "Pyrrhic War" c. 280 BCE. At the time, Pyrrhus was the King of Epirus (a powerful Greek state). As part of the war, Pyrrhus took leadership of the Greek cities of Eastern Sicily, and attacked the western (Carthaginian) half of the island. However, Pyrrhus was ultimately unable to defeat the Carthaginians and so withdrew. He was also subsequently defeated by the Romans at Beneventum (Southern Italy). The end-result of this war was Roman de facto control over the entire Italian peninsula.

The first Rome-Carthage treaty, and other subsequent ones, had left the Romans with a relatively "free-hand" in Italy — as long as they did not interfere with Carthage's Mediterranean trade. This allowed the Romans to aggressively expand in mainland Italy, conquering the peninsular by c. 272 BCE. All the while, Rome and Carthage grew increasingly suspicious of each other's intentions. Things would come to a head over the divided island of Sicily, beginning the first of three Punic Wars c. 264 BCE.

During this war the Romans invested a great deal in building and replacing war ships, so despite their inferior skills at sea, they soon matched the Carthaginians in number. As the war dragged on, the Romans got more and more naval experience. And so through a mixture of technology, resources and strategy — the Romans were eventually able to decisively defeat the Carthaginian navy.

This was not before over 20 years had passed, to the point where both sides were financially and demographically exhausted. At one point, Carthage even had to ask for a loan from Ptolemaic Egypt (a request which was quickly rejected). And so, Rome's "knack" for preservation, no matter what, eventually won them the war c. 241 BCE. In suing for peace, the Carthaginians were forced to cede Western Sicily, give up claims on the eastern half, and pay large reparations.

Economic exhaustion meant that Carthage was soon engaged in another war, a war against its own mercenaries — that had not been paid following the First Punic War. The mercenaries' ranks were further boosted by local peasants, who turned the situation into a full blown revolt. Hamilcar Barca was the leader that put down this revolt, in what is known as the "Mercenary War" (c. 240 BCE). But, not before the Romans had reneged on the earlier peace treaty — demanding that Carthage also cede Corsica and Sardinia to them. Carthage was certainly in no position to refuse, and promptly agreed to these new terms.

Despite this set back, Hamilcar Barca quickly set his sights on Southern Spain, launching a military campaign there c. 237 BCE — to compensate for the loss of some of Carthage's Mediterranean possessions. With the addition of more Spanish territory, Carthage would be able to strengthen both its economic and military base. In turn, this would enable it to challenge Rome once again — for supremacy in the Mediterranean.

Hamilcar Barca's successors followed in his footsteps, further consolidating newly gained lands in Spain, and founding a second capital city there called *Carthago Nova* (Cartagena) or "New Carthage". As envisioned by Hamilcar, the benefits of these Spanish holdings were soon apparent. By the time that Hannibal Barca (Hamilcar's son) assumed leadership, Carthage's coffers had been replenished, and it had sufficient manpower to stand up to the Romans (once more).

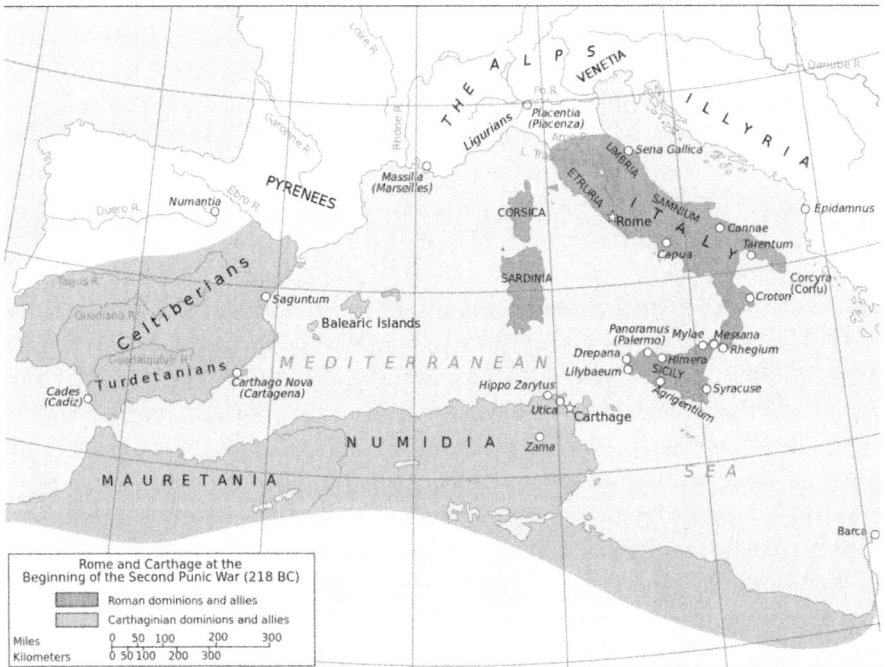

Map 17. Carthage and Rome at the start of the Second Punic War. Source: Wikimedia Commons/CC BY-SA 3.0 (Author: Rome_carthage_218.jpg: William Robert Shepherd, derivative work: Grandiose).

This Carthaginian revival worried the Romans. And so by the time Hannibal had captured the Eastern Spanish city of Saguntum (a Roman ally), Rome declared war — in 218 BCE. Hannibal quickly assembled an army estimated at some 50–60,000 troops. This army included Numidian light cavalry, and several dozen war elephants. Hannibal's strategy was to take the war to Rome — literally. He planned to march his army across the Pyrenees mountain range, cut through Southern Gaul (France) and then go over the Alps Mountains into Northern Italy. By doing so, Hannibal hoped to surprise the Romans.

This expedition cost Hannibal up to half of his men, many of his elephants, and a lot of supplies. The passage over the cold and snowy Alps, in particular, was not easy — in fact, it was one of the greatest military feats in history.

Five months later and Hannibal's army had arrived at the plains of Northern Italy. From here, Hannibal won a quick succession of victories, as he marched southwards towards Rome itself. The Romans soon refrained from full engagement, adopting the so-called "Fabian Strategy". And so the Romans resorted to hit and runs. Hit and runs that aimed to disrupt Carthaginian supply trains, hoping to lower their morale in the process. This remained the Roman strategy, until the Battle of Cannae c. 216 BCE.

In the lead up to the battle, Q. Fabius Maximus (who the Fabian Strategy is named after), had been replaced as dictator by two Roman consuls — G. Terentius Varro and L. Aemilius Paullus. Both of these commanders were far more aggressive, than Fabius, in policy. They assembled over 80,000 troops, to directly engage Hannibal in battle. Though smaller in number, the Carthaginians managed to surround the Roman armies, and virtually annihilated them. This was a classic military maneuver — the double envelopment or pincer movement. Military historians regard Hannibal's use of such, as one of the greatest tactical moves ever.

With this victory, Hannibal had hoped that the Romans would capitulate, and sue for peace. However, as was typical of Rome, it did not know when it was defeated, and so refused to give in. In total Hannibal spent around 15 years in Italy, while winning a string of other victories, none of which made the Romans surrender. The Romans simply had the manpower and supplies that the Carthaginians did not. The Romans could stay in Italy (home turf) forever, but Hannibal could not, not without sufficient supplies.

This Roman manpower enabled them to both contain Hannibal in Italy (Fabian Strategy) and field other armies elsewhere — in one case in Spain. Cornelius Scipio (Scipio Africanus) was the general that helped Rome defeat the Carthaginians in Spain (c. 206 BCE), after which Scipio turned his attention to Africa and Carthage itself.

Hannibal was forced to return to Africa and engage Scipio at the Battle of Zama (c. 202 BCE). Zama was located a few miles south of

Carthage. Although the battle was evenly matched, Hannibal was eventually defeated, and Carthage was made to surrender.

Under the terms of the peace treaty, Carthage was to pay another indemnity, cede Spain and its other Mediterranean possessions, its navy was restricted in size and it was not allowed to possess elephants. Hannibal did remain a leading figure in Carthage. And like before, the city soon started to prosper — due to its agricultural and trade activities.

The Romans became worried and perhaps rather jealous at the same time. Hannibal's enemies also plotted against him, enemies that he had gotten through a raft of new political/economic reforms — that had "cleaned up" the Carthaginian government. And so, he was soon forced to flee into voluntary exile, before the Romans could demand for his arrest (for allegedly plotting against them with a foreign power). A decade or so later, the Romans would catch up with Hannibal and demand for his extradition. Hannibal committed suicide in order to avoid capture.

"Carthago delenda est" (Carthage must be destroyed). So said Cato the Censor, after which came the Third Punic War in 149 BCE. The pretext for this war, was said to be the Carthaginian violation of a clause, in the earlier peace treaty with Rome, whereby Carthage was required to get Rome's consent, before taking any military action — in this case against Masinissa the King of the North West African Kingdom of Numidia.

Just over three years later, and the Romans had captured Carthage. The city was plundered and razed to the ground. Surviving occupants were sold into slavery, and it was said that the Romans ploughed and salted the earth — to prevent its regeneration. Carthage and the African territories it once controlled became a Roman province — Africa Proconsularis. Later of course, this term "Africa" would be used to refer to the whole continent — of which the Romans only knew a part of.

11. The Garamantes and Saharan Africa

Unlike the rest of Africa, it is in early ancient times that Saharan people, societies and civilizations had what you might call a "Golden Age". A Golden Age before the lands finally became much too barren, for any form of permanent settlement. Of course, the Nile Valley was the exception to this. Thanks to the yearly monsoon rains, in the Ethiopian Highlands, and the resulting floods, urban life could go on — along the green banks of the Nile River.

To the west of the Nile is Egypt and Nubia's Western Desert. This vast desert region is but a small part of what can be referred to as the Central Sahara — stretching all the way to Africa's Atlantic Coast. This desert is home to a number of oases. Today, you can still find people living at some of these oases — courtesy of vast underground reserves of water (inherited from Ancient times). An example of an "urban oasis" (today) is the Siwa Oasis in Egypt (near the border with Libya).

More than 3000 years ago, in pharaonic times, there were many more oases to be found in the Central Sahara. There were not just more oases, but these oases were larger — giving people access to greater water resources. Accordingly, the oases were fairly fertile — accommodating both plants and animals. And as a result, these oases formed part of extensive trade routes across the Sahara — east to west, north to south and vice versa. Said another way, this was the earliest form of Trans-Saharan trading — which the Garamantes eventually took some part in (as did the Carthaginians).

Who were the Garamantes?
The Garamantes, a desert people of the Central Sahara, can be described as a "lost civilization". Lost in the sense that until recently, we knew very little about them, apart from small accounts we get from authors like Herodotus (*Histories*):

> ...there is yet another hillock of salt and springs of water and many fruit-bearing palms, as at the other places; men dwell there called Garamantes, an exceeding great nation, who sow in earth which they have laid on the salt...

Herodotus also mentions that they herded cattle, and used horse-drawn chariots to hunt people (presumably slaves). This mentioning of chariots is quite interesting, given the number of Saharan rock art paintings of such. In this section of his book, Herodotus mentions the Garamantes along with several other groups — found along the Mediterranean Coast and further inland (the Sahara). Prior to the above passage, Herodotus does again refer to the Garamantes — in a way that kind of contradicts the quote above:

> ..the Garamantes dwell in the wild beasts' country. They shun the sight and fellowship of men, and have no weapons of war, nor know how to defend themselves.

So the Garamantes went from being a people that cannot "defend themselves" to a "great nation" most experienced in the use of chariots? This discrepancy may arise because the Garamantes may have not been one specific group of people, in the same way that the Nubians were not. Rather, the term Garamantes was perhaps just a generic one— for a variety of different Saharan groups.

Like with the Phoenicians, scholars are not sure of what the Garamantes would have called themselves, and so we rely on the Greek name i.e. Garamantes. This reliance on classical sources (Greek and Roman) has meant that prior published work tended to view the Garamantes exclusively through "classical lenses". Which basically boils down to — here are the (civilized) Romans. And here are the (uncivilized) Garamantes, on the fringes of the so-called civilized (Roman) world. For an example of this, we can refer to Roman historian Tacitus (*Histories*):

> the Garamantes, an ungovernable tribe and one always engaged in practicing brigandage (highway robbery and plunder) on their neighbors

Most Roman sources only mention military conflicts with the Garamantes. For more information, and to get a more Saharan point of view, we must turn to archaeology.

Archaeological findings

New archaeological research has confirmed the account of Herodotus, proving that the Garamantes were very much a "great nation". Fortified farms, villages, castle-like structures and towns, have all been discovered in South Western Libya (Fezzan). This Garamante civilization is said to have lasted from roughly 900 BCE to 600 CE.

Figure 12. Ruins of the ancient city of Garama. Source: Wikimedia Commons/CC BY-SA 3.0 (Author: Franzfoto).

Garamante society went through a few stages of development. The early stages (up to 500 BCE) saw settlements located near easily defendable positions (in Wadi al-Ajal). Material culture found shows the transition from a pastoralist-based culture, to a sophisticated irrigation-based one. Saharan surface water by this time was very low, and so irrigation would have been the only way for the Garamantes to effectively cultivate crops. Both Mediterranean and Sahelian crops were grown. That is, barley, figs, grapes and wheat — as well as cotton, pearl millet and sorghum.

Later a new capital was built at Ancient *Garama* (modern Germa/Jarma), replacing the older one at *Zinchecra*. By this time, the Garamantes had grown increasingly prosperous from their agricultural and trading exploits. Much of this success can be specifically attributed to their irrigation techniques. The Garamantes were able to tap into the vast "aquifers" of Saharan underground water, by constructing foggaras (qanats). These foggaras were basically gently sloping underground channels, which transported water to the surface — for irrigation and drinking. Put another way, foggaras were underground aqueducts, which artificially greened the desert, and supported dense populations in the process. As highlighted before, Libya's Great Man-Made River serves a similar purpose today.

To construct these irrigation systems, just like with the irrigation systems used by the Egyptians and Nubians, you needed organized labor. And so a hierarchy was likely established, with elites or kings at the top. Some of these kings may have been buried at the "Hatiya Pyramids", a cluster of small mudbrick tombs — a few miles west of Germa. As you may expect, many of these tombs and burial structures made space for grave goods. There is also evidence that burial orientation customs (and other funerary practices) were similar to those practiced throughout the Sahara (including in Egypt and Nubia).

At sites in and around Germa you can find abundant inscriptions. These inscriptions are often found either cut and/or painted on Garamantian burial structures. The script has not been deciphered, although it is thought to be similar to the "Libyco-Berber" script. The "Tifinagh" script, still used in North and West Africa, has its roots in Libyco-Berber. Incidentally, this Lybico-Berber like script has been found cut onto rocks throughout the Canary Islands. Scholars still do not know the hows and whys relating to how Saharan Africans effectively — first colonized the Canary Islands (by the first millennium BCE).

The 2nd century BCE saw the Roman arrival onto the North African scene. Despite Rome's conquest of Carthage (and other parts of North Africa), the Garamantes retained their independence. Records show that Garamante-Roman relations fluctuated, between good and bad — with hostilities breaking out at times. From around 300 CE the Garamantes began constructing walls around their towns. This suggests a period of increased insecurity. Also during this period, foggara-based irrigation seems to have stopped, and instead wells were more heavily relied upon. As such, good agricultural land became more scarce, and the range (and quality) of imported goods decreased.

This decline in Garamantian culture was likely due, in part, to ever worsening climatic conditions in the Sahara. Remember, the Garamantes were an urban society, which was established in a desert environment — where there was no Nile i.e. no river. Easily reachable groundwater levels, likely fell, and thus food could not be grown like before. Neither could life continue as before. And so, with the coming of the Arabs, the Garamante civilization fell (c. 600 CE).

Ancient Trans-Saharan trade network

Herodotus's description of the Garamantes, comes as part of what one can argue is an early "desert trail" or Trans-Saharan trade route. This was a route that began in Southern Egypt, running through Southern Libya, and onto the Hoggar Mountains (of Algeria). The Hoggar Mountains are not far from Algeria's border with Mali, and thus the river Niger "bend".

Nevertheless, some modern scholars are not convinced that there was such a Trans-Saharan trade network, in ancient times i.e. before the coming of Islam. These scholars cite the fact that there is little to no archaeological evidence — for imported West African goods in Garamantian lands (or anywhere else in North West Africa).

Scholars in favor of this ancient trading network point to sites like *Wadi Tanezzuft* (in South West Fezzan). This site appears to have somewhat of a "fortified" nature, and it is located on a commercial route definitely used in the Middle Ages. And thus, it potentially acted as a checkpoint, which allowed the Garamantes to control the flow of trade. This is similar, in a way, to how the Nile cataracts enabled both Egypt and Kush to regulate the Nile Valley trade.

Moreover, at Wadi Tanezzuft, pottery has been found that is decorated in manners seen in other parts of Sahelian West Africa (roulette decoration). This however, does not necessarily mean that the pottery was imported from West Africa. In fact, there is enough archaeological evidence to suggest that local Garamantian ceramic traditions are part of the West African roulette ceramic tradition or culture. This would confirm contacts between West Africa and Garamantian territory, even if we do not know the precise nature of these contacts.

Archaeological finds of valuable foreign goods (from the Mediterranean and Indian Ocean), in West Africa, and pre-dating the Arab conquests, have also been made. This clearly suggests that there must have been some form of established trade going-on, into and out of West Africa, well before Islam arrived. Ultimately, more archaeological expeditions need to be undertaken, to map out a clearer picture of how this proposed ancient trading network functioned.

Having said all this, archaeology may not provide all the answers. Archaeologically "invisible" goods could just have well been traded — like was the case in medieval times. Often scholars fail to appreciate theories that do not fit in with the "norm". This is fairly understandable, as if there is no "hard evidence" (metals, pottery etc.) do we ever truly know?

One can take a look at the goods commonly traded during the Islamic Trans-Saharan trade period — salt, slaves and gold. Salt and slaves cannot really be recorded as hard evidence. Gold has somewhat of a better chance — of finding its way into the archaeological record (though even this is still difficult).

For our knowledge of Islamic Trans-Saharan trade (from c. 700 CE), we tend to rely on written Arabic sources (which describe this trade network in some detail). It is these same sources that even tell the famous story of Mansa Musa. Here, on his pilgrimage (Hajj) to Mecca (1324 CE), Mansa Musa spent and gave away so much gold, in Cairo, that the value of gold crashed and did not recover — for many years to come.

How can one test this archaeologically? The answer is one cannot. Neither can we test Herodotus's account of the Carthaginians engaging in "silent trade", with other peoples off the coast of West Africa. Not being able to archaeologically prove either of these two events, does not mean they did not happen.

Further, one has to remember that the mid-first millennium BCE was a time of significant change in Africa, and the wider Mediterranean. New cities rose up, and new trade routes were established, partly as a result of the Bronze Age Collapse. And so you had the rise of Carthage, various Greek city-states and eventually Rome. All of who would have required resources to develop industrial capacity for themselves. Together with the Sahara reaching the final stages of desertification, and the resulting permanently settled societies that developed in Africa, the early emergence of a Trans-Saharan trade route does make sense.

On a final note, there is definite archaeological evidence for significant Garamantian trading relationships with both Egypt, and the Mediterranean Coast (Carthaginians and then the Romans). This comes as no surprise, given the Garamantes strategic location, right in the heart of North Africa. Being part of such trade networks i.e. acting as middlemen in much the same way as the Nubians (in the Nile Valley), would have made the Garamantes very wealthy.

Put differently, the Garamante civilization emerged precisely to take advantage of lucrative trading opportunities (across the Sahara), which arose (by the first millennium BCE) thanks to the coming of agriculture and (specialized) manufacturing towns or production centers, in more inner parts of Africa (and the Levant/Mediterranean). These towns produced things like leather, cotton (textiles), ceramics and metals. As we will see later, the Middle Niger River and the Lake Chad Basin are areas where such towns developed.

12. Greeks in Ancient Africa

Before the Greeks took control of Egypt, there was a long period of trade and interaction between the two. This period of interaction goes back to the 3rd millennium BCE, first with the Minoans (Mediterranean island of Crete) and then with the Mycenaeans (mainland Greece). The Minoans were technically a non or pre-Greek people, who were absorbed into the Mycenaean civilization and Hellenized (became Greek). Following the Bronze Age Collapse the Mycenaean civilization fell, and the Greeks entered into a 400 year Dark Age — known as the "Greek Dark Ages".

The Greeks emerged from this Dark Age in the 8th century BCE, and subsequently experienced both a structural and an intellectual revolution. It was a structural revolution in the sense that, the political maps of Greece were redrawn, with the coming of the *Polis* (city-state), and the subsequent adoption of *demokratia* (democracy) by such city-states like "Athens".

Various Greek thinkers and scholars travelled to Egypt, with the goal of expanding their knowledge. And this relates to the "intellectual" part of the Greek revolution, with the Greeks making important contributions to astronomy, mathematics, medicine and philosophy. Lastly, it was during this period (c. 800–300 BCE) that the Greeks established a physical presence in Africa.

Greek colony of Cyrene — Eastern Libya

Like Carthage (or Tunisia), Libya's Mediterranean Coast is also home to fertile land. These lush fertile parts can be found in Eastern Libya, in the historical region of Cyrenaica. More specifically in an area called *Jebel Akhdar* (The Green Mountain). Being one of the wettest parts of Libya, a variety of agricultural products can be grown here, including potatoes, rich fruits and cereal crops. No doubt that it was this agricultural potential, which attracted the Greeks to settle the lands in the first place. And so, by c. 630 BCE, the Greek colony of *Cyrene* had been founded.

Given the fertile nature of Cyrene, the Greeks that arrived from the island of *Thera*, did not meet land that was unoccupied. The land was already populated by various groups of Africans (Libyans) that interacted with the Egyptian state to the east. These Libyans were more nomadic in nature, and so any organization that they had was loose. This likely contributed to the Greeks being able to permanently settle the lands. We get more information from the Ancient Greek geographer Strabo (*Geography*):

> Cyrene was founded by the inhabitants of Thera, a Lacedæmonian island which was formerly called Calliste, as Callimachus says, "'Calliste once its name, but Thera in later times, the mother of my home, famed for its steeds.'" The harbour of Cyrene is situated opposite to Criu-Metopon, the western cape of Crete, distant 2000 stadia. The passage is made with a south-south-west wind. Cyrene is said to have been founded by Battus, whom Callimachus claims to have been his ancestor. The city flourished from the excellence of the soil, which is peculiarly adapted for breeding horses, and the growth of fine crops.

Apart from Cyrene other towns were also founded, along the Libyan coast, including Apollonia, Barca, Berenice and Taucheira — all being part of the larger Cyrenaica.

Greek colonies were founded in an organized manner, sometimes founded by a single mother city, and other times founded in collaboration with several cities. Despite this, and once established, the colonies remained more or less independent — although they did maintain ties with their respective mother cities. You can liken this to how Carthage maintained ties with its mother city (Tyre).

After a period of coexistence, and as the Greeks slowly expanded their Libyan colonies, there was an influx of settlers from other Greek islands. Consequently, native Libyans were driven off their lands. In response, the then Libyan King Adicran asked for Egyptian help. Herodotus (*Histories*) gives us an account of what happened:

> So a great multitude gathered together at Cyrene, and cut off great tracts of land from the territory of the neighbouring Libyans. Then these with their king, whose name was Adicran, being robbed of their lands and violently entreated by the Cyrenaeans, sent to Egypt and put themselves in the hands of Apries, the king of that country.

> Apries mustered a great host of Egyptians and sent it against Cyrene; the Cyrenaeans marched out to the place Irasa and the spring Thestes, and there battled with the Egyptians and overcame them; for the Egyptians had as yet no knowledge of Greeks, and despised their enemy; whereby they were so utterly destroyed that few of them returned to Egypt. For this mishap, and because they blamed Apries for it, the Egyptians revolted from him.

After this Egyptian defeat, the then Pharaoh Apries was replaced by Pharaoh Amasis II in c. 570 BCE. While on the throne, Amasis II had more peaceful relations with the Greeks of Cyrene (who grew increasingly prosperous). Following the Persian conquest of Egypt c. 525 BCE, Greek Libya also submitted to the might of the Persian Empire — paying tribute to King Cambyses II.

Subsequent to the retreat of the Persians (c. 404 BCE), Strabo in his account (*Geography*), goes on to discuss how the once (again) independent Cyrene went on to be conquered by the Macedonian Greeks, who were already in control of Egypt. The Macedonians, in this instance, refers to the Ptolemies, who controlled Egypt from c. 305–30 BCE. And thus Cyrene, and the other Greek Libyan towns, became part of the Ptolemaic Kingdom — before eventually falling to the Romans.

Although neighbors, there was seemingly no Carthaginian-Greek Libyan hostilities, except when the Spartan King Dorieus was rebuffed in his attempts to establish another Greek colony in *Cinyps* (Western Libya).

Greek settlers in Ancient Egypt (before the Ptolemies)

Well before Egypt fell into the hands of Alexander the Great (c. 332 BCE); Greek-Egyptian trading relations were well established. The Greeks had been granted what can be described as a "free economic zone". This economic zone or trading place, was established in the Western Nile Delta, at a place called *Naukratis* (Naucratis) — just over 40 miles south east of modern Alexandria. You can view Naukratis as a sort of Greek/Egyptian "Hong Kong".

The exact date of the city's founding is not known, given the rather contradictory ancient accounts and archaeological evidence at hand. However, it is likely that this was not before the reign of Psamtik I — who ruled Egypt between 664–610 BCE (26th dynasty). At the time, Psamtik I and Egypt were what you could term vassals of the Neo-Assyrian Empire. The same Assyrian Empire that had defeated the Kushite Kings of the Egyptian 25th dynasty. Before cutting ties with the

Assyrians, Psamtik I recruited Greek mercenaries. This helped him maintain some stability in his 54 year reign as pharaoh.

The link between Psamtik I and Greek mercenaries, has led some scholars to believe that Naukratis may have initially been a military outpost (for such mercenaries). This was before the city went on to develop a commercial nature, during the reign of Amasis II. Naukratis was thus subsequently used as a place where Greeks could reside and trade. No other place in Egypt explicitly allowed foreign traders to settle. By doing this, the Egyptians were able to better regulate the trade of goods coming into and out of the state. And it meant that they could simply use these foreign merchants to trade on their behalf (outsourcing), while still maintaining a degree of control. Remember, during this period of time, the power of the Egyptian state was limited, and so direct state-sponsored trading missions were both uncommon and expensive.

The Egyptians supplied grain, linen, papyrus and fine ceramics. Imports included silver as well as timber, olive oil and wine. Eventually, Naukratis became a Greek polis (city) or colony within Egypt itself. Temples were built, and pottery unearthed suggests that Naukratis was a destination for Greeks from all-over — who brought pottery to dedicate or trade. This links to the idea of Naukratis acting as a sort of center for interchange, of Greek and Egyptian art, ideas and culture. The city would later be overshadowed by the port city of Alexandria.

What the Greeks learnt in Africa

There are many examples of what the Greeks learnt from their interactions with Ancient Egypt (and other non-African civilizations) — stretching back to the time of the Minoans. The fact that the Greeks learnt from the Egyptians, does not belittle in any way their own subsequent achievements. Culture and knowledge do not exist in a vacuum. And it is the ability to build on prior knowledge, which has allowed humans to develop over time. In other words, new knowledge is built on old knowledge — without which there would be no "new" knowledge. Thus at the end of this book, you will see a list of other texts and journals (references) that have been consulted, in order to produce this book itself. Without these prior records, it would have been almost impossible for any decent account of Ancient Africa to be written.

The following passage in the book *Library of History* by Diodorus Siculus, outlines some of the notable Ancient Greek scholars who acquired some knowledge from Egypt.

We must enumerate what Greeks, who have won fame for their wisdom and learning, visited Egypt in ancient times, in order to become acquainted with its customs and learning. For the priests of Egypt recount from the records of their sacred books that they were visited in early times by Orpheus, Musaeus, Melampus, and Daedalus, also by the poet Homer and Lycurgus of Sparta, later by Solon of Athens and the philosopher Plato, and that there also came Pythagoras of Samos and the mathematician Eudoxus, as well as Democritus of Abdera and Oenopides of Chios. As evidence for the visits of all these men they point in some cases to their statues and in others to places or buildings which bear their names, and they offer proofs from the branch of learning which each one of these men pursued, arguing that all the things for which they were admired among the Greeks were transferred from Egypt

This should not surprise anyone, because the Egyptians had a prosperous civilization well before (2000+ years before) the "Classical Age" of Greek culture (beginning c. 500 BCE). And so, being so close to each other, one could say that it was fairly inevitable, that the much older Egyptian arts, religion, literature, sciences, and laws would have influenced Greek thought and culture. A fact that is well-documented. As the cycle of civilization goes, the Greeks then influenced the Romans, and the Romans went on to influence "Western civilization".

13. Land of Punt

Punt, sometimes referred to as "God's Land", was a place known to be rich in myrrh, frankincense, ebony, gold, gemstones and more — all of which were goods highly treasured by the Ancient Egyptians. These treasures had many uses, for example — perfumes were used in religious ceremonies (like mummification), and for medicinal purposes. Perhaps the most famous of all such scents was *kyphi* — a compound incense. That is to say, and depending on the exact recipe in question, kyphi was made up of several different ingredients including resins, herbs and spices.

Egyptian Pharaohs, such as Queen Hatshepsut, are the ones to have left us with the "puzzle" of Punt. I call it a puzzle as there are so many unanswered questions, with regards to this both legendary and mysterious land. We have clues, but not the full picture, giving rise to multiple theories — with some even questioning if Punt existed at all? Other questions include:

Where is Punt actually located?

How did the Ancient Egyptians travel to Punt?

Why are there no recorded military campaigns to Punt?

And much more.

Evidently, Punt was too far away for it to pose a military threat to Egypt, with Egypt being protected by its natural barriers. Of course, these natural barriers also made it difficult for Egypt to go on the offensive i.e. to directly take control of Punt itself. Therefore, one can assume that Egypt had only commercial interests in Punt, contrasting with its interests in Nubia and Syria-Palestine (which were both commercial and militaristic in nature).

Nothing is known of what the Puntites referred to themselves as. Neither do we know much about their homeland. Said another way, we have no first-hand written records from Punt itself. For what we do know, we refer to Egyptian records. These records primarily occur in the third and second millennium BCE.

Analysis of such records show that Punt was an exotic land, the emphasis on such, leads us to believe it was exotic in a way that completely differed from Egyptian land. This exotic nature comes in the form of not just the land, but the inhabitants and the nature of the resources acquired from the land.

Clearly, journeys to Punt involved travelling by sea, probably a journey that would have taken place via the Red Sea. Given such a sea journey, it is likely that Punt would not have referred to any part of Nubia or Kush. Given the nature of Egyptian geography, any Red Sea voyage had to begin by crossing the Eastern Desert, before actually going south (down the sea). This gives rise to two very important questions:

How far south did they go?

And.

Was Punt located on the eastern or western side of the Red Sea?

In tackling the latter question, we seek an answer to whether Punt was located in Africa or on the Arabian Peninsula. Being on the eastern side of the Red Sea would put Punt in Arabia, while being on the western side would put Punt in Africa. Of course, it is also more than possible, that Puntite territory referred to land on both sides of the Red Sea. Accordingly, we have the candidate (modern) countries of Saudi Arabia, Yemen, Sudan, Eritrea, Ethiopia, Dijbouti, Somalia and Kenya.

For a subject (Egyptology) or land (Punt), relatively well-studied, or at least well-described (by the Egyptians), one can begin to wonder why it is so difficult to locate Punt? However, it is important to remember that for the Egyptians, and many other ancients, writing was mostly reserved for religious or administrative purposes. Writing, for "writings sake", was not really a thing. Consequently, the pharaohs left behind little by way of maps, travel directions, distances and/or other things — which would have helped scholars in directly pinpointing the location of Punt.

Initially, based on the mention of aromatics in Egyptian records, scholars suggested that Punt was to be found on the Arabian Peninsula. However, later discoveries, particularly in the memorial temple of Queen Hatsehput (near Luxor) suggested otherwise. According to temple reliefs, at the time of Hatsehput's expedition (15th century BCE), Punt was ruled by chief Parahu and his wife Ati. Puntite houses were raised on stilts and they herded cattle. Temple illustrations of the wild animals and products found in Punt include giraffes, baboons, rhinos and palm trees. These are mostly only found in Africa, suggesting an East African, rather than an Arabian Peninsula location for Punt.

Figure 13. Egyptian relief or scene of Puntite Chief Parahu and his wife Ati (top right). Source: Wikimedia Commons/CC BY-SA 4.0 (Author: Maksim Sokolov (maxergon.com)).

Today, most scholars agree on East Africa, even if the precise location is still argued. Earlier opinions of Punt being in Somalia, has lost some support — in favor of Punt being nearer the coastal regions of South Eastern Sudan, Eritrea or Ethiopia. This Sudan/Eritrea/Ethiopia homeland is backed up by recent scientific studies, where analysis of mummified baboons points to such origin.

Journeys to Punt may not have always involved going via the Red Sea, especially if Punt was actually located in East Africa. Thus, Punt could have been reached via the Nile and through Nubia, before arriving in Eritrea/Ethiopia. However, going through this Nile and land route, would have meant going through middlemen — as the Egyptians would have been unable to trade directly with the Puntites. As it was back then (and as it is today) trading through a middleman almost always involves higher costs. So one can assume, in periods of Egyptian strength at least, expeditions directly to Punt would have been far more cost effective — allowing the Egyptians to purchase goods in bulk.

Having said all this, it is also possible that the Puntites themselves were simply middlemen that dwelled on the coast — trading goods obtained from inner Africa. This would be in a similar manner to the Swahili traders, off the Swahili Coast, who traded between East Africa, Arabia and India (as briefly touched on before). The fact that the inhabitants of Punt also sent their own trading expeditions to Egypt provides some evidence for a potential middleman role.

It is also important to highlight that Punt may not necessarily have been linked to one specific geographic location. To explain, as Punt was so closely associated with the luxury products the Egyptians so desired, it may have been a term that simply referred to any land from which those products could be obtained. This is feasible as Punt was a term used for around 1500 years, and so the term could have been used to refer to different localities at different times. Evidence for this theory also comes from the fact that, Punt would not be mentioned in Egyptian texts for relatively long periods of time. Between those stretches of time, the sources of exotic goods such as myrrh potentially changed. And so to put it simply, Punt may have just meant "a source of myrrh" (or other aromatic resins).

The fact that historical references to Punt pretty much cease by the end of the Egyptian New Kingdom (c. 1100 BCE), adds further weight to this theory. As we already know, the Egyptian New Kingdom is when the state reached its zenith — after which Egypt entered a period of terminal decline. With this decline would come the severing of direct trade links — as Egypt could no longer afford to sponsor large trading expeditions. Therefore, any mention of Punt stopped.

This severing of trade links relates to the wider idea of permanent changes in the direction of global trade (at the time). Remember, it was the ability to control the flow of trade that partly made civilizations prosper, as seen with not just the Egyptians, but with the Carthaginians, Garamantes, Kushites and other civilizations after them — all leading up to this modern-day.

Future archaeological evidence may indeed point to a potential Puntite homeland. Nonetheless, even this would not really mean that Punt can be limited to one such area, definitely not without a lot of concrete evidence. And thus, the search for the Land of Punt continues.

14. Before there was Aksum — D'MT Kingdom

As previously gone over, with its rather cool and temperate climate, the Ethiopian Highlands region has favorable conditions for agriculture. And so, by the end of the African Humid Period (c. 5000 BP), local Afroasiatic speaking peoples began to form small little settlements in the area. Here they practiced mixed farming i.e. growing crops and raising livestock. As suggested by some scholars, later cultural practices may have been influenced by interactions with the Nubia region, and/or the movement of peoples south from said region. This movement, from lowlands to highlands, may have been encouraged by worsening ecological conditions (droughts) and/or changing trading relationships in the Mediterranean, Nile Valley and Red Sea — with the latter becoming increasingly important (in terms of trade).

One of the first identifiable cultures, in the highlands, is the Ancient "Ona" culture. Excavations at Sembel (Greater Asmara, Eritrea) reveal some of the earliest settled agro-pastoral communities known in the Horn of Africa, dating back to at least 900 BCE. Ona people lived in villages and small towns made of solid stone walls. The pottery found here is somewhat similar to such found in Kassala or the Gash Delta region of Eastern Sudan, providing evidence for an early Ancient Ethiopia/Eritrea link with Nubia. In addition, various "bulls' heads" (figurines) have been found at sites of this culture — suggesting that cattle, like with both Egypt and Nubia, were an important part of the economy and religion.

Furthermore, some of these bulls' heads appear to relate to "humped" cattle species. This is significant as these species of cattle are able to tolerate drier conditions, resist diseases and are highly productive (when it comes to milk production). Remember by around 3000 BP, in the mid-late Holocene, conditions in the wider area had generally become more arid. And so, arid-adapted cattle (and crops) would have provided a fairly reliable subsistence base — from which relatively large towns could develop i.e. urbanism. These Greater Asmara communities both pre-date and exist at the same time as Pre-Aksum settlements in Northern Ethiopia (e.g. D'MT Kingdom).

By the mid-first millennium BCE, smaller societies (to the south of Asmara) had become increasingly centralized. No doubt, relations would likely have already been firmly established with the Nile Valley. In fact, as seen in the previous section, this Ethiopian Highland area is a likely candidate for the location of the famed "Land of Punt". As we already know, Puntite trade with Egypt declined after the fall of the Egyptian New Kingdom. And perhaps with such, came the need for reorganization and changes in trading strategy. Accordingly, a new political system developed, centered specifically on the northern edge of the highlands (Tigray region — Northern Ethiopia). This new system was controlled by a kingdom known as "Da'amat" or "D'MT". It existed from around the 8th to the 4th century BCE.

Although there are few surviving written records, about this kingdom, some limited archaeological work has taken place. The evidence unearthed shows D'MT's trade links and connections with Southern Arabia (across the Red Sea). Like its potential predecessor, Punt, scholars suggest that DM'T also acted as a middleman — a middleman that brought in African goods from the interior, and exported them overseas. Goods such as frankincense, myrrh, gold, gemstones, ivory, rhinoceros horn and tortoise shell were likely exchanged for — olive oil, wine, textiles, jewelry, metals and tools (similar to what Aksum would subsequently export and import).

Apart from the trade links, there were also cultural similarities between D'MT and the South Arabian Kingdom of Saba (Yemen). Incidentally, it is believed that this Kingdom of Saba is the same "Kingdom of Sheba", mentioned in both the Hebrew Bible and the Quran. We can see these similarities from the architectural styles, imagery, inscriptions and more. For instance, one of the religious symbols extensively used by D'MT is the crescent-and-disc — a symbol also used in Yemen. While there were Sabaean cultural influences, the people of D'MT would have already developed their own cultural identities, on top of which Sabaean ideas were "Africanized".

A proposed location for the capital of DM'T is at Yeha. Here you can find the oldest standing building in Ethiopia, dating to approximately 700 BCE. This temple was dedicated to the deity Almaqah — the moon god (also worshipped in Yemen). Although old, it is still remarkably well preserved. The temple once had two floors, and was constructed on top of a hill — expertly designed and built with sound engineering practices. It is rectangular in shape, around 18 x 15 meters, and it is built of large, very-well dressed, blocks of limestone. Even after the disappearance of D'MT, the temple would continue to be used as a religious site, precisely as a monastery (by Ethiopian Christians).

The limestone used to construct the Great Temple at Yeha likely came from a place called Wuqro (to the south of Yeha). Here, specifically at a village called Meqaber Ga'ewa, a completely preserved carved stone altar has been discovered. Made of limestone, the altar is superbly decorated, and its design suggests that it may have been used to offer animal sacrifices (to the god Almaqah). This altar sat in the center of what was undoubtedly another temple of the Pre-Aksum era — with its unique layout and number of religious objects recovered. An example of such religious object is the ceramic incense-burner. This incense-burner suggests the use of aromatics in worshipping the gods (just like the Egyptians).

Inscriptions (written in Sabaean or Sabaic) found at Meqaber Ga'ewa refer to a king (Wa'ran) and both his father (Radi'um) and mother (Shakkatum). The reference to the king's mother is noteworthy, as it demonstrates the importance of women in the society. The prominence of women in African politics is also something that we see with the Kushites of Nubia, which again suggests links between the Nile Valley and the Ethiopian Highlands.

Using religious evidence as an argument, among other things, some scholars have argued that the Sabaeans may have crossed the Red Sea, and founded the D'MT civilization. This was in line with the old way of thinking about African civilizations, where most things or "advances" would be credited to external (non-African) influences. Nowadays, the purely African origins of D'MT are more widely accepted, with some scholars viewing it as an indirect predecessor to the Kingdom of Aksum. It has been suggested that South Arabian immigrants simply settled in D'MT to work, in a similar fashion to how the Hyksos came to live in the Nile Delta, or the way Nubians lived peacefully in parts of the Egyptian heartland. Alternatively, the Sabaeans may have established a presence in D'MT, precisely to develop and maintain trading links across the Red Sea i.e. they were primarily merchants.

As to what eventually happened to the Kingdom of D'MT — there is no consensus among historians. There is very little evidence, archaeologically or literary, for the time of D'MT's decline or in the subsequent years preceding the coming of Aksum. Some historians believe that the kingdom may have gradually declined and ended, before the Kingdom of Aksum emerged. Like stated previously, others believe that D'MT indirectly developed into the Aksumite kingdom. Lastly, some argue that Aksum rose independently — going on to conquer D'MT itself.

If we assume that D'MT was considerably centralized, then perhaps the former argument makes sense — a period of decline which led to less centralized control. This would mean that the land came to be dominated by an unknown number of successor chiefdoms or polities. Perhaps one of these successor polities was Aksum, who went on to expand their territory and found a new capital at "Aksum".

This new state of Aksum, named after its capital, had another important city under its control. This was the port city of Adulis (Eritrea). Due to its position, off the coast of the Red Sea, Adulis grew very wealthy — in a similar way to the city of Carthage (in the Mediterranean). Ships coming from India, via Arabia, could stop at the port of Adulis — bringing in valuable goods (cotton, silk and spices of the East). They could then go on to pick up valuable African luxuries — exporting them to Arabia, India and beyond. The city of Aksum itself could be considered as somewhat of an inland port — at the crossroads of many trade routes from interior Africa. Goods arriving at Aksum would then be sent to Adulis for export.

The Aksumite kingdom would later go on to mint its own coins, with such coins being subsequently found in foreign lands (like India), demonstrating how interconnected Aksum was with the long-distance — Africa-Arabia-Asia trade network. The kingdom is also famous for converting to Christianity, relatively early on, when King Ezana made Christianity the state religion (4th century CE). A *Ge'ez* script, had already been developed by then, and was soon used to translate the Bible. Ge'ez, a Semitic language, is partially related to modern Ethiopian and Eritrean languages — Tigrinya and Tigre. It was the same King Ezana that led Akusmite armies into Nubia — the end-result of which was the fall of the Kingdom of Meroe (although some scholars believe it was not a militaristic takeover per say). As mentioned before, by this time, Aksum was already regarded as one of the four great powers of the time (along with the Romans, Persians and Chinese).

15. Middle Niger River — Sudanic empires and Tichitt civilization

As discussed earlier, apart from the river Nile, the river Niger is also one of Africa's great rivers. From the start of the Iron Age (c. 1000 BCE), and well into the first millennium CE, the "Middle Niger" region (including the Inland Niger Delta) was home to a number of urban communities — each characterized by its individual craft and productive capacities. Some of these communities grew to become very large — and in the process went on to stamp their names in history.

Map 18. River Niger. Source: Wikimedia Commons/CC BY-SA 3.0 (Author: author of Niger_river_map.PNG, derivative work: Wizardist (talk)).

And so we have historic cities such as Gao, Jenne-Jeno and Timbuktu. These cities were all part of the so-called "Sudanic Empires" — centered on the Middle Niger River. To be more precise, that is the empires of Ghana, Mali and Songhai. Ghana (also known as Wagadou) flourished from c. 300–1100 CE, Mali c. 1230–1670 CE and Songhai c. 1460–1591 CE. These Sudanic states developed extensive commercial ties, as exampled by the famous Trans-Saharan trade network. Without these states, this trade network would likely have not been possible, as only such organized states could handle the purchase, transport and exchange of commodities — from interior Africa to the Mediterranean (on such a large scale).

West African gold was the main commodity sought, from this Saharan trading network, demand for which would rise with the increased need for minted coins — by the end of the Ancient era (c. 500 CE). These kingdoms were written about, in quite some detail, by Islamic travelers and geographers. As a result, these states would go on to adopt Arabic and Ajami (Arabic alphabet for writing African languages), as a means of record keeping.

The story of how these empires were formed is a familiar one, familiar in the sense that the same climatic changes that forced (or encouraged) some Africans to settle the Nile Valley — are what forced others to settle the Middle Niger and its floodplains. These climatic conditions were of course, related to the drying of the Sahara.

Scholars often see the drying of the Sahara as a gradual event that "forced" people to move. However, we can also think of it in other ways. Drier climatic conditions would have in fact opened up new lands for people to exploit, ones that had been previously inaccessible. For example, bush and woodland would have retreated, becoming grassland, which is more suitable for grazing and cultivating savanna crops. This same phenomenon may have also opened up a passage, through the Congo rainforest, enabling the proposed "Bantu Migration" (from Western to Southern Africa).

Although there were prior settlements in the Middle Niger region, a major influx of people was experienced between c. 300 BCE and 200 CE. This influx corresponded with a further sharp decline in rainfall in Saharan West Africa. Despite being located in a relatively hot and dry region, the Middle Niger was still able to support large populations. One of the reasons it was able to do so, was the nature of the river itself.

The Niger's source is in the Guinea Highlands (modern Guinea), from where it runs a crescent shape, reaching its northernmost point in and around Timbuktu (modern Mali), before making its way to the Niger Delta (modern Nigeria). This means that large amounts of water (from the high rainfall areas of the Upper Niger) flow to the Middle Niger area (yearly). And like with the Nile, huge amounts of fertile silt come with it. Unsurprisingly, this made the Middle Niger a great place for agriculture — be it crop cultivation, raising livestock or fishing.

One of the first cities that developed, as a result of this agricultural potential and the subsequent beginnings of sedentary life, was Jenne-Jeno (Old Jenne) — permanently settled in around 250 BCE. The productive capacity of the Jenne-Jeno floodplains allowed it to export its agricultural surpluses to other nearby regions — that is the export of products like rice and fish. In exchange, for resources that was scarce on the floodplains such as iron, salt and stone.

This exchange network relates to the idea of specialized towns or manufacturing hubs, appearing across large parts of West Africa by the early first millennium BCE. Scholars, like Christopher Ehret, have termed this phenomenon the "West African Commercial Revolution". And as alluded to earlier, many of these towns exported their products beyond Africa itself (to the Mediterranean and further afield) — with the help of merchants and trading civilizations like the Carthaginians and Garamantes.

The key thing to understand, with this commercial revolution, is that it materialized due to people being able to specialize in non-food generating activities — instead relying on others to produce the food for them. And having it distributed, by boat and donkey, to the regions in need e.g. Saharan salt and copper mining centers, as well as Saharan oasis towns.

Moreover, the development of relatively large cities, like Jenne-Jeno (and subsequently of such like Gao and Timbuktu), was the culmination of centuries of prior agricultural and trading developments. In other words, the emergence of these cities (and the Sahelian kingdoms to which they were a part) came about due to trade being conducted on an ever increasingly large scale — helped by the consolidation of both political and economic power, the increased global demand for African goods, the introduction of the camel — as well as an influx of people from other parts of Africa, the Arab world and beyond.

And to stress again, this means that the history of towns and long-distance trade in West Africa (as in other parts of the continent) goes back to well before the arrival of Islam. The expansion of the Trans-Saharan trade network, with the coming of Islam, was only possible because these trade networks were already in place — trade networks that were controlled by already highly organized African societies.

Going back to the first cities, archaeological work has also been carried out at sites like Dia Shoma, which is much older than the better known Jenne-Jeno (and Timbuktu) — dating to c. 900 BCE. Dia itself is said to have been settled by peoples associated with the "Tichitt" ceramic tradition.

Tichitt civililzation

For those looking for some of the oldest villages and settlements in West Africa, they can be found at the archaeological sites of Dhar Tichitt in Southern Mauritania (near the border with Mali). Here you can find evidence of stone architecture and storage facilities (granaries) — with some being built almost 4000 years ago. To put that in some context, c. 2000 BCE corresponds with the start of Ancient Egypt's so-called Middle Kingdom.

The origin of these Tichitt villagers is not so clear. As there are no written texts, we simply have to rely on archaeology — to draw conclusions. Before the beginning of Tichitt culture, the region would have already been somewhat populated, but not on a permanent basis. Instead you would have had mobile groups of herders, hunter-gatherers and fishermen. A sort of "pre-Tichitt" phase if you like. This was much like the rest of the Sahara (in the same time period).

We know that there was a gradual decrease in surface water (lakes) in the wider area from around 4000 BCE. With this decrease in water supply, also came a decrease in wild grains. From science, we also know that Dhar Tichitt received more rainfall then — than it does today. Accordingly, Tichitt would probably have acted as some sort of sanctuary or haven — away from the harsher conditions in the Sahara. Thus, by c. 1900 BCE, a more settled culture had developed in the area — one which cultivated pearl millet. Incidentally, this is not the earliest record we have for domesticated pearl millet, that record goes to a site around 1000 km east of Tichitt, in the Lower Tilemsi Valley (Mali) — dating to c. 4500 BP.

Pearl millet is very well adapted to growing in harsh conditions — such as drought, poor soil fertility, and high temperatures. These are conditions under which other crops would not be able to survive e.g. barley, wheat etc. Therefore it is in the Sahel, where you had such conditions, that pearl millet was domesticated. Even today millet remains an important crop in the Sahelian region. For instance, it forms part of a popular beverage called *fura* in Hausa language (Niger/Nigeria).

A four tier administrative/settlement hierarchy, for Dhar Tichitt itself, has been proposed — consisting of hamlets, villages, district centers and regional centers — with there being a flow of tribute and prestige goods between them. Such hierarchy may form the basis of a fairly credible argument — that there was some form of political centralization in Tichitt culture. Having said this, there appears to be little material evidence for "extreme" social differentiation or inequality i.e. Tichitt having an elite ruling class (like seen in early Nubia and Egypt). This suggests that Tichitt relied on a more cooperative form of social organization.

Once initially settled at Tichitt, settlements quickly expanded to Dhar Walata, and even as far as Dhar Tagant and Dhar Nema, all of which sit in Mauritania — along escarpments i.e. on top of long cliffs. Below these cliffs is the "Hodh depression", which used to host the various lakes that aided the permanent settlement of the area. Despite these other settlements, the Dhar Tichitt escarpment appears to have played a particularly important role ideologically and in ritual life — seeing as the vast majority of burial mounds are located here.

The many hundred Tichitt settlements all show clear signs of economic and spatial (site layout) differentiation, according to their settlement rank (regional center, district center, village or hamlet). Likewise the compounds within each settlement were organized, with space being allocated for both private (e.g. residential units) and public use (e.g. streets, alleyways, squares, livestock pens, tombs, watchtowers etc.). These compounds varied in size, according to their function. Many of such operated as workshops, that produced a variety of goods i.e. you had craft specialization. There were workshops to produce stone tools (e.g. scrapers), arrows, quartz beads, grindstones and more.

Around the start of the first millennium BCE, probably in conjunction with further Saharan environmental degradation, Tichitt sites became smaller as people began to permanently settle in the Mema region of Mali (just over the border). Prior to this permanent settlement, there would have likely already been some form of Tichitt seasonal pastoral presence in the Middle Niger — especially in the dry season. At the Mema floodplains, the people from Tichitt interacted with another group of people, with contrasting material culture (pottery), who earlier appeared to occupy the area much more intensively.

From the evidence at hand, this other group relied mostly on fishing and hunting — with much aquatic remains appearing in the archaeological record. Accordingly, some have suggested that there may indeed have been an early exchange network at play — with perhaps fish being exchanged for grain, rare stones or even cattle. It is thought that these same populations may have contributed to the rise of the Ghana Empire, a few centuries later — with many of the Tichitt organizational systems or traditions being seemingly "inherited" or advanced upon. Of course, this Ghana Empire was positioned in the Mauritania/Mali area — and not where the modern country of Ghana sits.

As stated earlier, one of the subsequent urban centers that developed, dating to c. 900 BCE, is found at Dia Shoma. Here, archaeologists have found various Tichitt ceramics, suggesting that the Tichitt "diaspora" are likely to have participated in its development. Therefore, scholars have been able to argue continuity — between Dhar Tichitt and the civilizations that would develop in the Middle Niger region (like the Ghana and Mali kingdoms). Having said this, much more archaeological work is required, to get a clearer picture of the West African Sahel and Sahara, in the first millennium BCE.

Dia Shoma itself reached the height of its urban development much later (late in the first millennium CE). And so by then, the principal settlement had more than doubled, from an original 20 hectares or so. Of course, there were also many satellite settlements — linked to Dia. Research also suggests that there was a "mixed" group of Africans living in the area (at its zenith). This is rather unsurprising, as people probably flocked to the town from across a wider part of West Africa — perhaps looking for work opportunities, and/or in line with the growing idea of territorial boundaries.

16. Nok culture of Nigeria

As you may have already noticed by now, in the absence of written records, archaeology is the main source of information on early African cultures. In relation to this, and throughout this book, I have mentioned pottery as a key source of archaeological evidence. Other important archaeological artifacts include charcoal and slag (byproducts of smelting metal). Dating such artifacts enables scholars to paint a picture of life in early West Africa — with one of the earliest known societies being the so-called "Nok culture".

The Nok culture, with its sites scattered across Central/Northern Nigeria is among the earliest centers of fairly organized African society — one with a tradition for sculptures. These sculptures are some of the oldest artistic representations of humans — in the whole of Africa. With Nok, one can also find evidence of early African metalworking — in the form of iron implements (tools). Nok's cultural development began around 1500 BCE, extending to the beginning of the Common Era.

Both the sculptures and iron implements can be found in areas just north of the Niger and Benue River confluence. Examples of Nok villages include the village of Nok itself, and other centers like Kachia, Kafanchan, Shere and Wamba. At these different locations, objects and figurines that resemble those discovered at Nok, in the 1940s, have been found. It is for such reasons that all subsequent finds, are seen as belonging to Nok culture or Nok civilization. This Nok cultural sphere covers an area of up to 70,000 square kilometers — an area larger than modern Togo.

The first figurines date back to the early first millennium BCE. And this is when the "main" cultural phase began, lasting until c. 400 BCE, during which iron production also commenced. Prior to this main cultural period, there was an "early" phase of Nok culture — without figurines. In this early phase, it was similar pottery styles and continuous occupation of certain sites, which underpinned the Nok culture. The "late" cultural phase is marked by a sharp decrease in actual Nok sites, up until the early centuries CE — when the material culture appears to change completely.

Despite similarities in material culture, it is important to remember that Nok civilization may not necessarily represent one particular group of people, as is often implied i.e. there may have been no concept of "Nokness" as there was of "Egyptianess". Instead, it is possible that Nok material culture and artwork simply represented artistic styles, which came to be adopted by several somewhat distinct iron-using West African communities — all of who had their own unique cultural traits. We cannot confirm either way, as we have no written records to go on — like we do have with say the Egyptians or Carthaginians.

Economy and art

The earliest evidence for iron use in Nigeria can be found a few hundred kilometers south west of Nok, at a place called Taruga. Excavations carried out in the region; prove that smelting took place here. Archaeological finds include charcoal, iron slag, and wrought iron — as well as some domestic pottery and figurines. With regards to the ironworking, dates go as far back as c. 500 BCE. As this find is one of the earliest known ironworking sites in Nigeria, it is possible that knowledge of iron metallurgy may have spread from Taruga, to other parts of the country, and beyond. This links back to the earlier discussion on the origins of iron metallurgy in Africa.

Iron implements such as arrow points, axes, hoes, knives, spears and swords — in general — were much more effective than stone and wooden tools. They enabled improvements in the efficiency of hunting and warfare, made it easier to clear forests and made agricultural land preparation less time consuming — with the end-result being an increase in food supplies and thus population levels.

And as previously touched on, iron deposits were fairly accessible — being distributed widely across West Africa. Wood, in the more forested regions, was also abundant — with it of course being used to produce the charcoal that fueled the metal-producing furnaces. Predictably, well-wooded areas with large reserves of iron ore later became mining villages and centers for iron production — supplying the wider area with this key metal. For instance, we go on to see such villages spring up in and around Oyo (South West Nigeria). This all helps to explain the rise of some of the West African kingdoms of the first and second millennium CE.

The artifacts found at Taruga suggest that as well as being able to smelt iron, Nok people planted some crops (pearl millet, cowpea etc.). Evidence for meat processing, in the form of animal bones, and whether or not the Noks kept domesticated animals is generally lacking — primarily due to the acidic soils of Central Nigeria not preserving organic matter well. This led to a chemical study; to determine what exactly Nok pottery was used to do — be it cooking, storage or other things. Results from the chemical analysis reveal that some pots were used to process or store beeswax — suggesting that Nok people exploited honey.

The exploitation of beeswax/honey itself is not really surprising, given the fact that rock art depicting bees, honeycombs, and honey-collecting, goes back over 40,000 BP — to Didima Gorge in Namibia. It's more that evidence of honey-related activity is largely invisible to the archaeological record.

Beeswax has multiple uses, one of which is as an adhesive (glue), with evidence for this also stretching back 40,000 BP to Border Cave, South Africa — where it was used to haft a bone point. Honey of course also had and still has many uses in Africa — sweetener, food source, beverage making and medicinal purposes. As for the meat eating habits of the Nok, if they did eat much meat at all, researchers are still unsure of this (although the honey could have been used to help preserve meat for extended periods of time).

The clay sculptures that they made, indicates that the people of Nok took to fashion — wearing beads, bracelets and nose rings. These sculptures were of high-quality, which shows us that the Nok were master artisans — with a flair for style. The smooth surfaces that once finished these figurines have all but worn off, leaving behind a coarsely grained underlayer. Most of the figurines have missing parts, which is unsurprising, given that some were made close to 3000 years ago. The fact that some of the sculptures have lasted so long, in good condition, is proof of high-quality craftsmanship.

In terms of the production process, the sculptures were handmade, from coarse-grinded clay. Many Nok pieces were formed by the "subtractive" technique i.e. material was removed to form the final shape. This suggests that sculpting techniques may have been influenced by prior wood carving. After drying, the clay would have been covered with slip (a mixture of clay and water) and polished, to give a smooth glossy finish.

*Figure 14. Nok sculpture, Louvre Museum. Source: Wikimedia
Commons/CC BY-SA 3.0 (Author: Ji-Elle).*

The artifacts made were hollow, with several aesthetic openings
(eyes, mouth, nostrils and earholes), which aided in both the drying and
firing process. This firing process was likely similar to what is
traditionally done in Nigeria today. To explain, firing would have taken
place on the ground (flat or slight depression). The pieces would have
been covered with twigs, grass, leaves and other organic matter —
before being burned in a controlled manner.

The Noks produced a variety of figurines. Some were naturalistic,
while others were more creative in nature. Figures were even made of
people with illnesses — such as elephantiasis (severely swollen limbs),
which suggests disease may have been common at the time. As they

were made of terracotta (baked clay), the figurines tend to be a brownish orange color. Sculptures of both people and animals were made — that were near "life-sized" (though much smaller ones were equally produced).

The classic Nok look was more of an "elongated" figurine, with heads that tended to be disproportionally large (compared to the rest of the body). This emphasis on the "head" is something we see throughout the art of some later African peoples — where it is said to often signify respect for intelligence. Apart from this, another notable feature in most figurines is the semi-circular or triangular shape of the "bulging" eyes. The hands or the chin would often be placed on the knees, with some sculptures. Despite sharing common features, almost every carving was individualized (at least to some degree).

Scholars know very little about the functions of these sculptures. Things are not helped by the fact that many Nok terracotta, have been looted from their original sites (Nok figurines are very valuable). A number of theories have been made, as to the purpose of the Nok sculptures — like they portrayed the ancestors or that they were simply deities to be worshipped (rituals). Others suggest that they may have been grave markers. And another popular opinion is that the sculptures could have functioned as charms — used to prevent crop failure, illness and/or infertility.

Origins and legacy

Despite the knowledge obtained through studying Nok ceramics, many details of Nok culture, society, social organization and origins are unknown. And so for example, did the Nok migrate to Nigeria? Or have they always been there?

A lack of early evidence for permanent settlement, going back more than c. 3500 BP, suggests that Nok culture may have arisen as a result of migration. This migration may have involved people with pearl millet as a staple food, coming from upstream river Niger, in and around the Tichitt cultural area (as discussed earlier). A migration from the east is also possible, as too is the theory that Nok was an indigenous culture that arose independently. As of today, there's no concrete proof either way.

A quick discussion, on the possible eastern origins of Nok civilization is in order. Some art historians have argued that the Nok sculptures are remarkably similar (in style) to artwork produced in the Nile Valley. This could be as a result of some sort of migration, subsequent to the Egyptian New Kingdom, or it could be that the artistic styles were more of a Sahara-wide convention — that was spread and linked through ancient trade routes.

As a matter of fact, some scholars have even suggested that copper and tin were exported, from the Nok cultural area, to the Nile Valley (from the 2nd millennium BCE). Ancient Egyptian trade routes to the oases of the Western Desert are already well documented. And ones that go even further, to the vicinity of the Niger River bend, have been suggested (going back to the section on the Garamantes, and the desert trail described by Herodotus). Therefore the question is — how far south did these routes go from here?

It should be noted that trade routes that did not go directly through the Sahara are also a possibility. The Middle or Nubian Nile Valley could have been reached, from Northern Nigeria, via the Lake Chad Basin and the Darfur region of Sudan. This route could have been travelled both overland and by river. To further this point, another tributary of the Nile, the Yellow Nile, ran from the Ennedi Plateau (Eastern Chad) through Darfur and on to the vicinity of Kerma (Nubia).

Incidentally, this Ennedi Plateau is another significant Saharan rock art location — with cattle extensively portrayed in the paintings. The Yellow Nile River had mostly become dry by the start of the first millennium BCE, with its remnants being known as the *Wadi Howar*. Undoubtedly, the death of this Yellow Nile River led to the dispersal of several groups of Africans — who so depended on it (Nilo-Saharan speakers and perhaps Nok people?).

Like their origins, what eventually happened to Nok civilization is also up for speculation. We do know that there was a sharp decline in the amount of pottery produced by the final century BCE. Subsequent to this decline was the disappearance of Nok cultural markers, and the appearance of seemingly unrelated ones. Put differently, new ceramics appear, very different in style and decoration to the Nok ones. In addition, Nok figurines are no more, and there seems to be a greater variety of agricultural products produced (e.g. with the addition of fonio and oil palm). This all indicates a cultural change, marking the end of Nok civilization by the early first millennium CE. Climate change, overexploitation of resources, in-fighting or the coming of rival kingdoms — are all valid theories for Nok cultural decline. Perhaps it was a combination of all such reasons?

Having said this, it is evident from figurine dress and hair styles, that Nok culture somewhat influenced the people that live in the Nok cultural area today. For evidence of this, one can look to modern

Nigerian states like Benue, Kaduna and Plateau — among peoples like the Tiv and Ham. Further, several of the distinctive features of Nok artwork can be linked to the art produced in other parts of Nigeria (at later dates). For instance, art of the Yoruba Kingdom of Ife.

Apart from a material culture influence, Nok perhaps also had a wider social organizational influence. It was a few centuries after the apparent disappearance of Nok culture, that you had the emergence of various other organized societies (in Nigeria specifically). Like seen with the empires of the Middle Niger River, these societies did not develop overnight — instead they were the results of prior social and economic developments. And so, even if Nok did not directly lead to cultures like Ife and Igbo-Ukwu, perhaps it laid the foundations for their development?

After all, it is with Nok that we get relatively high site densities, sophisticated artwork, productive agricultural systems/economies, and ironworking — with the latter three especially linking to the idea of specialization and trade (arguably the things that form the backbone of civilizations/states).

Linked to this idea of trade is the River Niger, with there being ample evidence for interregional trade between the Middle Niger (Mali) and the Lower Niger (Nigeria). Case in point, the trade links that would later develop between Gao and Igbo-Ukwu (South East Nigeria). What is more, some of the material unearthed (beads) at Igbo-Ukwu appears to ultimately have Mediterranean origins — again demonstrating the extent to which trade links would develop across large parts of Africa.

Despite this idea of Nok being a potential "foundational" culture, it should be noted that there is little evidence for much Nok social complexity — not when compared to Tichitt settlements, or the early societies that emerged in the Lake Chad Basin. For example, if we take social complexity in terms of settlement size — there are few Nok sites that rise above village level. That is to say, though there are plenty of settlements, none of them are what you can (individually) consider dense or urban in nature. And so likely did not require the development of social stratification i.e. a ruling elite. In essence, Nok communities were small-scaled and probably organized on a local level — with some links to other nearby communities. These links were particularly strong and complex in relation to ideological and religious beliefs — as shown by the wide extent of Nok terracotta.

Such community links did not develop in a way that ended with Nok social inequality or a hierarchy (that can be clearly determined from current archaeological data). Perhaps the reason that this did not occur with Nok, like it did with Kush or D'MT, might relate to the fact that Nok culture sat (at the time anyway) in a less favorable mid-long distance trading position (few connected rivers, low population levels etc.) — from where vast wealth could be accumulated? In short, the Nok area was not or did not host a center of trade. Be that as it may, it is just as likely that Nok social inequality may simply have been displayed in ways that differed from other early African societies.

17. Lake Mega-Chad, Chadic societies and the Sao civilization

A way to understand how mobile cattle herding, in the Sahara, gave way to farming and more settled societies, is to study the history of Lake Chad. Lake Chad sits between the modern countries of Cameroon, Chad, Niger and Nigeria. Although now a shadow of its former self, in terms of size, Lake Chad was once the largest lake in the world, similar in size to today's Caspian Sea. And so scientists have coined the term "Lake Mega-Chad", in reference to what it once was, when the Sahara was green and lush.

In terms of numbers, Lake Mega-Chad spread over 350,000 square kilometers, c. 6500 BP (towards the end of the African Humid Period). This can be compared to Lake Chad's surface area shrinking from around 25,000 square kilometers in the 1960s, to less than 2000 square kilometers in the 1980s — a reduction of over 90%. Today, thanks to slightly more favorable rainfall in the Sahel, the surface water area has increased to around 14,000 square kilometers. Having said this, the size of the lake does still fluctuate significantly, primarily in relation to the wet and dry seasons.

Despite some "natural" revitalization, there are calls for human input. This could be done through the construction of a series of dams and canals, from tributaries of the river Congo — to the Chari River. This Chari River flows from the Central African Republic, through Chad, and then on into the lake.

Dufuna Canoe — the oldest surviving boat in Africa

Going back to the African Humid Period, Lake Chad then could be described as somewhat of a vast "inland sea", in the heart of the Sahara or Central North Africa. And so, the earliest archaeological evidence that we have of such large body of water, is the Dufuna Canoe. This canoe dates to around 6500 BCE, and was likely used for intensive fishing and trading activities.

The boat is named as such, because it was discovered in a small village (Dufuna) on the Komadugu Gana or Misau River (a tributary of Lake Chad), in what is today's Yobe State (Northern Nigeria). What is remarkable about this discovery was the fact that the boat was well-preserved — missing only a few fragments. As for its size, it was 8.4 m in length, with a height of 0.5 m. The ends of the boat were rather pointed, given it a noticeably stylish appearance. The boat was deliberately made from African mahogany, using highly specialized tools, as mahogany keeps especially well under water.

The elegance in design suggests that this find was not the beginnings of a water-transportation tradition or culture; rather it was a subsequent development from much earlier traditions. That is to say, the actual origins of water transportation, in Africa, go back much further in time. This is backed up by the fact that the oldest boat in the world, the "Pesse Canoe", discovered in the Netherlands, is much smaller and less sophisticated in design. This again demonstrates ways in which the cultural history and evolution of early African "tech" developed on its own, without Near Eastern or other external influences.

In addition, this begs the question, how exactly did these Africans carve out this sophisticated canoe? Remember this was supposedly a time (c. 8000 BP) well before the advent of metalworking. It is questions like this that highlight how little we do know about the ancient past. All we can say for sure is that its production must be credited to skilled specialists, and involved a considerable number of man hours.

Dufuna would have only been a few kilometers from the shorelines of the Lake Mega-Chad. The floodplains of Dufuna may even have been permanently flooded. Either way, what you would have had in the area, is an abundance of fish. And so there was likely, what you could call, a "mini" fishing and shipping industry (in this part of Africa). This was an industry that allowed people to exploit the rich aquatic resources of Lake Chad, and its connecting rivers.

It should also be mentioned that a terracotta model of a dugout canoe has recently been recovered in the Nok cultural area. This model appears to show two people on board a watercraft — accompanied by cargo. Although it is only a model, that is younger in date than the

Dufuna Canoe, it too is evidence for both an extensive shipping industry and related trading networks being in place (in wider West Africa).

Moving towards the Common Era and with the increase in population and subsequent trading activities, even longer boats would have been required — to efficiently transport cargo from region to region. The size of a dugout boat is only limited by the actual size of the tree from which it is carved. As noted by early Portuguese explorers like Pacheco Pereira, some of the longest canoes (globally) could be found in West Africa — thanks to the particularly long trees of the continent's tropical forests.

Rise of complex societies in the Lake Chad Basin

From available archaeological and geological data, the Lake Chad Basin appears to have been unoccupied (by humans) towards the start of the Holocene. This was because the Sahara was in a hyper-arid phase — with the desert being much larger than it is today. Accordingly, lakes and rivers (Lake Chad, Lake Victoria, White Nile etc.) were either dry or at very low levels. Hence the history of the most recent period of human activity, in the Lake Chad area, only goes back to the early Holocene or African Humid Period. During this hyper-arid phase, humans would have been living in what are termed "environmental refugia" i.e. areas that were still able to sustain life in the face of unfavorable climatic conditions (in the wider region).

Multiple waves of migrations to the Lake Chad Basin, in the last 12,000 years, has resulted in considerable linguistic diversity — with speakers of the main three African language families being in close proximity to each other (Nilo-Saharan, Afroasiatic and Niger-Congo). The idea of Nilo-Saharan speakers expanding westward (from the Nile Valley area) towards the Lake Chad Basin (and the Middle Niger bend/river), in line with the greening of the Sahara (start of the African Humid Period) is quite well accepted (and links to the idea of the aquatic civilization discussed later). Yet, the case of how the Chadic (Afroasiatic) languages later got to the same Lake Chad Basin is debated.

This debate links to the already highlighted issues with identifying the Proto-Afroasiatic homeland. If Chadic is most closely related to Berber, then its origins would lie to the north of Lake Chad (in the Sahara), and we would be looking at a North-South movement of Chadic speakers. However, if Chadic is most closely related to Cushitic, then this would simply imply an East-West movement (along the Yellow Nile or Wadi Howar). There is genetic evidence for both such Chadic migrations, North-South and East-West, with the North-South movement also being applicable when taking into account a possible Levantine origin for Proto-Afroasiatic (rather than the North East African one assumed here). But, there is little archaeological evidence, south of Lake Chad, for the early interactions that took place between ancestral Chadic and Nilo-Saharan speakers. The Dufuna canoe is pretty much the earliest archaeological evidence we have (which can indicate possible ways of life).

Nonetheless, before there was intensive food production, there was a pottery phase in the Chad Basin. Pottery unearthed at Konduga, which sits on the Bama Ridge (North Eastern Nigeria), is dated to around 5500 BCE — that is 1000 years after Dufuna. The Bama Ridge itself represents the shoreline of the former Lake Mega-Chad. Konduga pottery is decorated in a manner that is very similar to pottery found in parts of the Sahara (in the same time period). No animal bones were found at the site, and so scholars are not sure on the actual workings of the Konduga economy. All the same, the position of Konduga on the ridge, up to 12 meters in height, suggests that the ridge may have functioned as a "land bridge" — which gave access to the wider lake bed area.

A little over 80 km north west of Konduga, and south west of Lake Chad itself, is Gajiganna. Although we first find pottery at Konduga, it is Gajiganna that provides a much clearer picture of early settlement in and around the Lake Chad Basin. Having said this, the site is much younger — dating from c. 3700–2800 BP.

The settling of Gajiganna corresponded with falls in the water levels of Lake Chad. This allowed previously submerged areas to be settled. Thus these settlers brought domesticated animals and built villages in the area. Fish was an important part of the Gajiganna diet, as too were water birds and mollusks. Although they hunted wild animals, the majority of animal remains come from domesticated ones — cattle, goats and sheep. Wild seeds were also gathered, and the villagers eventually started cultivating pearl millet.

In terms of artifacts, pottery was by far the most plentiful. This pottery was finely finished — painted and then decorated with mat and comb impressions. The lack of stone, in and around Gajiganna, meant that it had to be imported from elsewhere — from places like the Mandara-Mora mountain range to the south. And so you had some, but relatively few stone artifacts like flaked arrowheads (Saharan-type), grinding stones, ground axes and hammer stones — compensated for by the extensive use of bone as a material (as exampled by barbed harpoons). Incidentally, this lack of stone indicates that early trade networks must have been in place, to enable the importation of the much needed stone.

Various artworks were also unearthed, to be precise, clay-fired figurines. Like with the Nok culture, these figurines represent both humans and animals. And like with the Ancient Ona culture (Ethiopian or Eritrean Highlands); cattle seem to be well represented — again demonstrating the importance of such to early African economies. Although relatively simple in design, the figurines are among the earliest found in the wider area — appearing before the use of iron. The dead were buried either in the settlement or around it, seemingly without grave-goods.

As conditions grew drier and Lake Chad retreated further, Gajiganna was eventually abandoned — although other larger and fortified "Gajiganna cultural" settlements, like Zilum, did emerge in the vicinity (with fortifications probably signifying increased competition for resources and a general increase in population levels i.e. semi-urbanism). This can be compared with Nok cultural settlements, in the same first millennium BCE, which — as already gone over — do not appear to show the same evolution in social complexity. It should be mentioned that some scholars subscribe to the view that — significant migrations and/or intrusions (from the north and east) played a bigger role (than climate change) in this sudden rise of "Proto-Urban" settlements in the Chad Basin.

As is often the case, when one door closes another door opens. As a result of Lake Chad's continued retreat, another area became open to settlement, specifically the *firki* swamps directly south of Lake Chad (and to the east of the Gajiganna area). The firki would flood during the wet season, and because the clay tended to retain water for long — the plains were ideal for both animal husbandry and farming. Many firki settlement sites have been identified, stretching from North Eastern Nigeria to Northern Cameroon and South Western Chad. Accordingly, these settlement areas are also termed the "Chadian Plain".

The most well-known of these firki sites is Daima. Its period of settlement spans from around 1000 BCE to 1500 CE. The people of Daima lived a life and produced art that was very much similar to that at Gajiganna, and at other Chadian Plain settlements. Later, around 2000 years ago, iron was introduced. Glass and carnelian beads also start to appear, which demonstrate potential trading links with outsiders. Not before long, these Chadian Plain settlements had started to become more urban in nature. And thus some were likely linked together as small polities or chiefdoms.

Chadic polities and the Sao civilization

It is these Chadic polities that were initially grouped together, by some scholars, as the so-called "Sao civilization", beginning around 500 BCE, and lasting until c. 1800 CE. This was due to the fact that the polities were very similar, and spoke one form of "Chadic" language or another. They engaged in art and manufactured a range of items in brass, clay, copper and iron. And they also built fortified or walled cities. Hence they were labeled as a "civilization". Subsequent archaeological work has given us a clearer picture, and so this notion of the Sao civilization has generally been dropped — in favor of (Ancient) Chadic polities or chiefdoms.

This term "Sao", coined by a Bornu scholar in the 16th century, referred to the fact that the original settlers in the Lake Chad area (e.g. the Kotoko) were non-Kanuri (Nilo-Saharan) speaking. As the Kanem migrated and mixed with the Sao (or Chadic people), the "Kanuri" language developed. This Kanuri language (along with Teda/Tebu) was the principal language of first the Kanem Empire (c. 7th century) and then the Bornu Empire (c. 14th century) — both of which were centered on the Lake Chad. They were both engaged in Trans-Saharan trading, and so embraced Islam, with Kanem's control extending into the Fezzan (Libya). The Fezzan was of course, once home to the Garamantes (discussed earlier).

The coming of this Kanem Empire is also linked to the desiccation of the Sahara, with the migration of Nilo-Saharan speaking people to the south. This migration displaced some of the Chadic polities, while others were simply absorbed and "Kanurfied". Other polities were forced to pay tribute, while others resisted.

Although some archaeological work has been done to try and understand these polities, what we know for sure is still very limited. One of the Chadic polities studied in detail is the Houlouf chiefdom, centered on the Houlouf region, in the extreme north of Cameroon. Its roots go back over 4000 years, to around 1900 BCE. Houlouf was connected to long-distance trade networks, produced specialized crafts, and developed social stratification i.e. it had an elite class. The Houlouf chiefdom rose to prominence after defeating a rival polity in around 1400 CE. A few centuries later, in the face of pressure from the Bornu

Empire, the Houlouf chiefdom would itself fall to another competing kingdom (the Lagwan).

"Hausaland" in North Western Nigeria, also developed in a similar manner — with its group of large independent city-states. These Hausa city-states sat between the Western Sudanic kingdoms of Ancient Ghana and Mali, and the Eastern kingdom of Kanem-Bornu. The city of Kano became the most powerful of the Hausa city-states, as it was the southern end of a Trans-Saharan trade route.

18. Lake Turkana and the Aqualithic or Aquatic civilization

Lake Turkana, in earlier times known as Lake Rudolf, forms part of the eastern branch of the East African Rift Valley (discussed earlier). It can mostly be found in North Western Kenya, with a small part of its northern-end crossing the border with Ethiopia. Like Lake Chad, it too was a much bigger lake in the early African Humid Period. It was bigger in terms of both surface area and depth. Consequently, it overflowed and drained into the Nile River. More specifically, it drained north westward, into the Sobat River (South Sudan) — with the Sobat River being a tributary of the White Nile. Quite extensive archaeological work has been carried out in the area, the results of which have made Lake Turkana an important part of African prehistory.

Archaeological findings

A number of noteworthy discoveries have been made around Lake Turkana — the world's largest permanent desert lake. You have some of the oldest human like (evolutionary) fossils ever found, some of the oldest known stone artifacts, possibly the oldest human use of fire, and some of the oldest known anatomically modern human skulls ("Omo Skulls").

In terms of the early Holocene, we can look to the early archaeological site of Lothagam. Lothagam sits on the western side of Lake Turkana, and it is here that a major fishing site was discovered. Excavations produced barbed harpoon points, tools, pottery, fish bones and buried skeletons. In fact, Lothagam was found to be among the richest bone-artifact sites on the continent. Further work carried out at another site nearby, unearthed wavy-line pottery — dated to the 6th millennium BCE. So again you have another instance of pottery finds, in Africa, without any evidence of food production (just like Konduga near

Lake Chad). What is potentially more significant, howevι
line pottery — found not in North Africa but in East.
wavy-line pottery is clearly similar to that which has been
Nile Valley, and other parts of the Sahara.

The earliest remains of domesticated livestock found in Ł   ℓfrica,
is also at Turkana — dating to around 2000 BCE. Bones of both cattle
and goats were recovered at Dongodien. This date is slightly earlier
than that for the domesticated cattle remains of Gajiganna (Lake Chad).
It is worth mentioning that the evidence for this early domestic
livestock, at Dongodien, is associated with a new decorative style of
pottery — Nderit ware. This differs from the plain and wavy-line
pottery of earlier times. This could be due to population movement or
simply the diffusion of livestock and new ideas. Put differently, a change
in subsistence strategy from fishing/hunting to pastoralism — bringing
about a new pottery tradition.

The dating of these finds at Dongodien correspond with drops in the
water levels of Lake Turkana, which may have opened up new grazing
areas — free from the tsetse fly (which can kill cattle). This also links to
the idea of "tsetse-free" corridors, via which cattle could be moved from
the then drying Sahara (c. 5000 BP), to more southern parts of Africa.

Around Lake Turkana there are several different "megalithic" pillar
sites, some of which seemingly demonstrate a mortuary tradition. In
other words, some were used for burials. Perhaps they also served as
assembly points like Nabta Playa, west of the Nile Valley, where distant
and related groups would meet from time to time (for ceremonial
purposes, to share information and more generally to assist each other
— in times of environmental uncertainty). Either way, the construction
of such pillar sites begins by c. 5000 BP, the oldest and the largest of
which being the Jarigole and Lothagam North pillar sites.

A wide variety of material culture has been recovered from such
sites. For example at Jarigole you have Nderit pottery shreds, ostrich
eggshell beads, flaked stone tools, clay cattle figurines and more. Some
of the artifacts unearthed are exotic and have origins nearer the East
African coast, such as shell beads and amazonite bead pendants —
suggesting some form of trade network was in place. This is quite
significant, as these dates are well before the much better documented
Swahili city-states and the related international trading network — that
developed across the Indian Ocean (by the first millennium CE).

Finds at the Lothagam North pillar site are similar to finds at the
Jarigole pillar site and the Dongodien settlement site — with all three

being "early herding sites". In contrast, and as of yet, there are no clear connections to the other smaller pillar sites — which differ in both their organization and material culture i.e. the purpose of these sites likely differed. Alternatively, this could mean that these smaller pillar sites may have been constructed by a number of different groups, with perhaps different lifestyles.

The early herding or pastoralist culture later spreads southwards, along the eastern rift into the savanna plains of Serengeti (Tanzania) and beyond. The spread further south (than Serengeti) is delayed somewhat, perhaps due to either tsetse fly or the need for regional pastoral adaptions to take place.

The Aquatic civilization

At Turkana we have some of the same cultural adaptations as seen in the Sahara — cultural adaptations at a time, in the early Holocene, when rivers, lakes and marshes were much larger. These waterways were very much interconnected, and so would have encouraged travel (using boats) and trading networks to develop. Remember, that a canoe dated to approximately 8000 BP was recovered near Lake Chad in Nigeria, and in the same Lake Chad area (Konduga), shreds of pottery similar in design to other (early) Sahara (and Turkana) pottery, dates to a few centuries later — providing strong evidence for this interlinked "wet" Sahara (and Nile Valley region).

Map 19. Aquatic/Aqualithic cultural area, Sahara-Sahel-Nile c. 7000 BP. Source: "A Feat of Crowds", https://indo-european.eu/maps/eneolithic-early / CC BY 3.0.

Not only may have higher water levels encouraged communication between fairly distant groups, there would have also been an abundance of aquatic food supplies. So crocodiles, hippopotamus, turtles — plus several varieties of fish. This would have gone with the land animals hunted, and any plant resources gathered. The end result of all this would have been fairly secure and predictable sources of food, found across the Sahara and up the Nile — all the way to Lake Turkana. Thanks to these favorable conditions i.e. the greening of the Sahara, there was a demographic expansion in the region i.e. population levels grew.

This relatively stable way of life encouraged a degree of "cultural uniformity" across this Nile-Sahara-Sahel belt, from the beginning of the African Humid Period to c. 6000 BP. By around this time, the Sahara started to dry up again, and thus, agriculture became more widespread as populations moved towards the remaining river sources — the Nile, the Egyptians and Nubians — the Niger, Tichitt and Sudanic civilizations — the desert Oases, the Garamantes and Kanem-Bornu etc.

If we take the Nile for example, during this Saharan green phase, it would have been far too wet and unsafe for human occupation. And so, population levels would have been low, with people instead occupying the wider Sahara. The drying of the Sahara would have reduced the Nile's water levels, and enabled people to return to the Nile — where surface water was still sufficient for human occupation. Therefore, you have the subsequent development of pharaonic civilization by c. 3100 BCE.

With regards to this aquatic cultural grouping, those Africans that thrived in the Sahara's recent wet phase have been grouped together as the "Aqualithic" or the "Aquatic" civilization. Most of their (archaeological) sites, across the Sahara and up the Nile, seem to be on the banks of rivers or near other water sources. Some of these bodies of water are still there, for example Lake Chad and Lake Turkana, while others have long since dried up. Despite drying up, scientists are still able to somewhat accurately pinpoint the margins or shorelines of these lakes and rivers, by looking for things like diatomite (remains of aquatic organisms). And so at these scattered sites, archaeologists have found similar remains of fish and other aquatic fauna, tools like harpoons, fish-hooks and of course pottery.

There are also ethno-linguistic or language arguments in favor of this Aquatic civilization. John Sutton, an archaeologist, who first proposed "The Aquatic Civilization of Middle Africa", also argues for a linguistic relationship across this aqualithic region. If you look at the distribution of the proposed Nilo-Saharan language family, you may notice that it kind of matches up with that of the archaeological finds for this Aquatic civilization i.e. it matches the aquatic cultural area.

As a reminder, it was discussed earlier how the Nilo-Saharan speakers expanded westwards from their wet homeland, in the vicinity of the Nile Valley, to the wider green Sahara (and southwards towards the Great Lakes) — precisely to places such as the Lake Chad Basin and the Middle Niger River. They were able to do this as they were able to thrive in riverine or wet environments i.e. they were culturally adapted to do so (as just discussed). It is this expansion that has resulted in the current distribution of Nilo-Saharan speakers in Africa.

Despite some evidence, this potential Aqualithic civilization has been criticized. Some scholars see it as too "general" in nature, over such a large area, without many "specifics". Further, in terms of linguistics, and as already stated, the Nilo-Saharan language family itself is not accepted by all linguists.

As to what happened to this Aquatic civilization, with the drying of the Sahara, subsistence strategies had to be adapted — to cope with the new environmental conditions. Alternatively, as already gone over, one could move to the now limited areas where aquatic subsistence strategies could be continued e.g. the Nile (and with that you had increasing population density and then the coming of the pharaohs).

In terms of adaptation the main strategy was to embrace pastoralism — hence you had the aquatic way of life giving way to cattle herding and then subsequently crop cultivation. Pastoralism became so widespread across Africa, and so important to ways of life and to the economy, that cattle became a fundamental aspect of both early African artwork and religion. The importance of cattle has been demonstrated across the continent, from Ancient Nubian culture (Nabta Playa) in the north, to Ancient Ona culture in the east, and Gajiganna culture in the west.

Lake Turkana itself can be considered the perfect case study of how this shift in subsistence strategy took place, in the face of constantly changing environmental conditions. As highlighted, it is precisely at Lake Turkana that we see first, aquatic ways of life, then pastoralism, and then (presumably) the coming of disease-resistant cattle that enabled the pastoralists to move into newer areas — to the south of the continent (potentially in combination with newer ways of manipulating the environment — to limit infection). Remember, in these early times, there were no borders per say i.e. the pastoralists pretty much had "free rein". Therefore, wherever cattle could go — so too could people.

As a final point, it should be made clear that the aquatic way of life was not the only subsistence strategy at play (in African prehistory).

There were many other strategies, as touched on earlier (the section on Niger-Congo speakers), some primarily relied on hunting (using bow and arrow) large land animals (elephants, giraffes etc.) — of which there were plenty in the time of the Green Sahara. While others, living in relatively arid areas (away from rivers), took up cattle raising very early on c. 9000 BP (and subsequently raised sheep and goats), as exampled by Nabta Playa (also discussed earlier).

By the way, we see all three subsistence strategies mentioned here (fishing-hunting-agriculture), at play when we look at the rise of pharaonic Egypt. This demonstrates how employing a mix of different strategies, can lead to a degree of stability (in unstable climatic times).

Aqualithic evidence from Japan

This aquatic way of life forms the basis for an explanation as to why we see pottery in Africa, well before food production (specifically the intensive cultivation of crops). Put another way, why archaeologists find early pottery in Africa, without domesticated plant remains.

A recent study of Japanese pottery vessels provides further evidence for the use of pottery in conjunction with aquatic resources (rather than crops/grain). Incidentally, some Japanese pottery (Jomon culture) has been dated as far back as c. 12,000 BP, to the end of the last glacial period or last "ice age" — a time that coincides with both the early Holocene and African Humid Period.

The three year study concluded that the ceramic vessels were used by these Japanese "hunter-gatherers" to store and process fish. Initially it was fish like salmon, but later it expanded to shellfish, freshwater and marine fish and mammals (as the fishing got more intensive). Accordingly, with more intensive fishing you had more permanently settled populations. These results also demonstrate a strong and long cultural association between pottery production, and fish processing. This tradition allowed the Japanese to withstand changes in climate for thousands of years.

Remember, scholars have traditionally linked the rise in pottery, to the rise in agriculture — as was the case in the Middle East. This study provides the basis for an alternative theory in Africa, one in which pottery was invented to firstly store fish and easily abundant wild plant foods — before finding other uses (agriculture etc.). This is what can be termed the aquatic lifestyle, from which we get the so-called Aquatic civilization.

A study similar to this Japanese one (or the Nok culture one discussed earlier), concentrating purely on early Saharan pottery, would provide us with more answers and help us to better explain Saharan Africa, at the end of the last ice age — going into the early to mid-Holocene. Studies that also focus on the linguistic aspects of the Sahel/Sahara would also give us a much clearer picture, in particular, the relationship between Nilo-Saharan, Niger-Congo and Afroasiatic languages.

19. Food production and early Eastern, Central and Southern African societies

In order to fully understand the urban settlement patterns of early Africa, south of the equator, it is helpful to quickly go over exactly how the ideas of African food production (as a whole) came to be. Although scholars do not fully understand all aspects of early African agriculture, some parts of the continent are better understood than others. The northern half of Africa is particularly well understood, partly because of the drier conditions preserving artifacts and remains better, and partly because of the ancient texts that help support theories.

We know that pastoralism or herding developed first, in the Eastern Sahara, by at least c. 9000 BP. This pastoralist way of life then spread westwards — across the wider Sahara. Later and following on from this original domestication of cattle — crop cultivation (millet, African rice etc.) was also added to the mix from c. 4000 BP. Such "agro-pastoralism" can be exampled with Tichitt culture. These initial crops of the Sahel and Savanna were not suitable for West Africa's wetter regions i.e. the rainforest areas, and so different food production strategies were called for. Consequently, in these wetter regions, the local domestication of other key plants occurred including cowpea, oil palm and yam.

Similar to Sahelian West Africa, herding (in particular cattle) was practiced in North East Africa before crop cultivation, as seen in the Lake Turkana area of Kenya. The same is also true for the Ethiopian Highlands area, with sheep and goats being introduced here and to the wider Horn of Africa — from the north.

As mentioned before, the Ethiopian Highlands region was somewhat of a center for indigenous plant domestication, with locally domesticated plants including teff, enset and coffee. Imported crops include wheat and barley. Perhaps strangely, for a region that accommodates such a wide variety of crops, there is very limited actual direct evidence for the early cultivation of such — be it the locally domesticated crops or the "foreign" ones. This is likely due to limited archaeological research in the region, as domestication of (local) plants or crops would have taken a (very) long time. Further proof of this "strangeness" is several African crops appearing in the Indian archaeological record earlier than they do on the continent's i.e. the wild ancestors of these plants were only to be found in Africa, yet the earliest evidence of domestication seemingly comes from Asia.

On a slightly different note, in line with the thought of population movement being responsible for the introduction of cattle to the Lake Turkana Basin (and beyond), there is linguistic evidence that some of these early migrants may have spoken Cushitic (Afroasiatic) languages — with Proto-Cushitic, of course, presumably originating somewhere in the Horn of Africa. Evidence of this comes in the form of linguistics (among other things), with words being reconstructed back to Proto-Cushitic (c. 8000 BP) that suggest its speakers herded cattle, and kept sheep and goats (and at least collected wild varieties of plants like sorghum).

The above is a simplified version of Ancient Africa's earliest food production history. As previously stated, the details are far more complex, principally due to the great diversity in climatic conditions (rainfall, temperature, soil etc.) experienced on the continent. All this diversity would have greatly influenced grazing and growing patterns (as too would have recurring seasonal patterns).

Completing the early food-producing picture — Kintampo complex

Differences between what can be grown in dry and wet Africa can be exampled with the so-called "Kintampo complex". With this Kintampo tradition (c. 2100–1400 BCE) we have the earliest evidence of (figurative) art, personal decorative items (beads, bracelets etc.) and semi-permanent village life — in the Late Stone Age of West Africa's forest or savanna-forest region.

Kintampo sites can mostly be found in modern Ghana. Here, at Birimi, evidence has been obtained for both domesticated crops and animals — going back to at least 1700 BCE. Birimi sits in Northern Ghana, in a region that can be described as savanna land, and so was suitable for cultivating pearl millet. Though evidence for it is lacking — shea butter is the major source of oil here (rather than oil palm).

Similar Kintampo sites to the south, at the edge of the forest region, have not produced much evidence of millet cultivation — due to conditions being unfavorable (too much rainfall). What you have instead is a "forest margin complex" of agriculture, with plenty of evidence for oil palm exploitation and possibly cowpea. Yams have not been identified, but this is likely due to the lower perseveration potential of yam tubers. Kintampo people also kept livestock; goats, sheep, and cattle remains have all been found. As well as such domestic food, they also hunted and gathered wild resources. Similar to other early farmers, their toolkit included ground stone axes (clear land/forests), grinding stones (process plants) and ceramics (storage/cooking).

Given such small scale food production, unsurprisingly, there is evidence for settled life at some of these sites. At such, Kintampo villagers made very distinctive artifacts known as "terracotta cigars" or "rasps" (though the purpose of such remains unknown), as well as a variety of other decorative or luxury items. These exotic materials suggest trade and communication networks were in place (at least regionally). By the end of the second millennium BCE, most Kintampo sites had seemingly been abandoned. Perhaps climatic conditions (increasingly dry periods) had an effect on the ability to continue growing oil palms.

The appearance of this Kintampo complex coincides with the final dryings of the Sahara. In addition, aspects of the Kintampo material culture (and the workings of its economy) are similar to that which is known in the Sahara. Therefore some scholars see Kintampo as a migrant culture (from the north). This Saharan migrant culture came to co-exist with the earlier and indigenous "Punpun foragers", and so you had two distinct socio-economic groups, with different styles of pottery, occupying parts of Ghana c. 3500 BP.

Other scholars are more skeptical, and suggest it was probably more of an influence from the Sahara, rather than large migrations southwards. Put differently, perhaps it was more of a trading relationship (to begin with) — with southern or tropical forest goods being exchanged for pearl millet (and other northern or Sahelian resources like cattle and sheep/goats). Subsequent to this, the "indigenous" Kintampo may have started to cultivate millet directly, on "home turf" (while also raising livestock).

Towards agriculture — south of the equator

We already know that before you have somewhat settled societies, you must have a means of feeding people. One way of achieving this is by sustainably producing food, either through rearing livestock or cultivating crops (another way, of course, is through intensive fishing — as seen with the Aquatic civilization). Therefore, in looking for the history of the first settled societies in Eastern, Central and Southern Africa, you would need to answer the question — how did agricultural practices spread to the southern half of the continent?

Evidence certainly points to the fact that farming techniques were introduced from outside the southern region. This is not surprising given the fact that farming was mainly (or initially at least) developed as a means of coping with scarcity in food. Where there was no such scarcity, there would have been no need to develop agriculture, and humans would continue with their hunter gathering ways. In parts of Eastern, Central and Southern Africa there were plenty of wild flora and fauna available. And so, even when farming was introduced, hunter gathering persisted for a long period of time — well into the second millennium CE (in some cases).

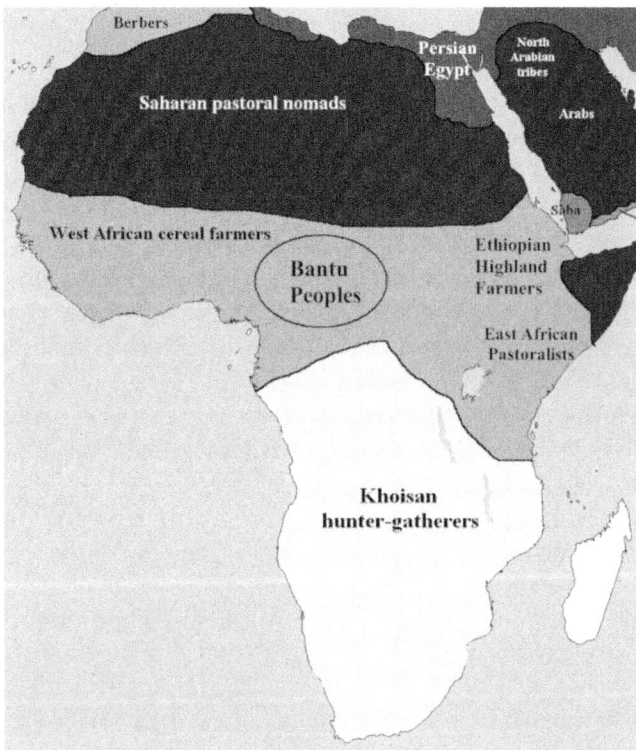

*Map 20. Africa c. 500 BCE. Source: Wikimedia Commons/CC BY-SA 3.0
(Author: Briangotts).*

While the technologies for food production came from a number of sources — Bantu Expansion, Ethiopian Highlands, Lake Turkana etc. — as exampled with the Kintampo complex, agriculture still needed to be adapted to local conditions. Through this adaptation, newer varieties of animals/crops were produced — varieties that were better suited to the African terrain south of the equator. Some of these crops appear to have even come from outside the continent — for example you have the banana (and plantain), which became a staple fruit crop in the wetter regions of the continent (Congo rainforest and tropical West Africa). Given the great diversity in African climatic conditions — the hows and whys are particularly complex.

By the time knowledge of ironworking was developed, Africans south of the equator were able to cultivate land much more effectively. This was particularly true in the wetter and more forested areas of the region, where earlier stone tools would have been inadequate for agricultural use. Of course, more efficient cultivation also enabled the production of more food. And more food allowed for permanent settlement and relatively high population densities — leading on to the earliest complex societies in Africa south of the equator.

The "late" adoption of farming methods (mainly due to geographic reasons outlined earlier), meant that settled communities below the equator developed much later — much later than they did in North and West Africa. And so too did its civilizations spring up at later dates, from the Middle Ages or Medieval times (beginning c. 500 CE) — the Kingdom of Kongo, Luba-Lunda Kingdom, Kingdom of Zimbabwe and more.

The earliest evidence of food production and ironworking cultures, only reached the southern end of Africa around the beginning of the first millennium CE. Once Iron Age cultures had arrived, across the region, consolidation would have taken place over a number of years. During this consolidation period, resources would have been developed and exploited, as they best could — despite any geographic and technological constraints. This then led on to more local advances, and subsequently some contact with external cultures, which influenced development in other ways — external cultures such as that of the Arabs, Dutch and Portuguese.

Bantu Expansion theories

As touched on earlier, the spread of farming and ironworking techniques may have been helped by Bantu-speaking farmers from West Africa (Cameroon/Nigeria). The actual routes they took, when moving through Central and Southern Africa, are up for debate. Further, their expansion could have been aided by climate change, whereby rainforest lands retreated, becoming savanna, and opening up new routes that had once been inaccessible. Routes through the savanna would have allowed for much quicker migration, than routes through dense forest cover. This is of course if one agrees with the idea of population movement, being responsible for the eventual spread of the "Bantu network", across vast parts of the continent.

As for the precise reasons for this potential migration — it's hard, if not impossible to say. Some experts have proposed that there were quite substantial increases in tropical West African populations, as a result of being able to produce more food (through farming). Therefore more land was needed. They could not go north, towards the Sahara, as there were already agro-pastoralists settled in the area. Hence, you have the expansion south, towards the rainforests, where there was less "competition". Their ability to outbreed, potentially along with having superior weapons, ultimately helped the Bantu people in displacing the hunter-gatherers below the equator.

Others suggest that it was not being able to outbreed the hunter-gatherers; rather it was the Bantu's "superior" technology that attracted people to their culture. This was a culture that embraced a settled way of life — that involved pottery making, farming and metallurgy. Hence the initial small numbers of Bantu were able to absorb different groups into their ranks, and with that you had various somewhat different (but related) Bantu cultures spread throughout the southern half of the continent.

Of course, it is almost equally possible that any actual movement of people (from West Africa) either did not happen, was limited at best, or happened much earlier in time (well before the coming of metalworking). And thus today's Bantu speakers were indigenous to Africa below the equator, living there together with other hunter-gatherers (including Khoesan speakers). Instead what you had was the later movement of agricultural, ironworking and perhaps Bantu language knowledge — which were all adopted by the indigenous locals. This adoption may subsequently have allowed the locals to greatly expand in number and permanently settle additional areas.

Which of these theories — migration, diffusion or adoption is correct? One cannot say with certainty. In fact, they may even all be part of the same story — a story that led to the wide distribution of Bantu speaking communities across Africa.

Routes to settled life

Like highlighted before (in the section on metals), African ironworking technology was varied, with many of such only being applied on a local level. These differences in ironworking techniques have enabled archaeologists to identify different cultures and spheres of influence. Differences in decorative pottery styles, has also helped distinguish cultures. As tends to be the case with archaeology, these differences only provide us with clues — with the rest being up for interpretation.

One of the earliest East African pottery finds, south of Lake Turkana, belongs to the so-called "Urewe group". This has been dated to c. 500 BCE, and was unearthed around Lake Victoria. Urewe pots incorporated such distinctive features as depressions or dimples in their bases, and elaborate grooved decorations on their rims. The archaeology of the larger African Great Lakes region is dominated by this Urewe culture — a culture which also smelted iron.

The Urewe tradition itself is but part of a larger tradition called the "Chifumbaze complex". This is due to the early iron-using communities of much of Eastern and Southern Africa being quite similar (at least archaeologically) — like was the case with the Aqualithic civilization. The archaeological sites for the Chifumbaze complex provide the first evidence for metallurgy, the cultivation of plants, the keeping of livestock, and for settled village life — in the southern half of the continent.

This Chifumbaze complex is not only made up of Urewe culture (and the wider "Eastern Stream" to which it relates), but also includes another stream of the Bantu Expansion, with noticeably different pottery, the so-called "Western Stream". It is this Western Stream, potentially originating in Northern Angola, which would ultimately form the basis for the emergence of the "Luba state" in the South Eastern Democratic Congo (around 200 years ago). This was an area especially rich agriculturally and in terms of raw materials (copper, iron, salt etc.). And so was a region that the Bantu could profitability "exploit".

If we are to assume that some sort of migration took place (from West Africa), the initial Bantu migrants would have had access to the very best farming lands, as they moved down (in small numbers — over several centuries) from more northerly areas. They would have chosen the most fertile of lands, with the best rainfall patterns, for the crops they wanted to grow. As a result, they would have stuck close to river valleys. Further, and at first, there was a clear focus on farming — rather than raising livestock (particularly true for the Eastern Stream). This may be related to the tsetse fly, which as we already know could harm cattle.

Given that they were the first permanent settlers, the ability to choose prime land meant that there was no need to go about clearing forests or adapting to a "new normal". In other words, the first Bantus would have looked for land that enabled them to practice what they already knew. Going back to the climatic conditions in Africa, the south east gets much more rainfall than the south west. Consequently, it is predictable that principal movements generally tended in a southeasterly direction (at first), avoiding the dryer south west — which explains the appearance of Urewe culture around Lake Victoria by c. 500 BCE.

By the time the Bantus arrived in the Great Lakes region, and as they subsequently moved from place to place — they would have come into contact with hunter-gatherers (Late Stone Age material culture) and early herding communities (Pastoral Neolithic culture — first seen in Lake Turkana). These Proto-Cushitic (and later Nilo-Saharan) herders, who had earlier been moving south from North East Africa, would have already interacted (or mixed) with indigenous foragers.

It is such interactions that resulted in the formation of a variety of somewhat related pastoralist groups — that spread beyond the Great Lakes to land nearer the East African coast. It is precisely such pastoralist groups (and the remaining foragers) that the Bantus came into contact with — towards the Common Era. Evidence for such interactions comes in the form of genetics, archaeology and linguistics. If we take linguistics for example, we find several Central Sudanic (Nilo-Saharan) loan words in Eastern Bantu languages — specifically words for things like cereals, livestock and other economic practices.

These interactions would ultimately result in a few things — as alluded to earlier (in the section on languages). Firstly, the Bantu and Nilotes (Nilo-Saharan languages/groups such as Dinka, Luo and Maasai) would gradually absorb or assimilate much of the earlier populations of East-Central and Southern Africa. Secondly, other (indigenous) groups, although remaining somewhat distinct, adapted and became herders themselves (complementing initial hunting and gathering). Thirdly, populations that were not absorbed were displaced or pushed to areas that were unfavorable for food production (deserts, dry plains, forests, mountains etc.). Some of the adapters and displaced people spoke

Khoesan languages — which of course used to have a much wider distribution across the southern half of the continent.

Like initial settlements above the equator, early Bantu settlements were small. No more than a handful of houses in a given area. And they were mainly self-sufficient (at first). Trading links between communities developed later. Villages close to abundant raw materials would likely have specialized, enabling them to trade their excess. For example, villages that were close to rich iron ore deposits — specialized in iron smelting.

This Early Iron Age period was also one of increasing craft specialization, and is one where we see a variety of material cultures (jewelry, sculptures, architecture etc.) and perhaps ethnicities develop. Material culture is only possible when you have access to the resources required to engage in a given culture. This has already been exampled with the Egyptians, who required certain resources to fulfill their duties to the gods.

The need for resources and trade was one of the contributing factors to the move towards more centralized control i.e. going from simple village based agriculture, to becoming chiefdoms and great empires. Resources could only be traded efficiently when society became more complex or well-organized. This was not just true in Africa, as shown in this book, but throughout the wider world.

Conclusion

Many of the early African societies mentioned in this book, ultimately laid the foundations upon which later African and non-African civilizations developed. As repeatedly highlighted, no civilization developed in a vacuum. Those closer to the centers of knowledge, or where things were done differently — had to adapt. Those further away had little to no need of doing so.

Africa's vastness as a continent meant that it had both groups of people — those that needed to adapt and those that didn't. This vastness, and resulting "pockets" of semi-isolation, is what gave rise to Africa's many cultures and its languages. Vastness and the lack of navigable rivers made it difficult to get around the continent — somewhat restricting trade and the spread of knowledge.

Knowledge, to a large extent, was developed out of necessity — in the face of climatic and geographic challenges. Africans back then did not wake up and suddenly decide they wanted to live in dense urban societies, develop writing or engage in architecture, these practices were all solutions to problems they faced at the time. Once the ball got rolling, newer problems arose — to which newer solutions were also needed. This is pretty much how the humans of today live — by researching and improving technologies that make life easier than before.

We have also seen how the acquisition of resources and the control of trade encouraged state formation. And along with this state formation, the concept of warfare developed. Armies needed to be equipped and trained, to protect what the state had (or forcefully take what it needed).

Most of the history discussed in this book, relates to a time before the coming of the Abrahamic religions of Christianity and Islam. Although most Africans today, follow one of these two religions, as we have gone over — there was a past before this. Elements of this past can still be seen today; in the way Africans combine elements of their traditional beliefs with the practice of these newer and more monotheistic religions. These are traditional beliefs very much linked to the African environment.

Please leave a review

Hope you enjoyed the read. It would be great if you could leave a review on Amazon. This will help other people seeking to learn about Africa's past. Thank you in advance.

And if you haven't already — sign up at muksawa.com/email-list to get free preview samples of upcoming books on Africa (and much more).

About the author

Adam Muksawa is simply a guy passionate about all things Africa. He believes that in order to understand Africa's future, one has to understand its past. This book is but a reflection of this belief.

Chronology of Ancient Africa

4600 mya (million years ago) – Planet earth forms.

350 mya – Pangaea begins to form, as the minor supercontinents of Laurasia and Gondwana are pushed together.

240 mya – Dinosaurs appear (before this you have fish, plants and shortly after you have mammals, birds).

200 mya – Pangaea starts to break up.

150 mya – Gondwana separates into multiple continents (Africa, South America, India, Antarctica, and Australia).

65 mya – Continents move to near modern positions.

30 mya – African and Arabian tectonic plates begin to separate, creating the Great Rift Valley.

2.8 mya – Stone ages — Homo habilis evolves, one of the earliest members of the homo family and early users of stone tools.

1.9 mya – Homo erectus — first known of our relatives to migrate out of Africa, and likely the first to cook food.

300 kya (thousand years ago) – Homo sapiens (humans) first appear in Africa — practicing a hunter-gathering lifestyle.

80 kya – Humans leave Africa and begin colonizing the world (eventually replacing Neanderthals in Europe and Western Asia — and Homo erectus in Eastern Asia).

13,000 BCE – African Humid Period (AHP) begins — most of Northern Africa is covered by grass, trees, and lakes (prior to this there was an Ice Age).

9000 BCE – Similar pottery starts to appear, and techniques of fishing-hunting-gathering are improved upon — across the Sahara and up the Nile Valley (Aqualithic or Aquatic civilization). Populations grow as a result.

7000 BCE – Knowledge of agriculture and pastoralism emerges.

6000–2000 BCE – End of African Humid Period — lakes dry up and vegetation disappears. Thus you have a slow move towards agriculture and pastoralism (instead of fishing-hunting-gathering).

5000 BCE – Pastoralists spread out across the Sahara. Fishers-hunters-gatherers move to the Nile Valley — increased population results in the rise of complex societies i.e. Ancient Egypt and Nubia.

4000 BCE – Trade intensifies between the various chiefdoms operating up and down the Nile Valley.

3100 BCE – King Narmer unifies Upper and Lower Egypt.

3100–2686 BCE – Egyptian Early Dynastic Period.

2685–2181 BCE – Egyptian Old Kingdom.

2500–1000 BCE – Egyptian expeditions to the Land of Punt.

2500–1500 BCE – Nubian Kerma Kingdom.

2500–500 BCE – Dhar Tichitt culture (agro-pastoral communities — Mauritania/Mali).

2134–1690 BCE – Egyptian Middle Kingdom.

2100–1400 BCE – Kintampo complex (agro-pastoral communities — Ghana).

2000 BCE – Herders move down (from North East Africa) to the Lake Turkana Basin (Kenya) — earliest signs of pastoralism in East Africa.

1800–400 BCE – Gajiganna culture (agro-pastoral communities — Lake Chad Basin).

1549–1069 BCE – Egyptian New Kingdom — Egypt establishes an empire in the Levant and Nubia.

1500–100 BCE – Nok culture (Northern Nigeria) — agriculture, terracotta sculptures and ironworking.

1100 BCE – Late Bronze Age Collapse — fall of several civilizations, and trade networks break down in the Mediterranean.

1069 BCE – Nubian Kingdom of Kush, centered at Napata, begins to form.

900–400 BCE – Kingdom of DM'T (Eritrea and Northern Ethiopia).

900 BCE – Beginnings of Garamante civilization (Fezzan — South West Libya).

814 BCE – Phoenicians settle at Carthage (Tunisia).

744–656 BCE – Kushite Kings of Nubia conquer Egypt, and form the 25th dynasty.

677–663 BCE – Assyrian military conquest — driving the Kushites out of Egypt.

653–332 BCE – Egyptian Late Period.

650 BCE – Greek trading port of Naucratis established (inside Egypt).

630 BCE – Greeks found colony of Cyrene (Cyrenaica, Eastern Libya).

525 BCE – Persia invades Egypt.

500 BCE – Urewe culture (Lake Victoria) — some of the earliest evidence for metalworking, the cultivation of crops, the keeping of livestock, and for settled village life — in the southern half of Africa. Also provides early evidence for the Bantu Expansion (across the continent).

400 BCE – Start of the Proto-Aksum period in Ethiopia.

332–30 BCE – Alexander the Great conquers Egypt — resulting in the Ptolemaic Kingdom.

264–146 BCE – Series of three Punic wars, ultimately resulting in Carthage being razed (by the Romans).

250 BCE – Jenne-Jeno (Mali) is founded — eventually becoming one of West Africa's first urban cities.

30 BCE – Death of Cleopatra and Rome rules Egypt (and most of Africa's Mediterranean Coast).

Bibliography and further reading

Ancient (primary) sources
In parts of this book, Ancient Greek and Latin authors have been mentioned. You can read (in English) a lot more of what they had to say about Africa here:

https://penelope.uchicago.edu/Thayer/E/HELP/Indexes/books.html.
https://www.perseus.tufts.edu/hopper/collection?collection=Perseus:
collection:Greco-Roman.

Works of particular interest include: Manetho (the Egyptian priest), Herodotus: The Histories, Diodorus Siculus: The Library of History, Dionysius of Halicarnassus: The Roman Antiquities, Polybius: The Histories, Aristotle: Politics, Tacitus: Histories, and Strabo: Geography.

General texts
Connah, G. (2004). Forgotten Africa: An introduction to its archaeology. Oxfordshire: Routledge.
Asante, M.K. (2019). The history of Africa: the quest for eternal harmony. 3rd ed. New York: Routledge.
Shillington, K. (2019). History of Africa. 4th ed. London: Red Globe Press.
Barker, G. (1994). The Archaeology of Africa: Food, Metals and Towns. London: Routledge.
Ehret, C. (2012). Africa in World History: The Long, Long View. The Oxford Handbook of World History.
https://doi.org/10.1093/oxfordhb/9780199235810.013.0026.

The African beginnings of human life / The Stone Ages in Africa
Morriss-Kay, G. M. (2010). The evolution of human artistic creativity. Journal of anatomy, 216(2), 158–176.

McBrearty, S. and Brooks, A.S. (2000). The revolution that wasn't: a new interpretation of the origin of modern human behavior. Journal of Human Evolution 39: 453–563.

Gowlett, J. A. J. (2016). The discovery of fire by humans: a long and convoluted process. Phil. Trans. R. Soc. B 371:20150164. https://doi.org/10.1098/rstb.2015.0164.

Backwell, L., Bradfield, J., Carlson, K.J. et al. (2018). The antiquity of bow-and-arrow technology: Evidence from Middle Stone Age layers at Sibudu Cave. Antiquity, 92(362), 289-303. https://doi.org/10.15184/aqy.2018.11.

de la Torre, I. (2016). The origins of the Acheulean: past and present perspectives on a major transition in human evolution. Phil. Trans. R. Soc. B 371: 20150245. https://doi.org/10.1098/rstb.2015.0245.

People and languages of Africa

Campbell, M. C. and Tishkoff, S. A. (2010). The evolution of human genetic and phenotypic variation in Africa. Current biology : CB, 20(4), R166–R173. https://doi.org/10.1016/j.cub.2009.11.050.

Keita, S.O.Y. (2015). History and Genetics in Africa: The Need for Better Cooperation Between the Teams. The Backbone Journal (W. Montague Cobb Research Laboratory - Howard University) Vol 1 Issue 1.

Schepartz, L.A. (1993). Language and modern human origins. Yearbook of Physical Anthropology 36:91–126.

Drake, N. A., Blench, R. M., Armitage, S. J. et al. (2011). Ancient watercourses and biogeography of the Sahara explain the peopling of the desert. Proceedings of the National Academy of Sciences of the United States of America, 108(2), 458–462. https://doi.org/10.1073/pnas.1012231108.

The First Agricultural Revolution

Petersen, M. B. and Skaaning, S-E. (2010). Ultimate Causes of State Formation: The Significance of Biogeography, Diffusion, and Neolithic Revolutions. Historical Social Research, 35(3), 200-226.

Mercuri, A.M., Fornaciari, R., Gallinaro, M. et al. (2018). Plant behaviour from human imprints and the cultivation of wild cereals in Holocene Sahara. Nature Plants 4, 71–81. https://doi.org/10.1038/s41477-017-0098-1.

Bowles, S. and Jung-Kyoo, C. (2019). The Neolithic Agricultural Revolution and the Origins of Private Property. Journal of Political Economy, 127:5, 2186-2228. https://doi.org/10.1086/701789.

Larson, G., Piperno, D.R., Allaby, R.G. et al. (2014). Current perspectives and the future of domestication studies. Proc. Natl Acad. Sci. USA (PNAS) 111, 6139–6146. https://doi.org/10.1073/pnas.1323964111.

Gifford-Gonzalez, D., Hanotte, O. (2011). Domesticating Animals in Africa: Implications of Genetic and Archaeological Findings. J World Prehist 24, 1–23. https://doi.org/10.1007/s10963-010-9042-2.

African geology, geography, climate and the rise of its civilizations

Dwayne, W. (2003). Bringing Geography Back In: Civilizations, Wealth, and Poverty, International Studies Review. Volume 5, Issue 3, September, Pages 343–354. https://doi.org/10.1046/j.1079-1760.2003.00503003.x.

Van Hinsbergen, D. J. J., Buiter, S. J. H., Torsvik, T. H. et al. (2011). The formation and evolution of Africa from the Archaean to Present: introduction. Geological Society, London, Special Publications, 357, 1–8. https://doi.org/10.1144/SP357.1.

Wilkie, B. (2020). "'What a Change When the Tide had Ebbed!': Rivers, Empire, and a Scottish Transport Company in Colonial Malawi." Environment & Society Portal, Arcadia, no. 18. Rachel Carson Center for Environment and Society. Available at <http://www.environmentandsociety.org/node/9040>.

Boggs, S. W. (1943). Africa: Maps and Man. The (US) Department of State Bulletin. September 18. 188-196.

Age of Metals — Copper, Bronze and Iron Ages

Herbert, E.W. (2003). Red Gold of Africa: Copper in Precolonial History and Culture. New ed. Madison: The University of Wisconsin Press.

David, K. (2016). A global perspective on the pyrotechnologies of Sub-Saharan Africa. Azania: Archaeological Research in Africa, 51:1, 62-87, https://doi.org/10.1080/0067270X.2016.1150082.

Holl, A. (2020). The Origins of African Metallurgies. Oxford Research Encyclopedia of Anthropology. https://doi.org/10.1093/acrefore/9780190854584.013.63.

Bandama, F. (2020). Preindustrial Mining and Metallurgy in Africa. Oxford Research Encyclopedia of Anthropology. https://doi.org/10.1093/acrefore/9780190854584.013.64.

Ancient Egypt

Schoville, K. (2001). The Rosetta Stone in Historical Perspective. Journal of the Adventist Theological Society, 12/1: 1–21.

Smith, W.S. (1960). Ancient Egypt as Represented in the Museum of Fine Arts, Boston. Boston: Museum of Fine Arts.

Creasman, P.P. and Wilkinson, R.H. (2017). Pharaoh's land and beyond : Ancient Egypt and its neighbors. New York: Oxford University Press.

Stevenson, A. (2016). The Egyptian Predynastic and State Formation. J Archaeol Res 24, 421–468. https://doi.org/10.1007/s10814-016-9094-7.

Ancient Nubia

Edwards, D.N. (2004).The Nubian past: an archaeology of the Sudan. London: Routledge.

Ross, L. (2013). Nubia and Egypt, 10,000 B.C. to 400 A.D. : from prehistory to the Meroitic period. Lewiston, NY: The Edwin Mellen Press.

Gatto, M.C. (2014). Cultural entanglement at the dawn of the Egyptian history: a view from the Nile First Cataract region. Origini: Prehistory and Protohistory of Ancient Civilizations XXXVI: 93-123.

Malville, J.M., Schild, R., Wendorf, F. et al. (2008). Astronomy of Nabta Playa. In: Holbrook J.C., Urama J.O., Medupe R.T. (eds) African Cultural Astronomy. Astrophysics and Space Science Proceedings. Springer, Dordrecht. https://doi.org/10.1007/978-1-4020-6639-9_11.

Ancient Carthage

Koffler, S. (1970). Carthage must not be destroyed. The UNESCO Courier. December.

Scott, J.C. (2019). Phoenicians: The Quickening Of Western Civilization. Comparative Civilizations Review: Vol. 81 : No. 81 , Article 4.

Broodbank, C., and Lucarini, G. (2019). The Dynamics of Mediterranean Africa, ca. 9600–1000 BC: An Interpretative Synthesis of Knowns and Unknowns. Journal Of Mediterranean Archaeology, 32(2). https://doi.org/10.1558/jma.40581.

Marquez-Grant, N. (2005). The presence of African individuals in Punic populations from the island of Ibiza (Spain): contributions from physical anthropology. Mayurqa, 30, 611–637.

The Garamantes and Saharan Africa

Magnavita, S. (2013). Initial encounters: Seeking traces of ancient trade connections between West Africa and the wider world. Afriques 4. https://doi.org/10.4000/afriques.1145.

Belmonte, J. A., Esteban, C., Betancort, M. A. P. et al. (2002). Archaeoastronomy in the Sahara: The Tombs of the Garamantes at Wadi El Agial, Fezzan, Libya. Journal for the History of Astronomy, 33(27), S1–S19. https://doi.org/10.1177/002182860203302701.

Mattingly, D. and Sterry, M. (2013). The first towns in the central Sahara. Antiquity, 87 (336), 503-518. https://doi.org/10.1017/S0003598X00049097.

Schörle, K. (2012). Saharan Trade in Classical Antiquity. Saharan Frontiers: Space and Mobility in Northwest Africa, Indiana University Press, pp.58-72, 978-0-253-00126-9. https://halshs.archives-ouvertes.fr/halshs-02966544.

Greeks in Ancient Africa

James, P. (2005). Archaic Greek colonies in Libya: historical vs. archaeological chronologies? Libyan Studies 36, 1–20.

Malouta, M. (2015). Naucratis. Oxford Handbooks Online. https://doi.org/10.1093/oxfordhb/9780199935390.013.114.

Lopes, H.T. and Almeida, I. (2017). The Mediterranean: The Asian and African Roots of the Cradle of Civilization. Mediterranean Identities - Environment, Society, Culture https://doi.org/10.5772/intechopen.69363.

Land of Punt

Phillips, J. (1997). Punt and Aksum: Egypt and the Horn of Africa. The Journal of African History. 38. 423 - 457.

Dominy, N.J, Ikram S, Moritz G.L. et al. (2020). Mummified baboons reveal the far reach of early Egyptian mariners. eLife, 9:e60860. https://doi.org/10.7554/eLife.60860.

Before there was Aksum — D'MT Kingdom

Munro-Hay, S. (1991). Aksum: An African Civilisation of Late Antiquity. Edinburgh: Edinburgh University Press.

Fattovich, R. (2010). The Development of Ancient States in the Northern Horn of Africa, c. 3000 BC–AD 1000: An Archaeological Outline. J World Prehist 23, 145–175. https://doi.org/10.1007/s10963-010-9035-1.

Matthews, S. and Büchner, S. (2016) Before Aksum: Excavating Ethiopia's earliest civilization. Current World Archaeology 79: 14 – 21.

Middle Niger River — Sudanic empires and Tichitt civilization
Kay, A.U., Fuller, D.Q., Neumann, K. et al. (2019). Diversification,
Intensification and Specialization: Changing Land Use in Western
Africa from 1800 BC to AD 1500. Journal of World Prehistory.
32:179–228. https://doi.org/10.1007/s10963-019-09131-2.
Holl, A.F.C. (2009). Coping with uncertainty: Neolithic life in the Dhar
Tichitt-Walata, Mauritania, (ca. 4000–2300 BP). Comptes Rendus
Geoscience 341: 703–712.
https://doi.org/10.1016/j.crte.2009.04.005.
MacDonald, K. (2015). The Tichitt tradition in the West African Sahel. In
G. Barker & C. Goucher (Eds.), The Cambridge World History (pp.
499-513). Cambridge: Cambridge University Press.
https://doi.org/10.1017/CBO9780511978807.020.
Kea, R. A. (2004). Expansions and Contractions: World-Historical
Change And The Western Sudan World-System (1200/1000 B.C. –
1200/1250 A.D.). Journal of World-Systems Research, 10(3), 723-
816. https://doi.org/10.5195/jwsr.2004.286.

Nok culture of Nigeria
Breunig, P. (2017). Exploring the Nok Culture. Frankfurt/Main: Goethe
University, Institute for Archaeological Sciences, African
Archaeology and Archaeobotany.
Franke, G. (2016). A chronology of the central Nigerian Nok Culture—
1500 BC to the beginning of the common era. Journal of African
Archaeology. 14(3), 257–289.
LAMP, F.J. (2011). Ancient Terracotta Figures from Northern Nigeria.
Yale University Art Gallery Bulletin, 48-57.
Dunne, J., Höhn, A., Franke, G. et al. (2021). Honey-collecting in
prehistoric West Africa from 3500 years ago. Nat Commun 12, 2227.
https://doi.org/10.1038/s41467-021-22425-4.

Lake Mega-Chad, Chadic societies and the Sao civilization
Breunig, P., Neumann, K and Van Neer, W. (1996). New Research on the
Holocene Settlement and Environment of the Chad Basin in Nigeria.
African Archaeological Review, Vol. 13, No. 2.
Holl, A. F. C. (2020). Adorning the Body, Asserting Status: Prestige-
Goods and Social Distinction at Ancient Chadic Chiefdom of Houlouf
(Northern Cameroon). International Journal of Archaeology. Vol. 8,
No. 2, pp. 22-31.

MacEachern, S. (2012). The Holocene History of the Southern Lake Chad Basin: Archaeological, Linguistic and Genetic Evidence. Afr Archaeol Rev 29, 253–271. https://doi.org/10.1007/s10437-012-9110-3.

Lake Turkana and the Aqualithic or Aquatic civilization

Wright, D.K., Forman, S.L., Kiura, P. et al. (2015) Lakeside View: Sociocultural Responses to Changing Water Levels of Lake Turkana, Kenya. Afr Archaeol Rev 32, 335–367. https://doi.org/10.1007/s10437-015-9185-8.

Lucquin, A., Robson, H.K., Eley, Y. et al. (2018). The impact of environmental change on the use of early pottery by East Asian hunter-gatherers. PNAS 115 (31) 7931-7936. https://doi.org/10.1073/pnas.1803782115.

Mohammed-Ali, A.S. and Khabir, A.M (2003). The Wavy Line and the Dotted Wavy Line Pottery in the Prehistory of the Central Nile and the Sahara-Sahel Belt. African Archaeological Review 20, 25–58 (2003). https://doi.org/10.1023/A:1022882305448.

Goldstein, S. (2019). Lithic technological strategies of the earliest herders at Lake Turkana, northern Kenya. Antiquity, 93(372), 1495-1514. https://doi.org/10.15184/aqy.2019.178.

Sutton, J.E.G. (1977). The African aqualithic. Antiquity, 51 (201), 25-34. https://www.doi.org/10.1017/S0003598X00100559.

Food production and early Eastern, Central and Southern African societies

Grollemund, R., Branford, S., Bostoen, K., et al. (2015). Bantu expansion shows that habitat alters the route and pace of human dispersals. Proceedings of the National Academy of Sciences of the United States of America (PNAS), 112 (43), 13296–13301. https://doi.org/10.1073/pnas.1503793112.

Bostoen, K. (2018). The Bantu Expansion. Oxford Research Encyclopedia of African History. https://doi.org/10.1093/acrefore/9780190277734.013.191.

D'Andrea, A.C., Klee, M., and Casey, J. (2001). Archaeobotanical evidence for pearl millet (Pennisetum glaucum) in sub-Saharan West Africa. Antiquity, 75(288), 341-348. https://doi.org/10.1017/S0003598X00060993.

Logan, A. L., and D'Andrea, A. C. (2012). Oil palm, arboriculture, and changing subsistence practices during Kintampo times (3600–3200 BP, Ghana). Quaternary International, 249, 63–71. https://doi.org/10.1016/j.quaint.2010.12.004.

Prendergast, M.E., Lipson, M., Sawchuk, E.A. et al. (2019). Ancient DNA
    Reveals a Multi-Step Spread of the First Herders into Sub-Saharan
    Africa. Science. 365(6448).
    https://www.doi.org/10.1126/science.aaw6275.

Printed in Great Britain
by Amazon

79214918R00132